WHO SPEAKS FOR YOU?

WHO SPEAKS FOR YOU?

THE INSIDE STORY OF THE PROSECUTOR WHO TOOK DOWN BALTIMORE'S MOST CROOKED COPS

LEO WISE

Johns Hopkins University Press

BALTIMORE

Johns Hopkins University Press
2715 North Charles Street
Baltimore, Maryland 21218
www.press.jhu.edu

Library of Congress Cataloging-in-Publication Data is available.

ISBN 978-1-4214-4650-9 (hardcover)
ISBN 978-1-4214-4651-6 (ebook)

A catalog record for this book is available from the British Library.

*Special discounts are available for bulk purchases of this book. For more information,
please contact Special Sales at specialsales@jh.edu.*

To Anne, Joe, and Claudia,
with hope for a more just world

Contents

PART III   THE TRIAL

Note to Readers

The author has received no compensation for the writing of this book.

Any opinions or points of view expressed in this book represent those of the author and do not necessarily represent the official position or policies of the US government, including the Department of Justice.

All quotations are from transcripts of proceedings in open court or from publicly filed documents not under seal.

Real names have been used if the person has been previously identified in a public filing not subject to an order sealing that document or if the person has been identified in open court. Pseudonyms are used for individuals who have not been identified in a public filing or in open court. These pseudonyms are a product of the author's imagination. Any connection between an individual identified by a pseudonym and any person with that name is coincidental.

Key Players

PROSECUTORS

Derek Hines, US Department of Justice
Leo Wise, US Department of Justice

INVESTIGATORS

Erika Jensen, Federal Bureau of Investigation
Scott Kilpatrick, Baltimore County Police Department
David McDougall, Harford County Sheriff's Office
John Sieracki, Baltimore Police Department and
Federal Bureau of Investigation

TASK FORCE DEFENDANTS

Thomas Allers
Momodu Gondo
Evodio Hendrix
Daniel Hersl

Wayne Jenkins
Jemell Rayam
Marcus Taylor
Maurice Ward

ADDITIONAL DEFENDANTS

Aaron Anderson
Thomas Finnegan
David Rahim
Antonio Shropshire

Donald Stepp
Antoine Washington
Glenn Wells

TASK FORCE AND SPECIAL ENFORCEMENT SECTION VICTIMS

Dennis Armstrong
Jimmie Griffin
Ronald Hamilton
Keona Holloway
Antonio Santiful

Oreese Stevenson
Sergio Summerville
Herbert Tate
Shawn Whiting

DEFENSE ATTORNEYS

William Purpura, counsel for Daniel Hersl
Thomas Rafter, counsel for Daniel Hersl
Christopher Nieto, counsel for Marcus Taylor
Jennifer Wicks, counsel for Marcus Taylor

Map labels:

Belvedere Towers ⑪ 134

⑫ Griffin robbery

The Barn ③ 138

The Alameda ⑦
Shopping Center 542 ② Stevenson robbery

Stevenson arrest 140 ⑤ 25 41

Burley and Matthews ⑬
crash 126 26

45

83

Shropshire's garage ⑩ 147

Danziger car ①
stop

Tate and Santiful ⑥
robberies

⑧ Armstrong robbery

North Gilmor Street ⑨ 129

Whiting
robbery

Baltimore

Summerville robbery ④ 395
(U-Store)

95

695 895

Legend:

1. North Longwood Street and West North Avenue intersection
2. Heathfield Road
3. West Northern Parkway
4. Ridgely Street
5. Jonquil Avenue
6. East Baltimore Midway
7. The Alameda
8. Sinclair Lane
9. North Gilmor Street
10. East 25th Street
11. Falls Road
12. Evesham Avenue
13. Belle Avenue and Gwyn Oak Avenue intersection

Scenes of Crimes Committed by the Gun Trace Task Force. Locations as positioned on the map are approximations due to scale.

WHO SPEAKS FOR YOU?

Prologue
Our Foreperson

"**M**embers of the jury, have you agreed on your verdict?" Karen Moye, the courtroom deputy, asked.

"Yes," the jurors answered in unison.

"Who shall speak for you?"

"Our foreperson," again, in unison.

Juror number two, a young African American man—the only one among the twelve jurors—rose to speak.

I had watched this scene play out many times before. The identity of the foreperson had never mattered to me. All I had cared about was the verdict. This time was different though. I had never had a case like this, and it had never occurred to me that the person a jury chose to speak for them would send a message even before announcing their verdict.

It did that day in the winter of 2018.

As co-counsel for the government, I sat at the prosecution table, the one nearest the jury, in the largest courtroom in the federal courthouse in Baltimore, Maryland. Courtroom 1A, also called the ceremonial courtroom, has two floors of stadium seating for the public. It looked packed.

On the walls, judges preserved in oil paintings looked down on the proceedings like saints in the stained-glass windows of a church. The art and architecture of courtroom 1A reflected the seriousness of what happens there. Following convictions in criminal trials, individuals lose their liberty, their property, and in the case of capital offenses, their right to life. In no other place in our society is the power of the state brought to bear more directly on the individual than in the courtroom.

A high bench runs the entire length of the courtroom, long enough to seat every federal judge in Baltimore. On that day, however, one judge, Catherine C. Blake, sat alone at its center. She wore the black robe traditional for judges; it cloaks their individuality and signals that the decisions they make would be the same regardless of which one of them is presiding. A decision is an expression of the law, not of an individual.

Immediately in front of Judge Blake, on a lower level, sat Moye, who as courtroom deputy made sure the trains ran on time. It was also her job to elicit the jurors' verdict in the stylized procedure of the court, asking every jury, "Who shall speak for you?"

That day, the answer had special meaning.

Next to me sat my co-counsel, Derek Hines. He had gray-flecked hair and a natural confidence that made it seem like he had tried cases many times before. But he hadn't. Derek was only in his early thirties, about ten years younger than me, but he was a natural trial lawyer. I never considered him anything other than a partner and a peer. Together, we stood out in one quite noticeable way: I'm six foot four, and Derek is even taller, coming in at six foot seven—earning us the nickname "the Twin Towers" in a *Baltimore Sun* profile. Although Derek had been practicing law for a relatively short time, his experience proved invaluable. Immediately after law school, Derek had gone to work at a firm where former FBI director Louis Freeh was a partner, rooting out fraud in the BP Deepwater Horizon settlement program, stemming from the 2010 oil spill in the Gulf of Mexico. So, even though in private practice, he was acting like a prosecutor. What he did next was even more unusual, especially for someone at a big law firm: he took a job as general counsel of the Cree Nation in Montana. In that role, he twice prosecuted the elected head of the Cree on corruption charges. For one of the trials, he needed police protection. Both those professional experiences reflected the qualities I came to see in Derek during the course of our case: confidence, toughness, and tenacity.

The two defendants, Daniel Hersl and Marcus Taylor, sat at separate tables with their lawyers. In 2018, most defendants being prosecuted in federal court were there for alleged immigration or drug offenses, but both Hersl and Taylor had been born in the United States, and neither of them was a drug dealer.

The two defendants were a study in contrasts. Hersl was almost twenty years older than Taylor and looked it, with thinning, close-cropped gray hair and a rough complexion. Taylor had a full head of black hair and a baby face. Hersl was white. Taylor was Black. Hersl had grown up in Baltimore; his mother still lived in the city's Little Italy. Taylor grew up in a military family and had moved around before settling outside Baltimore.

Hersl entered the courtroom with his typical swagger and smiled at his family seated in the gallery. I'm okay, he seemed to be signaling. I've got this. When he came into the courtroom that day, his eyes lit up. He looked happy, something that, given the context, was unsettling and memorable. Maybe he thought he was about to get off? It wasn't the first time I had noticed Hersl's eyes. In his booking photo he stared at the camera, his eyes unnaturally wide, with his head cocked back slightly. The intensity in his eyes was alarming.

Taylor quickly walked to his seat. Keeping his head down as he walked, I couldn't see his eyes. He had family in the courtroom, too, including his father, an Army veteran. We had hoped that Taylor's parents would eventually be able to persuade him to do the right thing and take responsibility for his crimes and cooperate with our investigation. He didn't. In the courtroom, Taylor betrayed no emotion.

For all their differences, Hersl and Taylor had two important things in common.

They were police officers.

And they were defendants.

Hersl and Taylor were on trial for crimes they had committed as police officers, charged with breaking the laws they had sworn to uphold, for using their guns and their badges to prey on the Baltimore City communities they had pledged to protect. They were both members of the Baltimore Police Department's Gun Trace Task Force, an elite squad of senior detectives assigned to take guns off the street. Instead, they robbed the people they stopped and arrested. They stole money, guns, drugs, Rolex watches, clothes, expensive cologne, practically anything they could get their hands on. Their sergeant, Wayne Jenkins, had even stolen prescription drugs from people who had broken into pharmacies during the violence that erupted in April 2015 following the death of Freddie Gray Jr., a 25-year-old African American, from injuries sustained while in the custody of the BPD.

Hersl and Taylor had undoubtedly been in courtrooms before—but not seated next to defense attorneys. As they awaited the jury's verdict, they were still sworn police officers, though on unpaid leave. Armed US marshals sat behind them. Each day, outside the presence of the jury, Hersl and Taylor were brought into the courtroom in handcuffs from small jail cells within the courthouse. This daily ritual demonstrated the uniqueness of their case: two police officers entered the courtroom in handcuffs and sat at the defense table, and men who sold drugs came through the front door of the courthouse to testify against them. It was usually the other way around.

Hersl cut a larger profile in the community than Taylor, but it wasn't a positive one. He had been in the news before this case, with Baltimore City having paid $200,000 to settle some of the dozens of complaints that citizens had made against him even before our case began.

The Task Force's victims were mostly people who sold drugs in Baltimore City plus people the Task Force officers *believed* sold drugs. Task Force members preyed on them because they had money to steal and most likely could be counted on not to complain. Even if they did speak out, no one would believe them.

But I did.

To be clear, I never had an epiphany. There wasn't a single "moment of truth." The truth also wasn't self-evident. Rather, the truth was a destination. When the investigation began, I didn't know where our team of prosecutors and investigators was headed. It was somewhere over the horizon. But for a series of breaks, we might have never gotten there.

The journey, the search, took me to Baltimore neighborhoods I had never set foot in—I had had no reason to go—to places where police officers and the community interacted in ways I had never experienced. In my overwhelmingly white, North Baltimore neighborhood, the chief complaint about the police is that they aren't around enough. In overwhelmingly Black East and West Baltimore, where the Task Force had operated (see the map, p. xiii), the complaint was that the police acted like an occupying army.

The Task Force created an upside-down world, where the drug dealers were the victims, and the police committed the crimes. Its members had flipped the script, and to catch them and to convince a jury to convict them, our team would have to flip the script, too. In the courtroom, we would have to convince the jury of what people in these neighborhoods had long known to be true: that sometimes the criminals wore badges.

This is a story of belief and disbelief, of how I came to believe that the Task Force's victims were telling the truth and the police officers were lying. Regardless of the jury's verdict, this case raised an inconvenient truth: sometimes the police were the ones not to be believed.

That truth was inconvenient for a number of reasons. It called into question all the cases the members of the Task Force had made. Ultimately, prosecutors would dismiss hundreds of their cases, not because the defendants were innocent, but because of the lost credibility of the police officers who made the cases and would have to testify in court about what had happened. To put it in the starkest terms, the guilty would go free, and perhaps, go back to the same neighborhoods where they had victimized people and victimize them again. But this was the cost of what the officers had done. As the case proceeded, one of my bosses would request updates on our progress, sometimes asking me, "So how many cases have you fucked up today?" He was only half kidding.

It was inconvenient because, perversely, by bringing the Task Force's crimes into the light, the public's confidence in the Baltimore Police Department would be further undermined. This was another way in which the Task Force victimized the city.

The context for this case included Freddie Gray Jr.'s death and the protests and violence that engulfed Baltimore after his funeral. The Baltimore City State's Attorney's Office—the local prosecutor typically called a district attorney, or DA, in other states—sought indictments against all six officers who arrested and transported Gray the day he sustained life-ending injuries in the back of a police wagon. None were convicted. After three unsuccessful trials, the State's Attorney's Office dropped the remaining cases, just seven months before our charges became public. If our case ended in acquittals, what message would that send? That the police could never be held accountable?

The question Moye asked the jury—"Who shall speak for you?"— had never struck me as particularly important before, but as juror number two rose to deliver the verdict, the question took on new meaning. Unlike the other members of the jury, juror number two looked like the Task Force's victims and the people who testified against them: young Black men. The jury had chosen him to speak for them.

What would he say?

6

PART I

THE INVESTIGATION

ONE

The Barn

The Baltimore City Public Safety Training Facility, a big, multistory brick building that looks like a school, is located in Northwest Baltimore near Pimlico, the racetrack that hosts the Preakness Stakes, the "middle jewel" of horse racing's Triple Crown. "The Barn," a long, narrow, single-story building with a pointed roof, runs alongside it. It's barely noticeable. I would pass the training facility on the drive from my home to the FBI's Baltimore Field Office, something I did frequently as part of my job as a federal prosecutor. I never paid it much attention. The only thing that caught my eye was an aging alpine tower, an enormous structure in the field next to the facility outfitted with ropes and walls to scale for training officers in climbing. The first time I noticed the Barn, a few years before our investigation even began, I had wondered what goes on in there. I would find out.

The Barn was home to the Gun Trace Task Force of the Baltimore Police Department. BPD had created the Task Force in 2007. While other US cities, most notably New York, had driven their murder rates down by the early 2000s, Baltimore's remained stubbornly high. A new commissioner announced a crime-fighting strategy that focused on drug dealers with guns, and as part of that new strategy, he created a gun-tracing task force. As the outfit's name implied, the Task Force was supposed to trace guns back to the criminals using them, and in this way, reduce violence. It consisted of eight or so senior plainclothes detectives at any given time. With the Barn as their home base and with citywide jurisdiction, they operated far from the eyes of BPD brass.

The Barn and the Task Force it housed became the focus of my legal career for three years, from 2015 to 2018. My path up to that point, in a real and metaphorical sense, had been an uncommon one for a federal prosecutor. In hindsight, however, it wound up preparing me for the Task Force case.

I joined the US Department of Justice in 2004 after clerking for a federal judge. My first case was the federal government's civil racketeering lawsuit against the tobacco industry. The trial began three weeks after I joined the department and lasted for ten months. The fraud charges at the heart of the case focused on lies the five major cigarette manufacturers had told the public for nearly fifty years. In that trial, I questioned expert witnesses and developed an interest in the intersection of science and the law, an interest that ultimately led to my prosecuting fatal overdose cases. In turn, those drug cases became one of the things that would lead me to the Task Force case.

After the tobacco case ended, I joined the Enron Task Force as a prosecutor in the securities fraud trial of Enron's two former CEOs, Jeff Skilling and Ken Lay, in Houston. From there, I went to Denver to join the team prosecuting the former CEO of Qwest Communications, Joe Nacchio, in the largest insider trading case ever charged by DOJ. Then I prosecuted Lance Poulsen, the former CEO of one of America's largest health care financing companies, National Century Financial Enterprises, for defrauding investors out of $3 billion.

After four years at DOJ, I went to Capitol Hill to set up the Office of Congressional Ethics (OCE) in the House of Representatives. The House created the OCE in 2008 after a series of high-profile scandals involving its members. The OCE's mission was to investigate allegations of misconduct by House members as well as staff and to do so in an independent and nonpartisan way. As I quickly learned on the job, going after the powerful doesn't tend to make one popular. The *National Law*

Journal published a profile of me at the time, writing that I was on my way to "becoming one of the least-liked lawyers on Capitol Hill." I took that as a badge of honor, but after about two years I missed the courtroom. In 2010, I returned to DOJ, this time to the US Attorney's Office for the District of Maryland in Baltimore.

I had first come to Baltimore fifteen years earlier to attend Johns Hopkins University as an undergraduate. I loved my time at Hopkins and came to love the city of Baltimore as well. Although I grew up in New Jersey, I took the Maryland bar when I graduated from Harvard Law School. My wife and I met at Hopkins, and we both wanted to make Baltimore our home, something we were finally able to do in 2014.

Based on my prior experience, when I joined the US Attorney's Office, I was assigned to its Fraud and Public Corruption Unit. On my first day on the job in 2010, US Attorney Rod Rosenstein assigned me to the trial of a sitting state senator, a case I would lose. It was a humbling experience, but I learned more from that loss than from some of the trials I'd won. One of the things I took from it was how hard it is to bring a successful corruption case without a wiretap. I never wanted to be in that situation again. After that case ended, Rosenstein asked me to work on an investigation into a leak of classified information to a *New York Times* journalist. Attorney General Eric Holder had assigned the case to him. At the end of an exhaustive eight-month investigation in 2012 and 2013, I along with two FBI agents interviewed Gen. James "Hoss" Cartwright (USMC), vice chairman of the Joint Chiefs of Staff, one of the most high-ranking targets there could be. Cartwright lied during the interview, and to our astonishment, when confronted with proof of his lies—his own emails—he fainted. He ultimately pleaded guilty, but that wasn't the end of the story. In the second presidential debate, in late September 2016, Donald Trump, the Republican nominee, mentioned the case, criticizing us for prosecuting Cartwright and not Hillary Clinton, Trump's Democratic opponent. Trump wouldn't be alone in coming to Cartwright's defense. Before Cartwright was sentenced, President Barack Obama pardoned him in the closing days of his administration.

What made my time at DOJ unusual was that when lawyers become federal prosecutors, they typically start with violent crime and drug cases. This means working with federal law enforcement agencies that specialize in these types of crimes, such as the US Drug Enforcement Administration (DEA) and the Bureau of Alcohol, Tobacco, Firearms and Explosives (ATF). They also work with local police officers, who are involved in federal cases in three principal ways: they serve on specialized federal task forces focusing on guns and drugs; they in the first instance investigate and then continue working on gun and drug cases subsequently "adopted," taken over, by federal law enforcement; and they conduct traffic stops, execute search warrants, and undertake other law enforcement operations in federal cases.

As a result of being assigned violent crime and drug cases, most federal prosecutors have a significant amount of experience working with local police officers, but because I had never done that kind of work, I didn't. I also obviously didn't have experience with defendants charged with drug and gun offenses. They, like local police officers, were largely unknown to me. Instead, I had prosecuted financial frauds, in particular, securities fraud, and public corruption, so-called white-collar crimes.

Federal law enforcement agencies, principally the FBI and the IRS, almost exclusively handle white-collar cases, without local police involvement. The agents who work on these cases typically have backgrounds in accounting and business. Sometimes the agents are lawyers themselves. The witnesses in white-collar cases are also different from those in drugs cases or cases involving violence. In the former, they are usually professionals employed at the company where the defendant worked or in a politician's office or by their campaign. In narcotics cases, key witnesses are often detectives or other police officers who, for example, while conducting surveillance saw a defendant engaging in hand-to-hand drug sales. Under such circumstances, the credibility of the police officer is paramount. Before the prosecutor puts the officer on the witness stand, she herself has to believe the officer. By contrast, I had seldom used law enforcement agents of any kind as witnesses in trials. In white-collar cases federal law enforcement collect and synthesize evidence to determine whether a crime had been committed and who was responsible for it, but that is often done after the fact and, as a result, they aren't witnesses to anything.

It also meant I had spent my career investigating and prosecuting authority figures, like politicians and federal officials, and other high-profile individuals, like corporate executives, who enjoyed a great deal of trust. They came into the courtroom cloaked in it, and they had other advantages that most defendants lacked: education, professional success, no criminal record, witnesses who would testify on their behalf about their (and others') good character. Of course, juries are much more likely to believe defendants in white-collar cases than someone who sells or sold drugs.

Prosecuting white-collar crime taught me that authority figures routinely abuse the public trust. I saw it firsthand, day in day out, for more than a decade. It also made me a contrarian—I had to disbelieve people that society believed. When we went to trial in the Enron case, the YMCA in Houston was still named after Ken Lay. Yet, there we were, having to convince a jury that Lay was behind one of the biggest corporate frauds in history. That contrarian streak would serve me well in the case against police officers.

The confluence of these trend lines in my career meant that on the one hand, I wasn't predisposed to believe police officers based on any personal experience I had working with them. On the other hand, I was predisposed to question whether they, like any other authority figure, should be believed any more than anyone else. I felt this approach probably put me outside the mainstream. In the ten years I spent as a prosecutor before the Task Force case, I had picked juries in more than a dozen fraud and corruption trials not only in Baltimore but also in

Houston, Texas, Denver, Colorado, and Columbus, Ohio. This process involved the court posing questions to thousands of jurors about their attitudes on law enforcement. Dozens, maybe even hundreds, of potential jurors, when asked, said that they were inclined to believe a police officer over other kinds of witnesses. That perspective didn't surprise me, but it was one that I didn't share. And to be clear, I didn't take the opposite view that police officers should be trusted less than other kinds of witnesses. Based on experience representing criminal defendants, some defense attorneys referred to police officer testimony as "testilying." I lacked that experience, too, and had no reason to think that was the case. The best way I can describe my outlook was a kind of radical skepticism. If CEOs of major corporations or politicians could commit crimes and lie to cover it up, why couldn't the police?

In this respect as well, my contrarian streak made me wonder why someone who sells drugs or has a criminal record shouldn't be believed? My approach to the victims in the Task Force case was that they deserved to be believed just as much as any other witness. Not more, but not less either. I knew this view was also probably outside the mainstream. Having said all that, I approached the case, fairly or not, with the expectation that most jurors would be inclined to disbelieve people who sold drugs when they testified against the police. Given this, from the start, I began looking for ways to break down the advantages the defendants, the police officers, would enjoy in terms of belief and to overcome the disadvantages our victim witnesses would suffer in terms of disbelief. I was aware that it was going to take a lot of evidence to overcome the former and the latter. As one senior prosecutor in the US Attorney's Office reminded me on more than one occasion, it wasn't every day that we went after the cops, so we better have the goods.

For me, the journey was not from believing police officers to not believing them, as one might expect or that you, as a reader, might anticipate occurring in this book. Rather, it was about finding the truth under very difficult circumstances and then convincing a jury to put aside their disbelief and believe the victims, people who sold drugs and had criminal records, and not believe the defendants, the police.

Figuring out what happened wasn't going to be easy. When the case started, we didn't know what we had on our hands. Fairly early on, however, we learned, to our surprise, that what we were investigating was much bigger than we had originally thought. In addition, the people we were investigating were investigators themselves. That meant they knew the very same techniques that we would use against them. With that knowledge, they also knew how to evade these techniques, and they did. As difficult as that made investigating the case, the hardest part would be trying the case in court, which required convincing a jury to believe the truth we had found. The question of whether we could successfully reach the jurors hung over me until the moment juror number two stood up to deliver the jury's verdict.

TWO

The Alameda

On an ordinary afternoon in the fall of 2015, the phone rang at my desk in the US Attorney's Office, in downtown Baltimore. It was Andrea Smith, who ran a regional drug enforcement task force for the Department of Justice. Andi asked if I could join a meeting in her conference room. She was two floors above me in the same building. I told her I'd be right there.

I had previously told Andi that I was interested in handling fatal heroin overdose cases. The nationwide opioid epidemic, driven by the proliferation of prescription painkillers and the introduction of fentanyl, which is more powerful than heroin, had pushed up overdose deaths in Maryland. As a result, our office was getting more and more such cases. Andi had given me a case in which the defendant, a drug dealer who had supplied the heroin that killed the user, ultimately pleaded guilty. Was this meeting about another one? Andi had hung up before I could ask.

When I got to the packed meeting, I only recognized one person, a DEA agent who'd worked my overdose case. The others looked like undercover police officers who worked drug cases. They had facial hair and tattoos and were dressed in jeans, t-shirts, and hoodies. Many of them wore baseball caps; one guy even had a man bun. They looked a lot different than the FBI agents I was used to working with.

Andi asked everyone to introduce themselves. The officers around the table were from Baltimore City, Baltimore County (the jurisdiction surrounding the city), and Harford County (half an hour up Interstate 95). They were talking about someone named Antonio Shropshire, a major heroin dealer who operated in and around a shopping center in Northeast Baltimore in the 5600 block of the Alameda, one of the city's three "parkways," meandering streets with tree-lined medians that link major city parks. In broad daylight, Shropshire and his crew sold heroin to people lined up in their cars, in full view of law enforcement.

The Alameda was developed at the beginning of the twentieth century when Baltimore was the sixth-largest city in the United States and growing. By 2015, like so many parts of Baltimore, the boulevard showed what disinvestment and drugs had done to the city in the second half of the twentieth century. Trees still stood along the Alameda, but many of the houses had been abandoned.

Shropshire's customers weren't just from Baltimore. They came from the surrounding suburbs and as far away as York, Pennsylvania. That's why the Baltimore County Police Department and the Harford County Sheriff's Office were there. Both jurisdictions lie north of Baltimore. Shropshire wasn't, however, the only one selling heroin on the Alameda. Another seller, Aaron Anderson, had been under investigation by some of the officers in the room. The theory was that Shropshire and Anderson had tolerated one another for a while, and maybe even had worked together. Prior to the meeting, however, confidential sources had begun reporting that Anderson had developed a higher-quality source of heroin, so now the two were in competition.

Confidential sources in drug cases are usually users or sellers who provide information to law enforcement. They do that, generally, for two reasons. The first is to "work off" their charges after having been arrested; that means exchanging information for having the charges against them dropped or reduced to less serious ones. Sometimes police departments or the local prosecutor's office even enters into a written contract with a confidential source that stipulates what they have to do. The second reason is money; the police get information from confidential sources by paying for it.

Regardless of whether Shropshire and Anderson were working together, they had something else in common: their customers were dying from fatal overdoses. In the meeting, we discussed working up a case against Anderson first. If he was arrested and decided to cooperate with law enforcement, he might help us build a case against Shropshire. Harford County and Baltimore County teams had already made undercover purchases from Anderson that could form the basis of federal charges.

I also learned in the meeting that Shropshire had been on law enforcement's radar for some time, but somehow always got away. In July 2015, a confidential source introduced Shropshire to an undercover officer, and Shropshire and that officer subsequently set up a drug deal. On the day it was supposed to take place, Shropshire left the scene as soon as the undercover officer arrived, and he didn't appear to be running late for something else. After the aborted meeting, Shropshire changed his phone numbers. The confidential source later told investigators that Shropshire had asked him if the buyer was a police officer.

The Baltimore County and Harford County police officers had a theory: Shropshire had a cop feeding him information and protecting him. If so, the drug case would also be a corruption case, too. After the meeting, I told Andi I'd like to work on the case, and we agreed to pursue it together with David McDougall, a corporal from the Harford County Sheriff's Office and Scott Kilpatrick, a Baltimore County detective. Andi was getting ready to retire, and later, when she began preparing for her last trial, Derek Hines was assigned to replace her.

The first major decision Andi, Dave, Scott, and I made was to charge Anderson, hoping that he would cooperate after we arrested him. For that to happen, we needed to keep Anderson's arrest a secret, so we took a sealed criminal complaint and arrest warrant to a US magistrate judge.

In federal courts, defendants can be charged in two different ways. The US Constitution mandates that all serious charges be brought by a grand jury. A grand jury, as the name suggests—grand, from French, meaning "big"—is a large jury, consisting of twenty-three members, sixteen of whom have to be present at any given time for the grand jury to conduct business. By contrast, a trial jury is formally called a petit jury—think petite, meaning "small," in French—because there are only twelve jurors. Grand jurors, like petit jurors, are members of the community called at random to serve. In Baltimore, a grand jury sits one day a week for eighteen months, while a trial or petit jury sits every day for the length of the federal trial, which is usually a week or two.

During their one-day-a-week of service, the grand jurors hear from witnesses, who might be civilians or law enforcement. The witnesses present testimony on a variety of cases, ranging from drug dealing to public corruption. The grand jury sits in the federal courthouse but not in a courtroom like a petit jury. Since their meetings are secret, they meet behind locked doors. No one is allowed into the grand jury room except the grand jurors themselves, prosecutors, the witnesses, and the court reporter, or stenographer, who takes down everything everyone says.

In most cases, federal prosecutors present an indictment to a grand jury as the culmination of an investigation. The grand jury, applying the standard of probable cause, then decides whether there is enough evidence to support the charges. Probable cause as a standard of proof is set out in the Fourth Amendment, but the Constitution doesn't expressly define what it means. Thus, federal courts, including the Supreme Court, have defined probable cause in a variety of contexts. A practical and flexible concept, it is sometimes analogized to "more likely than not," but that's admittedly an oversimplification. In this context, the grand jury decides whether it is more likely than not that the defendant broke the law. It's not the same high burden the government bears to prove that someone is guilty of a crime at a trial, where the standard of proof is beyond a reasonable doubt. The grand jury makes its decisions on whether there is probable cause that the defendant committed a crime based on witness testimony, documents, recordings, and other forms of evidence. If twelve members of the grand jury believe there to be probable cause, then they charge the person. This is another difference between grand and petit juries. At trial, the petit jury's decision must be unanimous.

In a smaller number of cases, a prosecutor will go to a US magistrate judge with a criminal complaint. In this scenario, the judge, rather than a grand jury, decides whether there is probable cause to believe the charges against the defendant. The evidence is presented to the magistrate judge in the form of an affidavit from a police officer or federal agent, who swears before the judge, under oath, that the contents of the affidavit are true.

Criminal complaints are used when speed is necessary, when there isn't time to go to the grand jury. I used one after learning that a suspect was attempting to flee the country, having booked a one-way international flight. They are also used when secrecy is necessary. Even though grand jurors take an oath not to tell anyone what they learn during their service, there's always the risk of leaks. If we want to propose to an arrestee that he or she work with law enforcement in an ongoing investigation, for example by making recordings of other people involved in the crime, or "wearing a wire," we have to keep the fact that they've been charged a secret. This was the case with Anderson, whom we were hoping would agree to cooperate.

The magistrate judge approved the criminal complaint against Anderson and also authorized a search warrant for an apartment on Marnat Road, in Baltimore County, where Anderson lived with his girlfriend, and for Anderson's Jeep. We got the warrant for his apartment and car because if drugs or guns were recovered from either location, that might provide an incentive for him to cooperate because it would greatly reduce his chances of getting off.

Dave and Scott had previously gone to a local judge to get a warrant to attach a GPS tracking device to Anderson's Jeep Cherokee. To get that warrant approved, they had to establish probable cause that the movement of the car would reveal evidence of a crime. Probable cause for a GPS warrant is often established by law enforcement conducting surveillance. What law enforcement typically sees is the suspect driving the target car to a drug sale. The judge would likely infer that it's probable that the suspect will use the car for that purpose again and that law enforcement might be able to identify others involved in his drug dealing business by tracking the car. Probable cause for searching a home is similar: if surveillance captures a suspect coming and going from his residence between drug deals, the judge can infer that the suspect stores drugs and cash from the sales at the house.

In the run-up to arresting Anderson and executing the search warrant at his apartment, investigators were monitoring the GPS device on his Jeep. They noticed that Anderson wasn't going home anymore. Instead, the GPS showed him going to a nearby motel. Law enforcement also saw Anderson and his girlfriend talking on cell phones on the hotel balcony, so they were clearly staying there. We added the motel to the search warrants. On October 19, 2015, Baltimore County Police, under Scott's lead, arrested Anderson coming out of his room at the motel and searched his car.

Dave called Andi and me after the arrest. Anderson was being held at Baltimore County's Cockeysville Precinct, a low-slung single-story brick building set back from the street. He was willing to talk. Scott met me at the door and led me to a drab conference room, where Anderson, hunched forward and looking down at his feet, sat at the table occupying most of the room. He was small and looked young, but at 27 he was already on the older end of the spectrum for heroin dealers. He wore a knit winter hat despite the room being warm. In the middle of the table sat a Chick-fil-A bag. One of the agents must have bought him lunch.

We interviewed Anderson for several hours that afternoon and made two surprising discoveries. The first explained Anderson's and his girlfriend's move to the motel. Dave explained to me that when the team went to execute the search warrant at Anderson's apartment on Marnat Road, they found the door damaged and the place torn apart. There were no drugs or money inside. Anderson told us why: the apartment had been robbed a week or two earlier. Anderson was north of Baltimore when it happened, but his girlfriend had been at home. A gunman threatened to kill her if she didn't tell him where the money was. She did, and the robbers stole $12,000 in cash, a Rolex watch worth approximately $10,000, a gold chain worth $3,000, and a large quantity of heroin worth about $64,000. For obvious reasons, Anderson never reported the robbery to the police.

Anderson suspected that Antoine Washington, a rival drug dealer in Shropshire's organization, was responsible for the robbery. That would be consistent with the theory that Shropshire and Anderson were in competition. Investigators later found a jail call that suggested that Anderson might be right. When someone is in a Maryland jail, he or she can make phone calls. Callers on both ends are told that they are being recorded, but despite this warning, arrestees routinely make incriminating statements. On January 4, 2016, someone called Shropshire from jail. The caller told Shropshire that he had heard that Anderson had been robbed. Shropshire told the caller he'd heard the same thing. Shropshire then said something that sounded ominous. He told the caller that Anderson was "lucky that shit happened that way," implying that Anderson might have been killed if he had been at home. Shropshire also knew that money and a Rolex, which is awfully specific, had been stolen from Anderson's apartment. Thus, maybe Anderson was right, and Washington, who sold drugs for Shropshire, had done the job.

The second surprising discovery was under Anderson's car. After we finished interviewing him, Scott walked with us into the hallway and told us that a second GPS tracker had been found on Anderson's Jeep. Scott had only put one tracker on it.

Who put the other one there?

Law enforcement maintains "deconfliction" databases in which police departments log targets under investigation to make sure multiple police departments aren't investigating the same person at the same time. According to the deconfliction database, we were the only ones investigating Aaron Anderson.

Later that day, Dave contacted the company that sold the second tracker. They gave Dave the name of the person who had bought it and was paying the monthly service charge using a personal credit card. Dave then checked a Maryland court database to see if the person had a criminal record and found the name listed dozens of times in court records—but not as a defendant. Instead, he was a BPD detective, Jonathan Crawford, assigned to something called the Gun Trace Task Force. Maybe he was investigating Shropshire but hadn't logged his investigation in the deconfliction database? That was my first thought. The tracker that Crawford put on Anderson's Jeep could be monitored using a smartphone app. Crawford or whoever was using the GPS device should have realized that it had stopped near a Baltimore County Police Department precinct on the day of Anderson's arrest.

Why hadn't we heard from him?

The situation was suspicious. The BPD had its own GPS trackers, so why would a police officer buy a tracker and pay the monthly service fee with his own money? Was he using an "off the books" tracker because he couldn't get a warrant for it? That was possible. My initial reaction to the second tracker's discovery gave law enforcement the benefit of the doubt—I presumed that the "good guys" were perhaps cutting corners to catch some real "bad guys." That seemed the most plausible explanation, but given what we were investigating—whether a police officer was helping Shropshire—we were also willing to consider something more nefarious. That's what made this case so different.

Sloppy police work happens. Prosecutors see it, and sometimes have to defend it in court, for example, when a defendant files a motion to suppress evidence seized in a search. We were going one step further, however, one big step. We were using our experience as investigators to consider whether the police were the ones committing the crimes. Specifically, was the tracker being used by a police officer to help Shropshire and his crew, in this case, to commit a home invasion? Why the second tracker had been placed on Anderson's car was an ongoing mystery—as was the identity of who committed the robbery at Marnat Road—until much later in the investigation.

Dave told the FBI about the second tracker and the fact that it had been bought and maintained by Crawford, a BPD detective on the Gun Trace Task Force. Within a few days, I got a call from the corruption squad supervisor, who told me the FBI was opening a corruption case to investigate whether a police officer was helping Shropshire. Now we had two teams working on the case: the Shropshire drug case, staffed with investigators from the Harford County Sheriff's Office and the Baltimore County Police Department, and the police corruption case staffed by the FBI. They worked largely in parallel because of the sensitivity of what the FBI was investigating. Erika Jensen, who had until recently been on the FBI's gang squad, was the lead case agent for the Bureau.

Before Erika joined the FBI, she had written code for encryption software. She brought the same degree of rigor and precision she had used in that work to the FBI. Before joining the corruption squad, Erika had investigated drug and gang cases in Chicago and Baltimore. These cases were built on the testimony of members of a drug organization or gang who had "flipped," that is, who had been charged and then decided to plead guilty and cooperate with law enforcement against other members of their group. Such witnesses don't enter the courtroom in business suits, like the witnesses I was used to handling. They arrive in orange jumpsuits and with long criminal records. The common attack on them from the defense side is that they would say anything to get their sentences reduced, so the jury shouldn't believe them. Working with these witnesses is challenging. To connect with them, agents and prosecutors often have to navigate racial, cultural, and class lines, and we had to do that in our case. Nearly all the witnesses we tried to interview didn't want to talk to us at first. Some adamantly refused, but Erika was able to convince most of them to speak with us, something she had done in previous gang cases.

Drug cases also involve the testimony of witnesses who live in the real and metaphorical borderland between the illicit economy and the legitimate one. These people—the girlfriends, wives, fathers, mothers, brothers, cousins, and friends of people who use or sell drugs—are also challenging witnesses. In the first instance, they can be very hard to find, sometimes having no fixed address or job. Just locating them takes a special skill. Once they're found, getting them to talk can be an even bigger challenge. They are deeply skeptical of law enforcement, and unsurprisingly, their loyalties tend to lie with their loved ones, not necessarily with the truth. Erika managed to convince these witnesses to talk to us, too.

Drug cases are also built using physical surveillance and, perhaps most importantly, wiretaps. Erika had written dozens of wiretap affidavits before joining our case, and it showed. The combination of the rigor and precision needed to write computer code and the street experience gained by a drug agent working with witnesses and wiretaps made Erika the perfect FBI agent to put together a case like this one.

Later, John Sieracki, a BPD sergeant specially assigned to the FBI's corruption squad, joined our investigation and became an indispensable partner for Erika. John was a task force officer, the name given to local police officers who work with federal law enforcement, including the FBI, DEA, and other agencies, on federal cases. Such an arrangement is common in federal law enforcement investigations of narcotics and violent crime. What was unusual in this case was that a task force officer, John, was working with the FBI to investigate his own agency, the BPD. John had worked his way through the BPD, ultimately landing in "internal affairs," officially the Internal Investigations Division. In addition to being a terrific investigator, John brought an insider's perspective to the BPD that proved to be invaluable. He knew the officers we would come to investigate, their reputations, and their allies in the department, among other things. John also knew how the BPD worked or didn't work. The BPD wasn't like the FBI or any other federal law enforcement agency with which I was familiar. Sometimes I felt more like an anthropologist than an investigator as we tried to make sense of what was going on in the BPD.

John was our guide.

Our first suspect in the hunt for the corrupt cop wouldn't be Crawford, who had bought the GPS tracker and paid its monthly service fee, but a BPD officer named Momodu Gondo, who served on the Gun Trace Task Force with Crawford. He had been assigned to the Task Force for a number of years. While Crawford had no apparent connection to Shropshire, Gondo had what can only be described as a suspicious relationship to him.

Gondo's nickname was "G-Money." He wore expensive clothes and drove a Mercedes, all on a police officer's salary. His relationship with Shropshire had not gone unnoticed within the BPD. In 2013, a BPD detective named Roger Gaines had complained to the FBI about Gondo. Although what he told them didn't sound good, it also didn't sound like a crime. In December 2015, Erika reinterviewed Gaines, and he told her what he had previously told the FBI. But the context had changed. She learned that Gaines and Gondo had bumped into Shropshire at a restaurant. Gondo introduced Gaines to Shropshire, vouching for Shropshire and even referring to him as "his brother." Gaines knew Shropshire was a drug dealer and was alarmed that Gondo seemed to be close to him, prompting him to contact the FBI.

Gaines also told the FBI that Gondo had a relationship with a man named Glenn Wells, who sold drugs for Shropshire. The Alameda connected Gondo and Wells. Gondo's childhood home had been on the Alameda, and Wells had grown up around the corner from him. Their backyards almost touched. Gondo and Wells's friendship continued into adulthood, even as Gondo went into law enforcement and Wells started selling drugs. Wells summed up their relationship in a phone call to Gondo, which we heard later in the investigation. Wells was set to report to prison to serve a short sentence, and he had called Gondo the night before to say goodbye. Wells said that he told people that his "best friend" had gone "right," but that he himself had "went left." Gondo chimed in, "Both still here getting money." The question we were trying to answer was how.

It turned out that Wells had introduced Gondo to Shropshire, and Gondo and Shropshire had become friends. Gaines had no information that Gondo's relationship with Shropshire was anything other than personal. Even so, I was surprised by it. I could understand that you don't pick the people you grow up with or who live around the corner from you, but if you're a police officer, would you start up a friendship with a drug dealer? I assumed that a police officer would cut off contact with someone who sold drugs, even if they had been close as children. These were assumptions that this case disavowed. What I thought was a sharp line between lawbreakers and law enforcement was blurred.

Two days before Christmas, I got a call from Erika late in the afternoon. I was at home with my kids, who were on holiday break.

"You're not going to believe who used to live next door to Anderson," Erika said.

I had no idea.

"Jemell Rayam," she revealed.

Rayam was Gondo's partner on the Gun Trace Task Force. Erika had pulled the personnel records of all the Task Force members. In Rayam's file she found a change of address form, something another agent might have ignored. Rayam had lived in the same apartment building on Marnat Road as Anderson from 2011 until April 2015, which was only six months before the robbery at Anderson's apartment. In fact, they had lived next door to each other, in the only two apartments on their floor.

"I had to read it twice. I couldn't believe it," Erika told me.

So now we knew the following: an illegal GPS tracker owned by Crawford, a member of the Task Force, had been put on Anderson's car; Rayam, another member of the Task Force, had lived next door to Anderson; Gondo was a friend of Shropshire, Anderson's rival drug dealer who seemed to know a lot about the robbery; and Anderson suspected Washington, a member of Shropshire's crew, was behind the robbery. All this suggested that the Task Force had been in on the home invasion at Marnat Road. But it wasn't proof.

That would come later.

THREE

East 25th Street

The first big break in the investigation came on East 25th Street, a strip of road cutting across the center of Baltimore and home to a number of auto body shops. A wiretap would lead us to one of the shops in particular. We felt that a wiretap—or "going electronic," as a colleague called it—was the only way to figure out if Gondo was really helping Shropshire, and if so, prove that to a jury. The latter held just as much importance as the former. The issues of belief and disbelief that the Gun Trace Task Force case raised applied to the jury that would ultimately decide the case just as much as they applied to us.

There is an elaborate set of rules for getting a wiretap, some imposed by statute and some imposed by the DOJ on itself. Working up to a successful wiretap application can sometimes take months. To get one, investigators have to establish probable cause to believe that the targeted phone is being used to commit a crime and that intercepting calls or texts, or both, will reveal evidence of the crime. It is the same standard used for criminal complaints and search warrants.

As with a search warrant, a law enforcement officer makes this showing through a detailed affidavit sworn out before a judge. In the case of a search warrant, the authorizing judge is a US magistrate judge; for a wiretap, it's a US district court judge, the same judges who preside over criminal trials in the federal system. That a district court judge, appointed by the president and confirmed by the US Senate, must approve a wiretap reflects the view that such an intrusion requires more oversight than a search warrant. This heightened level of oversight is reflected in other requirements as well. For instance, DOJ headquarters has to approve each and every wiretap in the country, which is not done for search warrants. In addition, after the tap is installed, the prosecutor must report to the judge who approved the wiretap on the progress, or lack thereof, that law enforcement is making. The prosecutor has to submit such reports every ten days, summarizing the calls and texts intercepted. If the wiretap isn't producing results, or if it has produced what the government sought in terms of evidence, it could be turned off.

In any event, the authorization to tap is only granted for thirty days. If the government wants to continue to tap the phone, it has to go through the whole process again. Because the end of a thirty-day cycle sometimes falls on a weekend, and because the intensive review process that wiretap applications undergo at DOJ sometimes doesn't finish until after the workday ends, I have had to go to judges at their homes to get a wiretap or a wiretap extension signed at night and on weekends. In the Task Force case, I had to make such home visits on more than one occasion.

Investigators must show that the specific phone they seek to tap will be used to commit a crime. It's not enough to say that people who sell drugs often use cell phones or have to use cell phones or some other inference like that—the wiretap applies to a specific phone involved in the commission of a crime. The path to getting a wiretap usually starts with identifying a specific phone number associated with the target of an investigation. In a drug case, this often comes from a confidential source who is a customer of the target drug dealer.

In our case, members of the Shropshire drug organization would arrange meetings via cell phone and then exchange drugs for money at a predetermined place in and around the Alameda Shopping Center. Often the buyer would remain in their car, and someone, "the hitter," would approach their window to give them drugs and take their money. To arrange these meetings, the customers had to call a number—the one for the "money phone," so called because that phone was how the drug organization made its money. The number changed often, usually on a monthly basis, but sometimes even more frequently, to try to stay ahead of wiretaps. These phones were also referred to as burner phones, because the drug organizations would "burn" or destroy them after a short period of time. To retain customers, when the number changed, texts would go out to all the numbers in the money phone giving them the new one.

There are numerous challenges to establishing that a phone number is associated with a drug dealer. Burner phones are prepaid and aren't registered to any particular user. They can be bought, anonymously, from phone stores or even kiosks in shopping malls. Also, drug buyers often don't know the real names of the people who sell to them; they just know them by street names or nicknames. Shropshire, for example, was "Brill"; Anderson was "Black." Complicating matters further, the money phone sometimes got passed between different members of the drug organization. In addition, the person who answers the call or text setting up a meeting isn't always the same person who shows up to hand off drugs and take the buyer's money. So, even if law enforcement has surveillance of a dealer selling drugs, it can be hard to establish that he is the person on the other end of the phone who set up the transaction—which is what you need to do to get a wiretap.

Another way to show that a phone is being used in drug sales is through analysis of the phone numbers calling the money phone and the phone numbers that the money phone is calling. To produce this kind of pattern analysis, a prosecutor can ask a court's permission to install a trap and trace device, which records incoming calls to a particular phone, and a pen register, which records outgoing calls. The two technologies are often referred to collectively as a "pen," because the pen register is the older of the two techniques. This technology allows law enforcement to see, in real time, the phone numbers calling and being called by a particular phone number and the duration of the calls.

It doesn't provide access to the content of the calls or text messages, but it allows law enforcement to potentially see a pattern consistent with drug trafficking activity. That pattern can then be described in the wiretap affidavit in support of a finding of probable cause.

Prosecutors have to get permission from a US magistrate judge to install a trap and trace device and a pen register, for which the evidentiary burden is a "reasonable suspicion," which is lower than probable cause. If a confidential source tells a police officer that he or she called a certain number to set up a drug purchase, that gives law enforcement reasonable suspicion that the number the purchaser called is being used in narcotics sales. Law enforcement might also conduct surveillance and see a known drug purchaser, someone whom the officer had previously arrested, going to a certain location, such as a house, for a brief period of time. If the officer knows that purchaser's phone number, again perhaps from a previous investigation or from a confidential source or some other way, the officer can look through toll records for the purchaser's phone, which can be obtained via a subpoena. If the officer sees that the purchaser made a call to the number that investigators want to put the pen on, the "target phone," before going to that location, that establishes reasonable suspicion that the target phone is being used to set up a drug sale. In general, a high volume of calls or text messages all with a short duration is also indicative of drug sales.

Once a phone number is identified as a money phone, the next step is often to initiate a "dirty call"—one setting up a meeting to buy drugs or ask for prices or involving something else related to the sale of narcotics. This, again, often is done by a confidential source or maybe an undercover police officer or both; a confidential source can be used to introduce an undercover police officer to a drug seller, after which the officer establishes a direct relationship with the drug seller. Confidential sources can be difficult to manage because they are, necessarily, a drug addict and may prove unreliable or unable to take direction well.

To get a wiretap that intercepts voice communications, the dirty call has to be an actual phone call. To get a wiretap that intercepts text messages, the dirty "call" has to be a text message. The authorization from the court is specific to the type of communication, so access to one doesn't allow access to the other. Sometimes law enforcement starts, for instance, with intercepting text messages and then expands to voice calls if, in the course of intercepting texts, the text messages show that the phone user is also communicating about drug sales through voice calls. The government also has to show that it has exhausted all other investigative techniques before applying for a wiretap. This is based on the view that a wiretap is more invasive than any of the other things law enforcement can do to gather evidence. So, in the application to the court, the government has to state everything it has tried in attempting to gather evidence up to that point and why they were insufficient.

It took the fall of 2015 and winter of 2016 to develop enough evidence to get a wiretap on Shropshire. On March 8, 2016, the tap on Shropshire's phone went live. Not long after that, we got permission to attach a GPS tracking device to Shropshire's car. The day after we attached it, investigators received an alert that the tracker had either been tampered with or moved. The signal was coming from somewhere around East 25th Street. Less than twenty minutes after the alert came through, investigators intercepted a call from Shropshire's phone. It was to Gondo.

Gondo didn't at first recognize Shropshire's voice. Shropshire quickly got to the point.

"Uh, I took the car, I took the car to the shop," Shropshire said. He then paused as if searching for words.

"Okay," Gondo said.

"And, uh, the thing was, the thing was lit."

Another long pause.

"Okay," Gondo responded, with a tone that said he understood what Shropshire meant.

We also understood what Shropshire meant. "It" was the GPS tracking device we had put on his car the day before. A mechanic must have found it, and the tracker was indeed "lit"; it had a red light that went on when in operation.

"What to do with it?" Shropshire asked.

It was a remarkable thing to hear—someone who sold drugs had found a GPS tracking device on his car, put there by law enforcement. Now he was calling a police officer to find out what to do next.

Gondo had a choice to make. Which side was he on?

He paused. We could literally hear him deciding.

"Uh . . . what time the shop close?" Gondo asked.

Shropshire said they closed at 8:00 p.m. It was after five o'clock, and Gondo was in Philadelphia. He'd be lucky to beat traffic to be able to see the device for himself at the shop.

"Is this an iPhone?" Gondo asked.

"Yeah," Shropshire responded.

"Just FaceTime me, yo," Gondo told him. Then they hung up.

FaceTime, the Apple video calling app, uses the Internet, not a cell signal, which meant our wiretap couldn't intercept it. As a police officer, Gondo knew this. He also knew the app would allow him to see the GPS device from Philadelphia.

Eighteen minutes later, the FBI intercepted a call from Gondo to Shropshire. Gondo confirmed to Shropshire that the device was indeed a law enforcement tracker, not one put on by a rival drug dealer.

"Ain't no question," Shropshire responded. "I'm gonna pop it on somebody else car."

"You know, I don't even know who I'm talking to, so whatever you do, you do," Gondo said.

This last statement seemed like a lame attempt by Gondo to cover himself or a signal to Shropshire that he would deny the conversation ever happened if it came to that.

"Just be mindful of that, brother," Gondo said. "You definitely gotta get rid of it."

At this point, whether Shropshire was mindful or not didn't matter. We had them on tape, and when Gondo said, "I don't even know who I'm talking to," it was too late. We knew.

The theory that Shropshire had a cop helping him was no longer just a theory. And our suspicions that it was Gondo had been confirmed. But while the call from the body shop answered some questions, it left more unanswered. At the meeting in Andi Smith's conference room at the very beginning of the case, investigators posited that Shropshire had stayed ahead of law enforcement for years because he had a cop helping him. That suggested a relationship that involved more than just the GPS tracker. In any event, the most important consequence of Shropshire's call to Gondo was that it was the kind of dirty call that could enable us to tap Gondo's phone.

On April 28, 2016, a wiretap on Gondo's phone went live. We hoped that spinning to Gondo's phone, as the practice of moving from one wiretap to another is called, would give us a full picture of what Gondo was doing to help Shropshire and Wells. It didn't take long.

Two days later, Gondo called his girlfriend, who worked at a high-end Washington, DC, nightclub.

"I don't make $1,200 in one day, you feel me, without me doin', you feel me, some other—I mean, I can, I do it," he said.

His assertion was convoluted and suspicious. What "other" thing could he do to make $1,200 in a day? Later in the conversation, Gondo returned to the topic of money.

"Just stack money and do what you have to do, you feel me?" he said. "You know me. That's just it; I'm good. I'm good. I'm good. I come from money, I have money, it's not even about that . . . I recoup it, I get it back quick, ten-fold, you feel me?"

What sideline would allow a police officer to "recoup" his money "ten-fold"? It sounded like he was selling drugs. It particularly made sense for a police officer who had relationships with drug dealers. Gondo gave us what we thought was the answer a week later, when the FBI intercepted another call from him to his girlfriend. It was 4:18 a.m.

"Where did you go today?" his girlfriend asked.

"I sell drugs. That's what I did today," Gondo said matter-of-factly, if a bit slurred, perhaps from being drunk.

Often people who sell drugs use code when they talk on the phone. Heroin is called "boy" and cocaine "girl." Ounces are "onions." Crack cocaine is referred to as "orange" or "blue," based on the color of the tops of the vials it's packaged in. For our case, we weren't going to need the DEA code breakers to tell us what Gondo had said.

To be clear, the focus of the investigation at this point was not yet about the Task Force. Even questions about Rayam raised by his having lived next door to Anderson related back to Shropshire.

All that was about to change.

FOUR

North Longwood Street

In 2016 as April turned into May, our investigation went in a different direction. It happened, without warning, at the intersection of North Longwood Street and West North Avenue, on Baltimore's west side.

Before May, my journey to find the truth had been moving in one direction. The theory presented in the first meeting in Andrea Smith's conference room at the US Attorney's Office in Baltimore was that a police officer was helping a drug dealer stay ahead of law enforcement. When Shropshire found the GPS tracker we put on his car, his call to Momodu Gondo confirmed the theory. When we later heard Gondo tell his girlfriend he sold drugs, it all made sense. I was about to learn, however, that Gondo had been up to more than that. Reaching that conclusion raised new questions of belief and disbelief.

The FBI had tapped Gondo's phone at the end of April. In a small, locked room at the FBI's Baltimore office, a team of monitors listened to Gondo make and receive calls in real time. We expected to hear him talking to Shropshire about police activities or maybe Shropshire telling Gondo about his drug crew, but that was before Erika told me about an arrest Gondo had made. It stood out because the police report Gondo had written contradicted what the FBI had heard on the wiretap. Why?

On May 9, the FBI had intercepted a conversation between Gondo and one of his confidential sources setting up a drug deal. The source was going to sell about $700 worth of Xanax to someone she referred to as "White Boy," who, according to her, always carried a gun and was going to bring another gun into Baltimore that he could sell to her. Guns were what the Task Force was after, so this sounded like a legitimate police operation, at least at first.

Two days later, on May 11, Gondo was back on the phone with the same source. Both were in cars, driving. The source was on her way to meet White Boy.

"They here, I just seen 'em behind me," the source said. When she gave Gondo the signal, he pulled White Boy over, and the call ended.

Five minutes later, Gondo called the source back. "We got them pulled over," he said. The source told Gondo that White Boy should have a gun in the right pocket of his jacket. He always carried a gun, she told Gondo, because he came with "so much money and they be scared." She added, "He be thinking he gonna get robbed, so that's why he comes every time with it."

White Boy was right to be scared about being robbed. Gondo and the source kept talking after White Boy was pulled over. He wasn't wearing a jacket, Gondo said, and the officer who had searched him didn't find a gun. The source insisted a gun had to be in the car because White Boy "never comes without it." She told Gondo to check under the seat and in the trunk. When the call ended ten minutes later, they still hadn't found a gun. Fifteen minutes later, Gondo called the source. They'd finally found a gun.

Gondo's police report on the incident claimed that members of the Gun Trace Task Force had conducted a traffic stop of someone named Nathan Danziger. The suspect, a.k.a. White Boy, was, indeed, white. Gondo wrote that after the vehicle had been stopped, Detectives Daniel Hersl and Jemell Rayam approached the car, and Hersl observed Danziger "reaching from his right pants pocket, placing a small caliber firearm into a camouflage backpack." After that, wrote Gondo, Danziger was "immediately placed into custody for officer safety."

We knew from the phone call between Gondo and his source that this wasn't what happened. In addition, we hadn't just heard what happened; we'd also seen it. A city-operated closed-circuit camera covers the intersection of North Longwood Street and West North Avenue, and footage from it confirmed what we had heard Gondo telling his source, which contradicted the police report: The police stopped the car. Hersl approached the passenger side. There had been no quick arrest, as Gondo wrote in the police report; the encounter played out over a much longer period of time. It was the discrepancies between what the FBI heard in the contemporaneous conversation and what Gondo wrote in the report that prompted the bureau to tell me about the incident.

Again, why did Gondo lie in his report? Did he write a phony report to make the arrest sound better? The law would have allowed the police to seize a gun if they had seen someone throwing it, as Gondo had written, but under the circumstances, searching the car for fifteen minutes without a warrant might have gotten the gun suppressed. If Gondo had written a false report once, maybe he'd done it on other occasions as well. What about Rayam and Hersl, the other two members of the Task Force on the scene? Were they in on whatever was going on? Had we stumbled onto a civil rights case? That would change everything. We couldn't let innocent people sit in jail while we conducted our investigation. We would have to get White Boy and his companion out of jail but without tipping off the Task Force that we were on to them. At this point, we still didn't know what we were dealing with.

Hersl had joined the Task Force earlier that spring. Gondo and Rayam had been working together for years. How did Hersl fit into White Boy's arrest? Gondo's report said that Hersl had seen Danziger put the gun in the backpack, which we knew didn't happen. Had Gondo told Hersl what the report said? It would seem risky not to because Hersl would have to testify about it if the case went to court.

Then there was Jonathan Crawford, the other Baltimore Police Department detective on the Task Force in spring 2016. He hadn't participated in Danziger's arrest, but he had bought the mysterious, second GPS tracker found on the dealer Aaron Anderson's car.

What had we stumbled upon? One bad cop or an entire Task Force of bad cops?

We wouldn't know until much later.

Erika wondered if Danziger had made any calls from jail, so we asked our paralegal, Matthew Kerrigan, a recent college graduate, to find any calls from Danziger in the days following his arrest. Matt found one: a call to his girlfriend from jail the day he was arrested. The two talked about the arrest, which was what we were looking for, but they also talked about something else we weren't expecting: money.

"What happened to my money?" Danziger asked. "They said they gave it to you."

"No, that's a downright lie," his girlfriend fired back. "They gave me my wallet with the money that was in my wallet. Your wallet was completely ransacked. They never gave me anything."

"No, it was in my pocket." Danziger practically shouted.

"Ok, so you have the money on you?" his girlfriend asked.

"No! It was in my pocket. It was the first thing they took out when I got out of the car," Danziger sounded desperate. He was trying to make bail, and his money was gone.

This was news to us. It was the first indication of the crime that would come to define our investigation and, ultimately, the case against the Task Force: robbery. The call, however, wasn't conclusive. It raised the obvious question: did the officers rob this man? The initial answer was that we didn't know. Finding the answer required us to look for new kinds of evidence and to look at old kinds of evidence in new ways. Specifically, it required that we believe people like Danziger, people who bought, sold, and used drugs, when they told us about their encounters with the police and disbelieve the police when they told us about those same encounters. Before we got there, however, other questions remained.

Maybe Danziger was just wrong. He could've spent the money but didn't remember that he had. He was using drugs, after all; that's why he was on his way to buy Xanax from Gondo's source. It was also possible that he was lying. Maybe he'd spent the money but didn't want his girlfriend to know. Alternatively, maybe his girlfriend took the money, and she was lying to him. I didn't know what to believe.

My first reaction wasn't that Danziger had to be lying. I suspected he might be, but I was operating in unfamiliar territory. I talked about this jail call with a senior prosecutor in the Narcotics Section of the US Attorney's Office. He told me that arrestees lied on jail calls all the time. I lacked the experience to know when and under what circumstances they did, so perhaps it was precisely my inexperience that made me more receptive to believing Danziger.

I could understand an arrestee telling his girlfriend he didn't have drugs or a gun when he was arrested. He would know that the call was being recorded. And if he needed his girlfriend's help, for example in hiring a lawyer, she might be more willing if he professed his innocence. But Danziger and his girlfriend were talking about money so that he could make bail. That would seem like a moment when he would tell the truth about how much he had had on him when arrested. Another fact that suggested he wasn't lying was that Danziger had been on his way to buy drugs when he was detained. That's when he'd have cash; you can't buy drugs with a credit card. If he had been arrested *after* the sale, it was entirely possible that he would have been broke, but certainly not before. With Danziger's call, our investigation entered a whole new phase. Now we were investigating a robbery, committed by the police.

The FBI pulled the arrest records of Gondo, Hersl, and Rayam, all three of whom had participated in Danziger's arrest. Our paralegal, Matt, started listening to jail calls from people the officers had arrested. He heard people like Danziger discovering that their money had gone miss-ing after an encounter with the police. There were also paper trails: at Baltimore's Central Booking and Intake Center, the local jail where all arrestees in Baltimore are first taken, arrestees get to see police reports that list any money or property seized from them at the time of their arrest. Matt found call after call in which arrestees at Central Booking, upon seeing their police report, discovered that the Task Force hadn't turned in the money they had taken off them. Jail calls weren't enough though. We needed to talk to these people, and I, and ultimately every member of our team, needed to determine whether we could believe them. We couldn't, however, interview them yet. If we did, word might get back to Gondo, Hersl, and Rayam. Only after we had finished with covert techniques, like wiretaps, could we run the risk that we might be exposed.

After Danziger's arrest, we listened again to some calls we'd inter-cepted on the wire. Calls that had earlier seemed run-of-the-mill now sounded different in light of what we'd learned about Gondo and Rayam. One of the calls was made a few days before the Danziger episode. On May 4, Rayam called Gondo at 9:00 a.m.

"Yo, you off today?" Rayam asked. Gondo said he was.

"I may got somethin' to where it may pan out," Rayam said. "The plan is, if I call you, then it's worth [it] for you to come in."

"Okay," Gondo replied.

To that point, the exchange sounded ordinary, at least in a world where you believed Rayam and Gondo were dedicated police officers try-ing to make arrests.

Rayam continued, "I know you got things, thing on, but feel what I'm sayin."

"Right, I got you," Gondo said.

Why didn't Rayam want to say what he meant? That made what he said sound suspicious.

Rayam laughed and then said, "Yeah, yeah, and I then I may just have it where it just me, you, and Sarge. All right?" Sarge was Thomas Allers.

"All right. I got you," said Gondo.

"You just . . . you come and meet, and then you leave in thirty minutes. You know what I mean?"

In light of what we now believe happened to Danziger on May 11, this call one week prior sounded like Rayam setting up a robbery. This was part of the learning process. We had to develop the ability to see, in the context of an arrest or the execution of a search warrant, whether the police were also committing crimes. Rayam wouldn't say what he wanted Gondo to do on his day off. If it had been real police work, he'd have told him, and Rayam made it clear that it would only be the two of them and Allers. That suggested Allers was either in on whatever it was or would turn a blind eye to what Rayam had in mind. And lastly, nothing in police work takes thirty minutes. An undercover drug buy of only a few minutes can take hours to plan and set-up.

So who was Rayam going to rob? Was Allers robbing people, too?

FIVE

The Winnebago Caper

After shifting from investigating Momodu Gondo's relationship to Antonio Shropshire to investigating whether the Gun Trace Task Force was robbing people, our team began feeling enormous pressure to bring charges or "bring the case down." We had evidence of a rogue unit in the Baltimore Police Department. What if someone the Task Force members tried to rob resisted, and the officers hurt or even killed them? People resist arrest all the time when the police are acting like they should. We worried that someone would be more likely to resist if they thought they were being robbed. If someone were to be hurt or killed, we would face justifiable scrutiny over why we hadn't acted sooner to arrest Task Force members. We didn't have the luxury of putting together the perfect case.

If we went to the BPD with the evidence that we had at that point, they probably would have suspended Gondo along with Thomas Allers, Daniel Hersl, and Jemell Rayam. That would incapacitate them, at least in the short term, but if they contested the allegations in a disciplinary proceeding, they might prevail. After a win, they'd be back on the street. The only way we could stop them was to convict them, and that required proof beyond a reasonable doubt. We weren't there yet, and that was the tension.

Even when we could interview the victims, which we hadn't done yet, we knew we'd have another problem; a jury might not believe them. We would later learn that the Task Force members were counting on just that. We, therefore, tried to design a scenario that would yield the kind of objective evidence—a video recording of the Task Force stealing money—that didn't rely on the credibility of any witness. That would bring the case to a conclusion and give us the kind of incontrovertible evidence we thought would win convictions. In other words, the case wouldn't turn on questions of belief and disbelief. At least that was the plan.

The FBI decided to rent a Winnebago, park it at a truck stop off Interstate 95 within Baltimore City limits, and put $4,500 in cash, "bait money," inside the motor home. We'd have the bills' serial numbers so we could track them. The FBI would put some seemingly personal items in the motor home, like dirty clothes, along with half-eaten food and some unused gelcaps (gelatin capsules), and other packaging material to make it look like someone had taken the Winnebago out of state to buy drugs and then driven around Baltimore distributing them.

Once the motor home was staged and in place, a real Baltimore County detective would call Gondo or Rayam and request their assistance. The detective would tell them that the Baltimore County police had arrested someone. The arrestee was cooperating, the story would go. He had told them that he had been driving a motor home, which was now parked in Baltimore City, and he had given his consent for the motor home to be searched. The key was hidden under the bumper. The Baltimore County detective would ask Gondo or Rayam to search the motor home and secure any evidence they found.

No FBI undercover personnel would be on scene. It was too risky. Gondo and Rayam knew how to spot surveillance. Instead, we asked a federal judge for permission to record the whole episode using cameras the FBI had installed inside the Winnebago. We needed a judge's permission because recording Gondo and Rayam inside the vehicle was more like tapping their phone than recording them on the street with CitiWatch cameras, which record public spaces where people don't have any expectation of privacy. We thought Gondo and Rayam might find the money in the motor home and steal it, thinking no one was watching.

Then we could arrest them. Inside the team, we referred to the operation as the "Winnebago caper."

The FBI's staging and the call by a Baltimore County detective to Gondo and Rayam went according to plan, but that's all that did. The Task Force immediately became suspicious. The tap on Gondo's phone revealed him and Rayam discussing whether it might be an "ethics sting," staged by Internal Affairs. Rather than heading to the Winnebago to search it, they sent a fellow detective, Jonathan Crawford, to a nearby hotel to see if it had closed-circuit TV cameras covering the parking lot where the Winnebago sat. If it did, they would be able to see that we had set up the whole thing. The FBI, acting fast, moved the Winnebago before Crawford could get there. Luckily, the hotel didn't have cameras covering the parking lot. The detective then called Gondo to tell him that they had found the Winnebago somewhere else and that an associate of the person they had in custody had moved it.

We barely avoided exposing the investigation. The Winnebago caper failed to produce the kind of incontrovertible proof we sought or bring the case to a swift conclusion. It did, however, show us what we were up against. These guys weren't just robbers, they were cops who knew how to catch robbers, and they didn't want to get caught.

Not long after the Winnebago caper, the team learned that the officer in charge of the Task Force, Sgt. Thomas Allers, was leaving it. Our understanding was that personnel moves took a while in the BPD, but this one didn't. We wondered if someone knew we were looking at Gondo and Rayam and had stepped in to protect Allers. At this point in the investigation, we weren't sharing any information with the BPD, so we were only surmising. That's how upside down things had gotten. A personnel move wasn't just a personnel move anymore. It might be a move against us. At this point, we confronted the issue of whom we could trust.

On June 15, we heard a call that gave us some insight into the overall situation. Gondo began a call to Rayam by asking if he was alone.

Rayam said he was. Gondo then said that someone in the BPD had called him and told him, "Yo, I heard y'all getting looked at."

Was there a leak? How did someone know Gondo and Rayam were getting "looked at"? The caller had also told Gondo that was why Allers had left the unit.

"So he's sayin' that's why he left?" Rayam asked. Gondo said he wasn't sure, noting that the special state-federal drug squad Allers recently joined had recruited him.

Rayam, as if trying to confirm what he was thinking, said, "And on top of that, he still part of it."

"Exactly, I said that as well," Gondo replied. "You get what I'm saying."

What was Allers still a part of? Robbing people with Gondo, Hersl, and Rayam? Turning a blind eye?

This conversation revealed that Gondo had at least one ally in the BPD who was willing to tip him off.

Regardless of why Allers was leaving, we now had a new Task Force sergeant to deal with: Wayne Jenkins.

Jenkins had grown up in Middle River, a blue-collar community in eastern Baltimore County, just outside the city. He had enlisted in the Marines after graduating from high school and after that joined the BPD. Short, stocky, and white, Jenkins had close-cropped hair and a thick neck. In his free time, he was an MMA (mixed martial arts) fighter, and he looked like one. Jenkins had produced a lot of arrests during his time with the BPD. The FBI's Erika Jensen told me that Jenkins was considered a "hard charger" and known as someone who operated "in the gray." I understood that to mean that his tactics fell somewhere between constitutional policing and conduct that violated people's rights. I heard the phrase more than once when I asked people about Jenkins. I didn't believe there was such a place.

Jenkins would be bringing three other detectives with him to the Task Force—Evodio Hendrix, Marcus Taylor, and Maurice Ward. With a new sergeant in charge, the rational thing for Gondo, Hersl, and Rayam to do would be to stop robbing people, or at least stop for a while. We worried what a pause in their criminal activities would mean for the investigation. We still needed more evidence to charge those involved, but how long could we afford to wait?

When Jenkins took over the Task Force, we also debated whether to tell him he had corrupt officers working for him. This turned out to be one of the most consequential decisions we made. The argument for telling Jenkins was that he might actually help us. He was an insider on the Task Force who could report on the activities of Gondo, Hersl, and Rayam and perhaps even wear a wire and record them. He could also help us stage a search warrant with a large amount of cash, like we had attempted with the Winnebago caper. Maybe if we tried again with an insider helping us, a ruse like that would work.

There was also an argument to be made that he needed to know that he had bad cops working for him. Their involvement in any law enforcement operation could taint it, causing potentially good cases and arrests to get thrown out of court. There was also the possibility that Jenkins might be in danger. We had no evidence that Gondo, Hersl, and Rayam were violent, but we had to at least entertain the possibility that they might harm Jenkins if he tried to stop them. We couldn't rule it out. This was another example of how upside down everything had become. We were worried about an officer getting hurt or even killed by men in his own unit.

The argument against revealing the investigation to Jenkins was, principally, that we didn't know if we could trust him. Would Jenkins tip off Gondo, Hersl, and Rayam? That was our fear at the time. Simply having this debate stood the normal way we approached investigations on its head. The police were supposed to be our allies. As we would learn, Jenkins wasn't. By this point, we had developed a healthy skepticism of anyone connected with the Task Force. We ultimately decided not to tell him anything. It turned out to be one of the most important decisions we made, as we learned a few weeks later.

SIX

Westminster and the U-Store

As spring turned to summer in 2016, our main objective was to get a recording of Momodu Gondo, Daniel Hersl, and Jemell Rayam conducting a robbery. Two incidents somewhat bookending the summer of 2016 gave us what we needed and took the investigation in yet another direction.

The first incident, in July, happened at a house in the Baltimore suburb of Westminster. Gondo, Hersl, and Rayam were there, and so was Wayne Jenkins. The second, in early September, took place in a grubby U-Store storage facility in an old industrial part of South Baltimore and involved the entire Task Force, including all but one of its newest members. The locations of the two incidents were miles apart, literally and figuratively. The house in Westminster represented success, the storage facility in South Baltimore the opposite, but one thing had brought the Task Force to both places: money.

Like the investigation in general, this phase started with a tracker. In early June 2016, Gondo and Rayam put an off-the-books tracker on the car of someone they referred to as "Big Dog." We didn't know who Big Dog was but suspected it was someone the Task Force believed to be a big-time drug dealer, somebody who would have lots of cash. Gondo and Rayam sounded excited as they discussed Big Dog on the phone. In a call on June 9, they talked about the car he drove and the house he lived in.

"Yes, Sir," Gondo said. "What about that Lexus?"

"That Lexus—now n***a, you know I save the best for last: that n***a out Westminster, yo," Rayam said. "He at this big ass mansion with a pool in the back."

Westminster, a small city in Carroll County, north of Baltimore City, has a population of about 20,000. It used to be surrounded by farm-land, but many of the farms had been carved up and turned into housing developments featuring large, single-family homes that some, derisively and perhaps unfairly, called McMansions. Big Dog apparently lived in one of them.

Several hours after Gondo and Rayam first spoke, they talked again. "You might wanna wait though, J," Gondo said. "You wanna know where the money house is before you grab him." Later in the conversation, Rayam said, "Damn, this n***a getting money, yo."

In a normal investigation, detectives might comment on things like expensive cars and fancy houses because they show that a drug dealer is selling a lot of drugs and making a lot of money. Drug dealers often have a "stash house," where they keep their drugs, and a "money house," where they keep their money. If the police search the drug house, they won't find the cash, too, and if they search the cash house, they won't find drugs that would give the police the ability to seize the cash. In this case, we would learn, Gondo and Rayam's comments turned out to refer to something else.

After these calls, we heard several others in which Gondo and Rayam discussed putting a tracker on Big Dog's car. After they did so, we heard calls during which they talked about where Big Dog was going, based on the tracker app that Gondo and Rayam had on their phones. The Task Force made its move on July 8, one of the most consequential days and nights in the investigation.

As we listened in real time, we still didn't know Big Dog's identity, but we were able to piece together that Gondo, Hersl, Jenkins, and Rayam had arrested him and his wife outside a Home Depot in Balti-more County, taken them from the store to the Task Force's office at the Barn, in Baltimore City, and then all four had traveled to Big Dog's house in Westminster. Various calls they made throughout the afternoon and evening charted developments. What happened after they searched the house would, up to that point, give us some of the best evidence in the case.

It all began at 3:00 p.m., when Gondo called BPD detective Jonathan Crawford. Rayam, who sounded like he was in Gondo's car, could be heard in the background.

"All right, so they both left Home Depot," Rayam said. "The guy and the girl. They're together."

"They're going home, yo. We can grab them now." Gondo remarked.

He then said, "Hey, Crawford, we're pulling them over."

Rayam added, "He gave the order. We pull them over, bring them back to the academy. That's per Sergeant Jenko."

The "academy" was another way they referred to the Barn, where the Task Force had its offices. Gondo called Jenkins.

"We ah, we headed down now," he said. "We got, um, got the package."

"All right," Jenkins replied. "Just tell them you gotta wait for the U.S. Attorney . . . And then introduce me as the U.S. Attorney."

I couldn't believe it. Impersonating the US attorney? That line was gold. Police officers impersonate drug dealers when they do undercover work, but I had never heard of a police officer pretending to be a US attorney.

Two hours later, at around 5:19 p.m., Crawford called Gondo. Crawford had been sent to execute a search warrant at a location in Baltimore City with the assistance of officers in the Southwest District. We knew from calls earlier in June that Big Dog owned houses in Baltimore City, and the Task Force suspected that he ran his drug business out of them. They must have gotten warrants to search one of the houses and sent Crawford to execute it.

The next call we heard made it sound like the search at the West-minster house might have been over. Gondo called Crawford at 7:38 p.m., and while Crawford's phone was ringing, Gondo could be heard talking to Rayam in the background. "I mean, if they're not gonna take the, it ain't that serious, just leave the fuckin' money."

Rayam said, "Was I loud?"

Gondo laughed and said, "Shit man! Who gives a fuck? Give it to us. We'll take it. Shit, n***a. Yeah, ah. Lemme, lemme, lemme git it. Give it back to me so I can take um, take one stack out of there." Crawford's voicemail answered and the call disconnected.

Gondo and Rayam were reenacting a dialogue they had with offi-cers from the Carroll County Sheriff's Office. We would later learn that the Task Force had called Carroll County to request that it execute the search warrant at Westminster because it wasn't in Baltimore City. Apparently, Carroll County wasn't as enthusiastic as the Task Force about seizing money. Rayam's remark to "just leave the fuckin' money" made it clear that money had been found, but Gondo's comment that he could "take one stack out of there" seemed to reference stealing some of it, not seizing it.

Several hours later, at 10:38 p.m., Gondo got a call from Rayam.

"Yo, real talk, I'm counting," Rayam told Gondo. Rayam sounded angry.

Gondo interrupted him. "No, negative. I would never, c'mon, man." Gondo sounded angry now, too.

"Hey, alright, again yo. Ima count it again, yo. I'm just lettin' you know," Rayam said.

Gondo didn't let Rayam finish, saying, "Hey, I would never."

Then Rayam cut Gondo off, "Hey bro, well, I'm just lettin' you know, if it's a mistake."

Gondo cut back in, "I don't make mistakes countin' money."

Rayam insisted, "I'm lettin' you know, yo. I don't got no reason to lie, man, I'm just lettin' you know, yo."

Gondo then got a call from a woman. "This n***a sayin' I'm three grand short, though," he angrily told her. "I'm just so mad about that."

Why would Rayam be counting money as he drove from a location where they had just executed a search warrant? The police go to great lengths to document what they recover in a search and where it was recovered. This is part of the chain of custody, and it's critically important to establish one so that whatever was seized can later be used in court. Typically, the team executing a warrant will take pictures of items where they are found, put them in evidence bags that are then sealed and marked, and make a detailed inventory of everything recovered. Rayam shouldn't have been counting the money while driving from the scene. On top of that, why would Rayam and Gondo be talking about a missing three thousand dollars?

Jenkins, Gondo, Hersl, and Rayam then met up at a bar in Baltimore called Looney's, in the Canton neighborhood. By 1:39 a.m., Gondo and Rayam were on the move again. After leaving Canton, they headed to the Maryland Live! Casino in Anne Arundel County, about halfway between Baltimore and Washington, DC. A late-night trip to the casino meant they had money to spend. On the way, a now drunk-sounding Gondo called his friend Glenn Wells, who sold drugs with Shropshire.

"Boy, I got in Stu Love butt for you, yo!" Gondo told him. "Stu Love" was a nickname we had heard Gondo and Rayam use for Jenkins.

"I appreciate it, Sir," Wells replied.

"You ain't have to appreciate shit, yo. You my brother," Gondo told him.

This sounded like Gondo had intervened with Jenkins to protect Wells. At 2:07 a.m., and apparently feeling generous, Gondo called his sister. "I'm just getting off, how much cash you need, yo?"

So Gondo had cash to spread around. Another sign that there'd been a robbery at Westminster. After we heard these calls, we went looking for the report the Task Force had written describing what had happened that night. We couldn't locate one. Instead, we found a report submitted by a detective with the Maryland State Police (MSP). He, along with officers from the Carroll County Sheriff's Office, had assisted in the execution of a search warrant with the Task Force on the night of July 8 at a house on Ships Quarter Road in Westminster. This was it.

Police departments often help each other in investigations. The Harford County Sheriff's Office and the Baltimore County Police Department had teamed up to investigate Shropshire, for example, but bringing in another department when robbing someone seemed really risky. What we learned from this incident and others, however, is that the Task Force used other police departments, without their knowledge, to cover up the fact that they were breaking the law, not helping them enforce it.

According to the report, the house in Westminster was owned by a man named Ronald Hamilton, "Big Dog," apparently. According to the report, Rayam had told the Carroll County officers that the Task Force had been waiting for their arrival before executing the warrant. The Carroll County officers searched the house. They found a heat-sealed plastic bag containing $50,000 in the upstairs master bedroom. The MSP officer seized that money, which meant that the $3,000 Gondo and Rayam were arguing about was money they weren't going to turn into BPD. That had to be part of what they stole.

The FBI also got an unsigned copy of the search warrant authored by Rayam for the house. In it, Rayam claimed to have been conducting physical surveillance of Hamilton. We knew that to be untrue because we had heard Gondo and Rayam say they were watching Hamilton's movements using the illegal tracker they'd put on his car. We couldn't find a report of an arrest that night, so we didn't know what had happened to Hamilton and his wife. The Task Force must have let them go. Were they robbed and then let go to keep them quiet? What could the couple tell us about the events of July 8? As in the case of Nathan Danziger and the theft of his money, talking to the Hamiltons would have to wait until after we'd finished using wiretaps and other covert techniques.

Even if we couldn't talk to Hamilton and his wife when we first heard these calls, what we learned from their case still represented a major breakthrough. The incident involving Danziger in May had raised the prospect that Gondo, Hersl, and Rayam had robbed someone they arrested. Now we had intercepted calls where Gondo and Rayam were talking about taking "stacks" of money and then, later, fighting over $3,000 as they sped from a search site. This was much more explicit evidence.

Hersl had taken part in both the arrest of Danziger and the execution of the search warrant in Westminster. Both were signs of his involvement as well. But what about Jenkins? He had only become the officer in charge of the Task Force in June. Had Gondo, Hersl, and Rayam gotten so comfortable around him in such a short time that they were robbing a search site while he was there or doing so without him knowing? Unlikely on both counts.

The more plausible scenario was that he was in on it, too.

The wiretap on Gondo's phone had proved its value in both the Danziger traffic stop and the search warrant for Westminster, but he seemed reluctant to talk on the phone except when he was drunk. We needed a new way to get inside the Task Force, so we decided to bug Gondo's BPD "take home" car.

The BPD gave senior officers like Gondo vehicles that they could use for their police work. Because it was a BPD car, we could obtain a key to it. The agreement that Gondo signed when he got the car informed him that the BPD could "monitor" its use. That meant we didn't need a court's permission to install the bug, like we had to do when we bugged the Winnebago. John Sieracki got BPD permission for us to proceed. The tricky part would be installing a bug without Gondo noticing.

Because Gondo's BPD vehicle was a take home car, it was never left at the BPD lot overnight, denying us easy access to it. An opening came in late summer 2016, when Gondo went to Las Vegas for the weekend. The installation was scheduled for the middle of the night. I went to bed with my cell phone on the nightstand. The phone rang around 2:00 a.m. It was the FBI's Erika Jensen. The bugging team was in Gondo's car and had found something of interest under the driver's seat: a clear plastic baggie containing twenty-seven gelcaps. Erika thought they contained heroin. We discussed what to do.

If we seized the capsules, they would be important evidence in a trial. We wouldn't just have recordings where Gondo talked about selling drugs, we would have "drugs on the table." In that case, however, after Gondo returned, he would know that someone had been in the car. Maybe he would think he'd been robbed. Then again, maybe he would suspect that he was under investigation, which would undermine the effectiveness of the bug. We ultimately decided to take one gelcap, so we could test it at the FBI's drug lab, and leave the rest. We would photograph the others but leave them where they were. That would give us drugs to use at trial without, hopefully, alerting Gondo to his being under investigation. Erika also called my partner, Derek Hines, and they reached the same conclusion.

Not long after the bug was installed, we picked up Rayam talking to Gondo late one evening. He talked about "taxing" an arrestee, which meant robbing him, and giving some of the money to Jenkins and Taylor.

The FBI was able to identify the person Rayam "taxed," because the Task Force Officers put in for overtime. On their overtime slips they claimed to have been conducting surveillance at a storage facility not far from the Baltimore Ravens stadium in South Baltimore. The FBI went to the storage facility and talked to an overnight manager. He told them that the police had arrested a customer named Sergio Summerville. He also gave the FBI video from the facility's CCTV.

The video surveillance showed Summerville leaving the parking lot at approximately 8:00 p.m. Two Chevy Malibus, one dark and one gold, blocked the exit. Six men in dark colored vests with "POLICE" across them in big white letters got out. It was the whole Task Force, except for Evodio Hendrix. This was the first time we saw Maurice Ward and Marcus Taylor, two of the officers Jenkins brought with him to the Task Force, involved in what looked like a robbery. This meant that not only were Gondo, Hersl, and Rayam robbing people with Jenkins, which was what we believed after Westminster, but Ward and Taylor were involved, too. The investigation now was into the whole Task Force, including its newest members.

The gold Malibu was Gondo's car. Then all three cars moved back into the parking lot. Rayam drove the car that had been stopped and searched it. About ten minutes after the stop, Rayam stood near the driver's door and appeared to put something into his left front pocket. We assumed it was money.

The bug picked up another exchange between Gondo and Rayam that caught our attention. Rayam had been talking to Jenkins. Rayam said that Jenkins had offered to "put me on some big shit" and that he had asked Jenkins, "What the fuck you doin' in pockets, it's a fuckin' waste of time man. But he's just like, yo, you know, um, I got Big Dude." The reference to "going into pockets" sounded like stealing small amounts of money from arrestees. "I got Big Dude" sounded like a bigger target.

Gondo asked if Jenkins had brought "his name up," which was what we wanted to know, too, along with Big Dude's identity. Rayam told Gondo that Jenkins had not mentioned him, but according to Jenkins, Big Dude would be good for $200,000.

Rayam said, "He was like if we do, you know, it'll be me and you, and I was like, all right, and G. He was like, yeah. And then I was like, well, what's up with the other dudes, your boys, you know, he was just like, nah, nah, they cool. I love them to death. Then he brought up the one where he, um, when they went outside after eatin' everybody put up 20 dollars, you know what I'm talkin' about? Everybody was, he talked about the time where everybody had 20 gs."

They were talking about a lot of money. A robbery where all three of Jenkins's "boys"—Hendrix, Taylor, and Ward—plus Jenkins would get $20,000 each would be the biggest robbery we had come across yet. This also meant, remarkably, that Jenkins, Hendrix, Taylor, and Ward had been robbing people *before* they joined the Task Force.

"He said that?" Gondo replied, sounding surprised.

"I asked him, how long you think it'll take to get us, 'cause you know, I need 50 gs, right now," Rayam responded. "So he say, how long do you think it's gonna take, I was like a month, naw, we do it right, a couple of weeks. I was like, all right, I'll be hittin' him on them slash days that you give us."

We later learned of an unwritten practice that some sergeants followed. When an officer seized a gun, he was given a day off. This was all off the books; no policy formally approved it. The sergeant would put a slash next to the officer's name in the roll book, as if he were working that day, but he wasn't. In short, Rayam was communicating his willingness to track Big Dude on his day off with the intent of robbing him. That's how motivated he was.

"All right," Gondo responded.

"I tell you, G. If I get somethin' like that, yo, I'm goin' to, I be done . . . I need a break, I need a big one."

So, Rayam needed a "big one." It sounded like a robbery to us, without a doubt.

SEVEN

East Baltimore

In the fall of 2016, our team's covert investigation became overt. The bug had yielded useful information over the summer but wasn't producing much anymore, so we decided to start finding and interviewing victims. That meant the Gun Trace Task Force members might find out about the investigation, but it was a risk we had to take. We needed evidence that we could only get from the victims themselves.

We had identified the victims by pulling the arrest records of Task Force members and then listening to the calls their arrestees made from jail. The jail calls were like time capsules; they told us what had happened and when it happened. If we ever got to trial, they could also help us convince a jury that the victims weren't lying. The victims would undoubtedly be attacked by the defense because they sold drugs or used to sell them or were in relationships with people who sold them. They'd be accused of making things up to get back at the cops. But these recordings—made when the arrestees had every reason to tell the truth about how much money they had or no longer had, because they were desperately trying to make bail—could save them.

The city of Baltimore is defined by an east-west divide. Someone is either from East Baltimore or West Baltimore, which are almost like two different cities. We found victims of the Task Force in both these Baltimores. I learned from interviewing victims that people tended to spend their entire life in the one or the other. As they moved, and our victims often did, it was within, not between, the two sides of the city.

In addition to this phenomenon, demographers have noted a racial overlay, described as the "Black butterfly" and the "white L," that correlates with a whole host of social and economic indicators. East and West Baltimore are the butterfly's wings and overwhelmingly Black. Meanwhile, Baltimore's white population clustered along the waterfront, forming the base of the L, and along a narrow north-south corridor between the two wings, forming the stem of the L, along the butterfly's spine. In terms of income, health (including life expectancy), crime, and other quality of life indicators, residents within the Black butterfly fare far worse than those in the neighborhoods in the white L. The Task Force spent most of their time in East and West Baltimore. This is where we went looking for the truth.

We interviewed victims who then testified in the grand jury. Their testimony was important for two reasons. First, in my experience, witnesses will lie to law enforcement, but not to a grand jury; the victims testifying increased the likelihood that we were being told the truth. Second, the rules of evidence allow for grand jury testimony to be used at trial even if a witness later changes his or her story. Witnesses are often reluctant to testify in open court. Sometimes it's because they're afraid of the defendants, who aren't present when they testify in the grand jury but are at the trial. Most witnesses overcome their reluctance, but some don't or can't. One of the things a recalcitrant witness will sometimes do is claim that they don't remember something, even if they do. Some will even change their story in an attempt to avoid angering a defendant in the mistaken belief that doing so will get them off the witness stand quicker. If any of those things happen, the witness's prior grand jury testimony can be read into the record and treated as evidence by the jury.

We usually interviewed victims and put them before the grand jury on the same day. People had jobs and issues with childcare, so we tried not to inconvenience them. Sometimes they had been hard to find, and we figured this was our one and only shot. We interviewed the victims at the federal courthouse, instead of the US Attorney's Office, because

Baltimore Police Department officers visit with prosecutors every day at the US Attorney's Office. We didn't want them to see any of the victims. Even at the courthouse we took care to avoid bumping into BPD officers as they went to and from hearings and other court proceedings. Usually, we tried to keep witnesses who were in custody but cooperating from being seen by other inmates in court for hearings. If word got back to the jail that someone was snitching, it could get the cooperator attacked or even killed. Now we were trying to keep police officers from seeing the victims. This was another way in which this case was upside down.

We met with the victims in a series of drab courthouse rooms, with empty walls and beat up furniture. There were two right outside the grand jury. They had no windows and got hot when the door was kept closed. The US Attorney's Office maintained a satellite office with four additional interview rooms on another floor of the courthouse. Three of them at least had windows, which was a plus, but one of those had a table that squeaked loudly when touched even a little. I always tried to sit back from it, which was awkward. Another room with a window in the satellite office, again a plus, had a glass-topped table, but the glass was cracked on one side. Someone had put duct tape over the crack, but you still risked getting cut when sitting at the table.

With each victim, we tried to, one, ascertain what they could tell us about the incidents we were investigating and, two, determine whether we could believe them. On the first issue, we had to evaluate each victim and each episode independently of the others, because if we got one wrong, if we bought a false story, it might cause a jury to disbelieve all the others. By this point, it seemed clear that Gondo, Jenkins, and Rayam were crooked and robbing people. But to conclude that they and other members of the Task Force had committed a specific robbery, we needed proof beyond a reasonable doubt because that's what a jury would have to conclude in order to convict them.

On the second issue, the victims we spoke to fell into two categories. The first consisted of victims where we had evidence—like a wiretap,

bug recordings, or CCTV footage—that would tell us if they were lying. That kind of evidence didn't rely on a witness's credibility. The
second category of victims were those where there was no objective evidence to corroborate them, just their jail calls and our personal and
professional assessments of their credibility.

Two of the first victims I met, Antonio Santiful and Herbert Tate, fell
into the second category. They had both been robbed by Hersl in the
same East Baltimore neighborhood on back-to-back days in November 2015. I met Santiful first, interviewing him in one of the small win-
dowless rooms outside where the grand jury meets. It had a small table
in it and a chalkboard with two rules written on it with a paint pen;
the rules had been there for as long as I'd been at the US Attorney's
Office, but I have no idea who wrote them there. Rule number one reads,
"Tell the truth." Rule two states, "Any questions, see Rule #1."

Santiful, in his late twenties, was dressed in loose, faded black clothes.
He spoke slowly, and seemed neither comfortable nor uncomfortable
talking to us. He just answered our questions. I spoke with Tate about
two weeks later. We met in the same small room where we had interviewed Santiful. Tate, almost a decade older than Santiful, wore a shirt
and tie. In further contrast to Santiful, Tate was a fast talker and seemed
not to want to be talking to us. His reluctance didn't involve an effort to withhold the truth, rather, he seemed to understand that he
was being asked to testify against the police and was appropriately
uncomfortable.

Santiful had a criminal record: a three-year sentence from a 2008
firearm conviction, and a month in jail for a 2015 drug possession conviction. When he got out, he took a job cleaning office buildings at night.
He had just come from work when his path crossed Hersl's. The company
he worked for paid him "under the table," the phrase he used and
something he told us without hesitation, which was a good sign. Witnesses who can't admit to minor wrongdoing rarely tell the truth.

Tate had a regular job as an HVAC engineer, a trade he had practiced for twenty-one years. He had a high school diploma, some college, and a master HVAC license. Unlike Santiful, he received an actual paycheck and had never done jail time. Tate was probably the best chance we had at convincing a jury to believe the victims. He would be like them: no criminal record, a regular job, some schooling. He may have grown up in East Baltimore, a part of the city that jurors might associate with crime, but by all outward appearances, he wasn't a part of that life.

Santiful still lived in East Baltimore; Tate had moved away. Hersl had arrested them in the East Baltimore Midway neighborhood. In the early twentieth century, East Baltimore Midway had been a segregated white neighborhood. In the 1960s, large industrial employers like the John Deere Company left the city, taking manufacturing jobs with them. Those jobs never returned. East Baltimore Midway experienced some of the most extreme white flight in the second half the twentieth century. In 1950, the neighborhood was almost 99 percent white. Ten years later, it was nearly 80 percent Black, and by 2015, almost 95 percent Black.

Santiful and Tate didn't know each other, but their stories were strikingly similar, which made it easier to believe them. What's the likelihood that two men who had never met would make up roughly the same story? Also making it easier to believe them was that they had both made calls from jail in which they talked about how they had been robbed. Santiful had called his girlfriend from jail hours after his arrest.

"Look, the police took all the money I had. You hear me?" Santiful said.

"Mhm," she responded, sounding unsurprised.

"They took all my shit just now, yo."

"So you got nothing in the house, no nothing?" she asked.

"I just had like seven hundred in my pocket yo," Santiful replied.

When we first heard this call, we didn't know why Santiful had $700 in his pocket. He could have made it from selling drugs, or he might have made it working. I frankly didn't care. We were listening for mentions of lost money. Obviously, if the money was legitimate, that would make the victim more sympathetic to a likely jury. But we would learn at trial that when a victim testified that they had a job and had honestly earned the money the Task Force stole from them, the defense would attack the victim as a liar. In a perverse way, claiming legitimate income opened the victim to credibility attacks that the drug-selling victims weren't exposed to. To be sure, the defense attacked the drug dealers, too, but not for lying about how they made their money.

Santiful's call was the most valuable kind because he said how much he had on him when arrested. We were then able to compare that amount to what the police reported seized and had turned into the evidence control unit after Santiful's arrest. With jail calls when the victim didn't mention a specific number, we anticipated the defense would argue that whatever was in the police report was the correct amount of money that had been seized. That put the word of the arrestee against the word of the police officers. In court, police officers occupy a special place. When they testify, they literally wear a badge of authority. Despite that, they are still supposed to just be witnesses. In fact, one of the standard instructions the judge gives to every jury is to not credit the word of a police officer above other witnesses. The need to give such an instruction suggests that believing the police more than other witnesses is the norm. We, however, had something that might help a jury see through all that: a recording from the day of Santiful's arrest in which he stated the exact amount of money he had on him when the police took him into custody. That recording corroborated the version of events Santiful described to us when we spoke to him in 2017.

Tate had also called his girlfriend after he was arrested. The first thing she did was ask what had happened.

"I don't know," he replied. "I was walkin' down the street; the police came up there. They lock me up, talkin' about some CDS but they didn't find no drugs or none of that shit. Took my money." CDS stands for "controlled dangerous substances," the legal term for drugs.

"What!" his girlfriend exclaimed. She was one of the few people we heard on the calls who seemed shocked when they learned that the police had stolen money. It was surprising to us that someone was surprised.

Hersl had arrested Santiful on November 28, 2015, the Saturday after Thanksgiving. It was unseasonably warm, and Santiful had driven his sister's car to East Baltimore to visit his friend "Goo" at Goo's Aiken Street rowhouse. In Baltimore, people gather on stoops all year long, and sometimes even put out some furniture. Goo had set up a TV on his porch to play video games with Santiful and about a dozen others.

Santiful didn't know why the police showed up. He wasn't selling drugs, and neither was anyone else on the porch. Four officers approached, shooed most everyone away, but put Santiful and another man in handcuffs. They then sat Santiful on the curb and searched him but didn't find anything—no drugs, no gun.

Hersl came up and searched Santiful again. He didn't find anything either, but he took Santiful's keys and kept them, which included the key to Santiful's sister's car. Hersl asked where the car was, but Santiful wouldn't tell him.

Santiful told us that he had $700 in his pocket as he sat on the porch. We hadn't told him about our recording of the jail call from a year and a half earlier in which he told his girlfriend the same thing. This made his story believable. Santiful couldn't remember what day he had been paid, but he knew it had been sometime the preceding week. His car had been impounded—which is why he was driving his sister's car—and he planned to use the money to get it out.

Santiful sat on the curb for about an hour and a half as three officers kept watch before a transport van arrived and took him to BPD's Eastern District. At the station, the police put him in an interview room. As Santiful waited, Hersl came and took him into the hallway, went through his pockets, took Santiful's $700, and returned him to the interview room.

A half hour later, the police took Santiful to Central Booking, where they charged him with nine offenses, including illegal handgun possession and distribution of drugs. Evidently, Hersl had used the keys he had taken from Santiful to find the car that Santiful had been driving. The car had electric locks activated by a smart key, so Hersl must have wandered around pressing the lock/unlock button until he heard a horn beep when he got within range of the vehicle.

Hersl claimed to have found a handgun and drugs in the car. Santiful told us that the drugs and gun weren't his and that other people also drove his sister's car, just like he had. Hersl had no warrant to search the car. When Santiful saw his charging papers, he learned how much money the police had turned in: $218, not $700. Ultimately, state prosecutors dismissed all nine charges against Santiful before the FBI even found him. We didn't know why. Also, he never got his money back—not even the $218 that had been turned in. We had no idea why that didn't happen either.

When we finished interviewing Santiful, we left him alone until his turn came to testify in the grand jury. When I went in to get him, he was asleep. After all, he had worked an overnight shift. When I saw him, it struck me that a man who intended to lie to a federal grand jury wouldn't be able to fall asleep. He wasn't worried about what he had to say because it was the truth.

Tate had grown up in East Baltimore Midway. Hersl had arrested Tate on November 27, 2015, the day before he robbed Santiful, making it the day after Thanksgiving. Tate referred to it as "holiday time" and said he had gone back to East Baltimore Midway to see old friends and some kids he was coaching in basketball at the neighborhood recreation center. Ironically, Hersl found Tate on a street called Robb Street.

A shopping center bisects Robb Street. The southern part, where Tate was walking when Hersl set upon him, is shaped like the head of a hockey stick. It runs due north and then bends back to the northeast until it dead ends at a retaining wall. On November 27, Tate was walking north on Robb Street when an unmarked police car pulled up. He hadn't seen it coming because of the bend in the road. Hersl told one of the other two officers to grab and search Tate. That officer didn't find anything illegal on Tate—no drugs, no gun. All Tate had was some cash, his pay stub, and receipts from bills he had paid. The officer took the money and sat Tate on the stoop of the rowhouse where they stood.

All the police wore plainclothes that day, but Tate recognized Hersl. He'd stopped Tate a few days earlier. It had happened on the same block of Robb Street. Hersl had approached Tate and made him sit down and take his shoes off. Then Hersl told him to stand up, and he unbuttoned the front of Tate's pants. Hersl proceeded to search around his waistline. Hersl also stuck his fingers in Tate's mouth and told him to stick out his tongue. He didn't find anything. All Tate had on him was $600 that he had earned from his job. Hersl didn't take his money that time. Instead, he let Tate go, but warned him, "Next time I see you, you're going to jail." It wasn't clear for what. Hersl wrote the date on a piece of paper and handed it to Tate. Just as a reminder.

Discussing November 27 with Tate, I asked what he had thought when the police stopped him even though he wasn't doing anything wrong.

"They jumped out aggressive," he said. "I mean, they known for being aggressive, so I ain't want to get in no trouble or get beat up."

It wasn't just that he knew not to resist the police in general, he also knew this particular group of police officers. That's how frequently they interacted with the community.

When Hersl stopped Tate on the twenty-seventh, the day Hersl robbed him, Tate had $530 left in his pocket from a $1,163 paycheck he'd gotten that morning. He'd already paid a day care bill—the receipt was in his pocket—and bought gas and groceries. He needed the rest to cover the next two weeks of expenses.

What I learned from interviewing victims in our case, again, nearly all of them from East and West Baltimore, was that carrying cash wasn't uncommon. Many victims told me they didn't have a bank account and had never had one. Instead, they used check-cashing stores to cash their paychecks, if they got a check, and paid bills at a check-cashing store as well. I had my first checking account when I was 18, when I went to college in Baltimore. The idea of not having a bank account seemed incredible to me, but I heard the same thing over and over. I then noticed something for the first time. In my neighborhood in North Baltimore, in one small row of shops alone, there were four bank branches. When I drove through East and West Baltimore, I didn't see any. That was another reason people that grew up or lived in those neighborhoods carried cash.

While Tate sat on the stoop, he watched Hersl go up and down the block looking into vacant homes, peering behind stoops, even breaking up some loose steps. Then Hersl disappeared down an alley at the top of the street for almost ten minutes. When he came out, his hands were empty. Tate had no idea what Hersl was doing, why he'd been stopped, or why he was cuffed and sitting on a stoop. Tate asked why he had been arrested.

One of the other officers told him, "Blue and Whites."

"What are those?" Tate replied, unaware that it referred to heroin packaged in blue and white gel caps.

"I don't have to show you a motherfucking thing," Hersl said, the first words he'd uttered to Tate during the arrest. "We just have to prove it in court."

When a transport van pulled up to take Tate away, the officer whom Hersl had told to search Tate asked Hersl, "What am I doing with the money?" Hersl told him to keep it. Tate asked them to count it, and he wanted to know what would happen to it. "Nobody's going to take your fucking money," one of the other officers said. "I make a hundred and something odd thousand dollars a year. I don't need your fucking money."

Tate later saw the police report describing his arrest. It said Hersl had seized $216 from him, not $530. At some point, the officer who searched Tate must have given Tate's money to Hersl and then Hersl turned some of it into the BPD. Between that officer and Hersl, we believed Hersl would have been the one to steal it. By this point, we had what looked like a pattern of robberies involving Hersl. The pattern was an important part of why we believed the victims. We hadn't seen any such pattern for the other officer.

The $216 figure struck me. It was two dollars less than the $218 in Santiful's police report. Would two men who'd never met have a nearly identical amount of cash on them one day apart? It seemed like Hersl was just putting numbers down in a report and not being very careful or creative. Like Santiful, Tate never got any of his money back. We didn't know why.

It took Tate four days to make bail. In the meantime, he lost his HVAC job because he hadn't shown up for work. A cascade of other consequences followed. He couldn't make his car payments, so his car got repossessed. He couldn't afford his rent, so his landlord evicted him. He had a criminal case hanging over his head, so he couldn't get another job. After months of borrowing money to make ends meet, he finally went back to work in April 2016. He also moved out of Baltimore. He didn't want to live there anymore.

Tate made a big impression on me. I found him utterly convincing. I had no reason to think, and still don't, that he made up what he told us. Even before I met him, I thought the Task Force was robbing people. We had heard enough on the wiretap and the bug for me to reach that conclusion, but after I met Tate, I remember thinking, "This is really happening." I also remember thinking that with a witness like Tate, we would be able to prove it to a jury.

EIGHT

West Baltimore

Antonio Santiful and Herbert Tate and the circumstances of their robberies were strikingly similar. Both were robbed by Daniel Hersl in the same East Baltimore neighborhood and were relatively young. Santiful had a minor criminal record. Tate had none. Neither of them appeared to be doing anything wrong when arrested, and the charges against them had been dropped before we met with them. If the victims we encountered were arrayed on a spectrum, Santiful and Tate would be at one end. Ronald Hamilton and Oreese Stevenson, a victim whom we would learn about in the fall of 2016, would be at the other end.

Like the similarities between Santiful and Tate, there were also things Hamilton and Stevenson had in common. They were both older than Santiful and Tate, had significant criminal records for drugs, and had served time in federal prison. In one major difference, the Gun Trace Task Force had caught Stevenson with drugs when it robbed him, and he admitted to my team that he had been dealing. Hamilton had not been selling drugs and told us he was no longer dealing.

We learned about Hamilton from the calls we intercepted on Momodu Gondo's phone the night he along with Hersl, Wayne Jenkins, and Jemell Rayam searched Hamilton's house in Westminster in July 2016. We identified Stevenson when we reviewed the arrest records for Jenkins, Evodio Hendrix, Marcus Taylor, and Maurice Ward. Stevenson had made a call from jail in which he talked about missing money after his arrest, just like Tate and Santiful, though the amount of money stolen from Stevenson, we would ultimately learn, was exponentially larger.

The FBI found Stevenson around the same time they interviewed Tate and Santiful. He lived on the opposite side of the city, in West Baltimore. We didn't have to find Hamilton. We knew from July 8 wire intercepts that he lived in Westminster, but he, too, had a connection to West Baltimore: he and his wife owned rental property there that brought him back into the city and thus into the Task Force's crosshairs.

We needed to talk to Hamilton and Stevenson to find out how much money was missing. In Hamilton's case, we knew the Maryland State Police had seized $50,000, but we also knew that Gondo and Rayam were fighting over a "missing" $3,000, which meant that they had stolen some money before MSP arrived at the house.

In Stevenson's case, we found a police report written by Hendrix, and approved by Jenkins, describing Stevenson's arrest. It said that Jenkins, Hendrix, Taylor, and Ward were patrolling in an unmarked vehicle near 5700 Jonquil Avenue on the afternoon of March 22, 2016. The four men were serving on a plainclothes unit led by Jenkins and had not yet joined the Task Force. The officers came across Stevenson and another man sitting in a parked car. They searched the vehicle and found half a kilogram of cocaine and $15,000 in cash in an oatmeal container, or so they claimed.

They arrested the two men and sent them to Central Booking. Stevenson called his wife, Keona Holloway, after arriving. She told Stevenson that the police had searched their home after they arrested him. The next day, Stevenson again called Holloway. She told him the officers had taken everything from the basement as well as his watch. They hadn't gotten a search warrant until one o'clock in the morning, she said. We would later learn that this was long after they had actually searched the house. Stevenson asked her to look in a bag with some jackets in it. "There should be money in there," he said. Holloway told him there wasn't any money in the bag. What we needed to know was how much money had been in the bag.

I first spoke to Ronald Hamilton in January 2017, a week after we interviewed Santiful. Hamilton didn't look or sound like the "Big Dog" that Rayam and Gondo described on the wiretap in the summer. He was soft spoken, and more than anything else, seemed tired, world weary. He wasn't reluctant to talk and didn't appear to have an agenda. No one had charged Hamilton after his run-in with the Task Force, so he wasn't trying to get out of jail or have a sentence reduced. On the flip side, he also didn't seem to have it out for the officers we questioned him about. To my mind, he didn't expect that anything would happen to them. He just matter-of-factly answered our questions. It became apparent, however, that what had happened to him that day had profoundly affected him and his family. We would only fully appreciate how much so later.

Hamilton's story about July 8, 2016, started at a Home Depot. From the wiretap, we had learned that Hamilton and his wife were there with a contractor who was working on their new house. They were shopping for blinds. At some point, Hamilton noticed someone staring at him. The way he put it was that a man made "visual contact" with him. The phrase "visual contact" seemed odd coming from a civilian. It sounded like something a police officer might say, but Hamilton's experience with the police was from the other side—being arrested and serving time in jail. The man and others with him watched the Hamiltons up and down every aisle.

The Hamiltons left the Home Depot and headed to the dry cleaners, but they never made it. A car cut them off in the parking lot in front of the dry cleaners. Men with guns jumped out and surrounded them, shouting, "Get out!" They were police officers, Hamilton could tell, even though they weren't in uniform. What he didn't know was that they were from the Task Force. Later in the evening, during the Westminster house search, they would be joined by Daniel Hersl.

One of the officers, Rayam it turned out, pulled Hamilton from the driver's seat and pushed him up against the car.

"Where your money at?" he demanded.

That was the first thing the officer said. Not "Hands up" or something else one might expect the police to say.

"Money?" Hamilton asked in disbelief.

The officer reached into Hamilton's pocket. He found no drugs or a gun but did find $3,400 in cash, which he snatched and put in his vest. That's when Hamilton knew something wasn't right.

"Why am I being stopped?" he asked.

They wouldn't tell him. Instead they put him in an unmarked car and his wife in another.

From the Home Depot in Baltimore County, the officers drove him to the Barn, where the Task Force had their office, in Baltimore City. After they arrived, the officers took Hamilton from the car. A man who hadn't been at Home Depot walked up to him and introduced himself as "such and such" from the US Attorney's Office. He was lying.

The man was Jenkins. He would go on to tell Hamilton that they had him on "three controlled buys," a staged drug deal, usually involving an addict working at the direction of the police or an undercover officer. Hamilton told him that that was a lie, and the officer responded by throwing some papers in his face and telling him he'd been under surveillance.

"I ain't doin' nothing," Hamilton responded.

"We got you," Jenkins told him.

Jenkins and another officer, Rayam, it turned out, asked Hamilton whether he had any guns or drugs in his house. Hamilton said he didn't. Then they asked him whether he had any money at his house. Money again. Hamilton told him he did. After twenty or so minutes of this, Hamilton became frustrated.

"If you got me, let's go down to the federal courthouse," Hamilton said. He'd been down this road before.

The men put Hamilton and his wife in an unmarked car, but as it left the lot, he noticed that they weren't heading toward downtown, the location of the federal courthouse. He asked where they were going.

"To your house," the driver told him.

"For what?" he asked.

At that point, Hamilton knew what was happening. He leaned over to his wife.

"Just don't say nothin," he told her. "They getting ready to rob. They trying to rob me. Don't say nothing."

When they got to the Hamiltons' large, Westminster home, which he'd just bought out of foreclosure, their children, ages 8, 9, and 18, were inside. The officers let Hamilton's wife call someone to take the kids away: three fewer witnesses.

The officers brought the Hamiltons inside and put them on the couch in the living room. They then fanned out through the house. After about an hour, one of them came to Hamilton and asked, "Where the rest of the money and stuff . . . Where the drugs at?" Hamilton told him there were no drugs. He didn't sell drugs.

A different officer took Hamilton downstairs to the basement.

"Listen, ain't nobody telling," the officer told him, "telling" meaning snitching. Hamilton cut him off.

"I don't be with no one," he said. "I be with my wife and my kids. Take me back upstairs."

Once back in the living room, he told his wife, "They playing good cop/bad cop." They were actually only playing bad cop. After searching the house and questioning Hamilton for more than an hour, the officers told Hamilton they were calling the Carroll County Sheriff's Office to bring in a drug-sniffing dog.

At this point Hamilton still didn't know who the police officers were or even their jurisdiction. The officer who had first pulled Hamilton out of his car now took him back downstairs, his second trip to the basement. He said, "Well, listen, if it's more drugs in here, just give it—just tell us. We'll put it up for you." In other words, the officers would hold on to the drugs for Hamilton. They'd obviously want a cut. Hamilton didn't say anything.

When Carroll County police officers arrived, they, too, searched the house. Hamilton estimated they stayed for about forty minutes. At the end of their search, one of the officers who had brought Hamilton home told him that Carroll County had found money. After the Carroll County officers left, the officers who had first arrested Hamilton remained. They took the handcuffs off him and sat him back down in the living room. The officer who had pretended to be with the US Attorney's Office told him, "Just be honest, man. If—you know, if you can help us, we can help you."

"Man, I'm not in the streets, man," Hamilton told him.

Then the officer asked him, "If you was doing bad, who would you rob?" Hamilton couldn't believe what they were asking him.

"I'd rob President Obama," he told them.

The officer laughed, replying, "You want to be a smart ass?" He wouldn't let up. "Man, you can wake up, man. You got 20 keys laying in your yard," he said, which Hamilton understood to mean that they could give him twenty kilograms of cocaine or heroin to sell.

It went on like this for some time, until the officers eventually gave up. After the Task Force officers left, Hamilton walked through his house and saw what they had done. They had robbed him. Just like he thought they would as they headed north from the Barn.

The next day Hamilton called the Carroll County Sheriff's Office. He spoke to one of the officers who had been at the search of his house. Hamilton wanted to know how much money Carroll County had seized. The officer told him $50,000. "Man, there was $70,000," Hamilton replied. "That's why I was trying to talk to you while you were there."

Hamilton had $50,000 in a single heat-sealed bag in his bedroom closet. This is what Carroll County found and seized. He made that money selling cars, collecting rent from his tenants, who mostly paid in cash, and gambling. He knew he had exactly $50,000 because he had just counted it. He had another $20,000 in a second heat-sealed bag. It had also been in his closet. He had earned that money selling cars and gambling, too. Both bundles contained $100 bills. The Task Force officers also stole two expensive watches, his, a Breitling with a yellow face, and his wife's, a Movado that he'd given her.

One minute, the Hamiltons were shopping for blinds, the next, they were in handcuffs. And no one told them why or who was even arresting them. They weren't read their rights; they weren't taken to a police station. Instead, they were driven against their will first to the Barn, then to their own house. Ultimately, they were let go. No charges were ever brought against them. The officers who did this to them walked away with $20,000 of Hamilton's cash.

After speaking to Hamilton, the FBI also interviewed the detective to whom Hamilton had spoken by phone the day after the robbery. The detective actually worked for the Maryland State Police but had been out with the Carroll County Sheriff's Office that night. He remembered being called to the Hamiltons' to assist with the execution of a search warrant. When he arrived, Rayam and three other officers, whom he described as two white guys and a Black guy, were already inside. We knew that the two white guys were Hersl and Jenkins, and the African American was Gondo.

While searching the house with the officers from Carroll County, the MSP detective found a heat-sealed bag of cash in the upstairs bedroom. This was consistent with what Hamilton told us. When it was later opened and the money counted, it totaled $50,000. This was the bag that was turned in. Even more important than the detective's memory of the night's events was his recollection of what happened afterward. He remembered getting a call from Hamilton, who told him that he had received a forfeiture notice stating that $50,000 had been seized at his house. Hamilton asked what had happened to the additional $20,000 that had been taken from him "earlier" by the members of the Task

Force. Hamilton told the detective that the other officers said they gave it to Carroll County. So why wasn't it on the notice? The detective told Hamilton that the only money he knew of was the $50,000 he had found.

We didn't have a jail call from Hamilton because he was never arrested, but the fact that Hamilton had complained about his missing money at the time, and that the detective he'd complained to corroborated his story, was strong evidence of his telling us the truth. We also had the argument between Gondo and Rayam about the missing $3,000 as further evidence of there having been more money at the house than the $50,000 recovered.

We obtained surveillance footage of the casino where Gondo and Rayam went late in the evening on July 8. A camera above the playing floor showed Rayam at a blackjack table betting $400, all in hundred dollar bills, the denomination of the missing $20,000. We also found a series of suspicious deposits made by Gondo and Rayam after the search. On July 11, the Monday after July 8, which was a Friday, Gondo deposited $8,000 in cash in his bank account. Specifically, he made three different counter deposits, in the amounts of $4,000, $3,900, and $100. We surmised that he broke up the deposits in this way to decrease the likelihood of the bank filing a Suspicious Activity Report. Banks file SARs, by law, anytime they register a cash deposit of $10,000 or more, and many banks will file them for deposits approaching $10,000, like $8,000.

On July 15, we intercepted a call to Gondo from a woman who complained about a $100 bill he had given her. It was counterfeit, she told him. Gondo pushed back telling her he had just deposited $8,000 in his bank account and, therefore, had no reason to give her a counterfeit bill. So, here we had Gondo passing out $100 bills in the days after July 8.

The FBI found Stevenson in November 2016, before we had spoken to Hamilton, but Stevenson didn't want to talk to us. I saw from the court records that Stevenson's attorney was Ivan Bates. I had never tried a case against Bates, but I knew him to have a good reputation. I called him and introduced myself.

I told Bates that I was calling about a former client of his, Stevenson, and that I needed his help because Stevenson wouldn't talk to us. He told me that he had gotten Stevenson's case thrown out in state court because Wayne Jenkins had conducted an illegal search. Bates explained that Jenkins had "jumped in" through the window and grabbed a backpack as Stevenson and another man sat in a parked car. Bates also said that this wasn't the only case he'd gotten tossed because of Jenkins's tactics. "I'm good, but not that good," he told me, acknowledging that he took on cases involving Jenkins because he knew how likely they were to get thrown out.

Bates agreed to talk to Stevenson and get back to me. A few days later, Stevenson reluctantly agreed to meet with us. Bates told Stevenson he'd "won the lottery" when the drugs in his case got suppressed and that he owed it to the system to cooperate with our investigation.

We met Bates and Stevenson at the federal courthouse. Stevenson wasn't nervous, but he was no open book like Hamilton. He clearly didn't want to be there. He answered our questions in short responses, sometimes a single word. Like Hamilton, he faced no charges and therefore had nothing to gain from talking to us. He didn't want to make small talk; we didn't waste his time trying to build rapport.

Stevenson had a criminal record for selling drugs. After his most recent release from prison, he started driving a truck to make a living. He also continued selling drugs. On March 22, 2016, he was sitting in a car on Jonquil Avenue in Northwest Baltimore. "I was sittin' there and the police car came up a one way and blocked me in and they all jumped out," he told us. Going the wrong way up a one-way street was the same technique Hersl had used with Tate. Stevenson recalled four officers jumping out. They were armed and dressed in plainclothes wearing vests marked "POLICE."

Hendrix came over to Stevenson's window, at the driver's seat. Jenkins went to the front passenger side, where the other person was sitting. Stevenson's passenger had a book bag in his lap. We would later learn that Jenkins kept an eye out for men carrying book bags.

Stevenson asked Hendrix what the problem was, and Hendrix told him that the tint on his front window was too dark. We would also later learn that Jenkins used tinting as an excuse for car stops. Stevenson said there was no tint. Jenkins then opened the door on the passenger side, "jumped in" according to Stevenson, and grabbed the passenger's book bag.

Stevenson admitted to us that the officers had interrupted a drug deal. The passenger was about to buy half a kilogram of cocaine from Stevenson, who expected the book bag to contain $21,500, the going price for half a kilogram at that time. When Stevenson saw the police report, he noticed that only $15,000 had been listed as recovered from the car stop. This was the first robbery that occurred that day.

After Jenkins grabbed the book bag, Hendrix pulled Stevenson from the car and handcuffed him. Jenkins did the same to the passenger. They sat both men on the curb while other officers searched the car. Police found the half a kilogram of cocaine in an oatmeal container, which they seized. A prisoner transport van arrived and took Stevenson to Central Booking.

At the time of Stevenson's arrest, he was living on Heathfield Road, in West Baltimore, but when the officers asked where he lived, he gave a different address, Presstman Street, as on his license. He and his wife were starting an assisted living facility in a house on Presstman. Stevenson had keys to both houses in his pocket. The police took them. There were no drugs or money at the Presstman Street house, but there were lots of both in the basement at Heathfield, Stevenson told us: $200,000 in a safe; $40,000 in a pair of black bags; a $4,000 Breitling watch; and ten one-kilo bricks of cocaine.

The Drug Enforcement Administration sent Stevenson a notice after this arrest that the money seized at his house was subject to forfeiture. The Task Force had called the DEA in to help them seize the cash, just as they had called in the Carroll County Sheriff's Office at Hamilton's house, in Westminster. It was easier to deny stealing the money if you weren't the last one to touch it. But of course, when you're the first one to touch it, that's a different story. The notice from the DEA informed Stevenson that they had only seized $100,000. Stevenson knew the safe contained twice that amount. There was no mention of the bagged $40,000 or the watch.

Unlike Hamilton, Stevenson didn't complain to the police, but he did tell Bates that money was missing, something Bates confirmed to us. But it had been Stevenson's word against the police. Why would anyone believe a drug dealer when he claimed to have been robbed by the police? Each of our victims said that to us in one way or another. The police enjoyed a presumption of truthfulness that the drug dealers didn't have. Being practical, Bates focused on getting the drugs from the car stop suppressed. When he did, the state dropped the charges against Stevenson, but Bates said he still expected a call from the Feds after Stevenson told him the amount of drugs seized at his house. It never came, and my call certainly wasn't the one Bates expected.

Stevenson's charging documents showed that the DEA had seized eight, not ten, kilos of cocaine on Heathfield Road. Stevenson had no reason to lie about having more drugs. Had the officers stolen drugs, too? This was the first episode we encountered where drugs were missing. At this point, I excluded nothing. If the police were stealing money, they could steal drugs, too. The truth was getting worse. Taking drug money off the streets meant less money to buy and sell drugs, but stolen drugs had to be sold to generate a return. This meant the cops had to become active participants in the drug economy, not just parasites siphoning off money from it.

Right after we interviewed Stevenson, we talked to his wife, Keona Holloway, whom he had called from jail. Like Stevenson, she was reluctant to talk to us. She was quiet and well-spoken, dressed in hospital scrubs. Holloway had been a nursing assistant for eleven years. She had been with Stevenson for fifteen years. While there is no common-law marriage in Maryland, they considered themselves spouses. They had two boys together, ages 3 and 12.

On March 22, around 5:30 p.m., Holloway's older son called her at work. He had been waiting for her on the porch at their home, but now someone else was at the house. She left work immediately and headed to Heathfield. On the way, she called her mother-in-law and asked her to go there, too. When she arrived thirty minutes later, two police officers were sitting in her living room. She identified Taylor and Ward from pictures we showed her.

Taylor told her that they were there because Oreese had been arrested. That was true. They also said that Oreese had sent them there. That was a lie. They told her she could stay in the house, but that she couldn't leave the living room. She sat there for about six hours, until around midnight. Taylor kept going from the living room to the basement. At the time, Holloway didn't know there was a safe in the basement; she also didn't know there were drugs in her house. At some point, two more officers showed up. She picked Jenkins and Hendrix out of the pictures we showed her.

Jenkins read Holloway her rights, showed her a search warrant, and told her she had to leave. While Jenkins was talking, Holloway saw Hendrix take out a set of keys. He put the keys in the door while another officer recorded him with a smartphone. In other words, they filmed a phony entry into the house. They had already been inside for hours. Holloway left—she felt she would have been arrested otherwise—but she didn't go far. Wanting to know what was going on, she sat in her car in front of the house. She remained there for four hours, eventually leaving at 4:00 a.m. because she couldn't stay awake any longer. The officers were still inside.

When Holloway returned the next day, she saw the safe in the basement, which had been broken into. It was empty. She had no idea what was missing much less that the safe even existed. She did, however, no-tice that Stevenson's watch was gone, as well as two bags of clothes they'd just bought. These were the bags that Stevenson later told her on the jail phone had contained money.

Stevenson and Holloway had a security system in their house. The cameras had been ripped off the wall. We asked Holloway if she knew Stevenson had been selling drugs. She said no, adding, "But, you know, you kind of have your suspicions."

One of the last victims we interviewed was Sergio Summerville, from the U-Store robbery we listened to on the bug at the end of the sum-mer in 2016. Summerville had been hard to track down. The FBI finally interviewed him in February 2017. I met him three days later. Sum-merville was small and wiry, his movements quick. He smiled easily but seemed nervous. It appeared he hadn't been able to take a shower or wash his clothes in a while.

Summerville, who had grown up in East Baltimore, had been unem-ployed and homeless throughout 2016, crashing "here and there" and keeping his possessions in a small unit at the U-Store, a storage facility in an industrial part of South Baltimore. To make money, he sold small amounts of cocaine and heroin, stashing the drugs and money in his storage unit.

On September 7, 2016, his friend "Fats" took him to his storage space just before 7:00 p.m. so he could change clothes. On their way out as Summerville punched an access code to open the gate, he saw headlights and noticed a car parked across the street. He didn't remem-ber the car being there when they came in, and he felt like he was be-ing watched. He was right.

As soon as the gate slid open, Summerville said, that car and another one pulled up and blocked the exit. Men jumped out of both cars. This matched what we saw on CCTV. Summerville remembered them shouting, "Get out the car, get out the car! Put your hands where I can see them!" One of the officers removed him from Fats's car and handcuffed him.

He identified Jenkins and Hersl from a photograph. He said that Jenkins claimed they were DEA agents, and Hersl said they had a search warrant. None of it was true, but Summerville didn't know that. Jenkins and Hersl said they knew what was going on. Then Jenkins asked him his name. To that, Summerville responded, "If you have a warrant and know everything that's going on, why you asking my name?" Good question.

At that point, Summerville heard an officer in the background say, "Fuck it. Take him down as a John Doe." In fact, however, they took nothing down. No police report exists for what happened that night.

One of the Task Force officers walked Summerville away and tried to reassure him that he knew who he was—that Summerville was from "the Avenue," and had several "bricks" of cocaine and thirty or forty thousand dollars in the storage unit. He then made Summerville an offer: if Summerville gave him a "number," which Summerville understood to mean money, he would let him go, or Summerville could meet him every week and pay him. Summerville described this as some kind of "extortion speech." Summerville understood the officer to be speaking for the whole group, which Summerville referred to as a "criminal gang or something."

Summerville declined the offer and refused to reveal his storage unit number. Then he saw several officers go to the storage facility's office. He figured they thought they could get his unit number by "scaring the guy" who worked there.

When the officers came out of the office, they took Summerville's keys out of his pocket. The key to the unit was on the ring. Then Summerville saw three of the officers—Rayam, Taylor, and Jenkins, it turned out—head toward his unit, where he had stashed $4,800 in drug proceeds, around a thousand dollars' worth of heroin, and a couple hundred dollars' worth of cocaine and marijuana.

When the officers came back to him, one of them, Rayam, was holding a sock, which he placed on the back of one of the unmarked police cars. The sock looked different from what Summerville remembered. He usually kept his cash in it, rolled up. Now the sock was flat. The video from the storage facility corroborated what Summerville told us. We saw Rayam emerge from the hallway with the sock, put it on the car, and walk over to Gondo's car. From the bug in Gondo's car, we heard Rayam tell Gondo that he only "taxed" Summerville a little bit.

The police then uncuffed Summerville. There would be no trip to Central Booking, no drug charge. No report. After they uncuffed Summerville, one of the officers made a recording with his phone, asking him his name and whether he'd been harmed. He said he had not. This was an insurance policy in case Summerville lodged a complaint, which he never did. Summerville chalked it up as a "loss," afraid he'd be charged for the drugs if he said anything about the missing money.

Because Summerville had seen the officers go into the storage facility office, we decided to talk to the man working there that night. The man, Gregory Thompson, remembered what had happened. Around 8:00 p.m., Thompson heard a "commotion." He went outside and saw a lot of police officers. One of their cars was at the gate, blocking another car attempting to exit. Thompson recognized Summerville, who he knew had a unit at the storage facility, in the car trying to exit.

At one point, two of the officers came to the office and wanted to talk to Thompson. He identified Jenkins and Hersl from photographs. Jenkins and Hersl told Thompson that they had found "a lot" of heroin in the car that Summerville had been in. A lie. Jenkins and Hersl asked Thompson for access to the storage unit's security cameras. Thompson told them they'd need a warrant. They didn't like that. They told Thompson he was impeding a police investigation. Thompson offered to call his manager to see if she would allow him to give them what they wanted. Before he could, one of them asked Thompson, "Do you know what you remind me of?" Thompson said he didn't.

"Somebody that needed to be robbed."

On this night, though, Thompson wasn't the one getting robbed. It was Summerville's turn.

NINE

Stealing from Everybody

By late fall of 2016, the FBI had been listening to Momodu Gondo for six months on the phone and in his car. Although looking for evidence of robberies, they also heard Jemell Rayam dropping off his kids at day care, Gondo going to the gym in the middle of the day, endless talk about where they were and what they were doing. As fall turned to winter and we began drafting the charges against the members of the Gun Trace Task Force, the significance of these seemingly mundane conversations struck the FBI's Erika Jensen: "These guys aren't working," she told me on a phone call.

Erika explained that typically the Task Force was supposed to work from 8:00 a.m. to 3:00 p.m. and that they could work overtime after that. But Task Force members were constantly talking about starting work late and sometimes missing their entire shift. Then they would work overtime but, in most cases, claimed more overtime than they had actually worked.

Erika's observation showed that she didn't have blinders on. We were investigating robberies, yet she noticed that the Task Force officers weren't at work when they should have been. That meant they were committing overtime fraud. Investigating fraud in a robbery case might seem like getting Al Capone on tax evasion, but this would add another dimension to our case. If they were committing overtime fraud, it meant that the Task Force officers weren't just robbing people who sold drugs. They were stealing from everybody, from every taxpayer.

The evidence of their fraud wouldn't come from the mouths of people some jurors might have a hard time believing. Instead, to clear that hurdle, it would come from cell phones, which the officers carried in their pockets, unwittingly tracking their own movements for us, and from the overtime slips they submitted supposedly detailing where they'd been and what they'd been doing. If the two didn't match, were jurors to believe that the overtime slips were somehow lying? We were counting on the ubiquity of cell phones as tracking devices to help make our case.

None of the Task Force officers lived in Baltimore. In fact, they practically had it surrounded. Everyone but Daniel Hersl and Marcus Taylor lived in Baltimore County: Gondo and Rayam to the northwest, in Owings Mills; Evodio Hendrix to the west, in Randallstown; and Wayne Jenkins and Maurice Ward to the east, in Middle River. Hersl was northeast of the city, in Harford County; he'd bought a house in Joppa in the summer of 2016. Taylor lived in Glen Burnie, south of the city, in Anne Arundel County.

Some police departments require officers to live in the jurisdiction they serve. The idea is that it creates better community relations and engenders the kind of trust that leads eyewitnesses to cooperate. Others say residency requirements reduce the pool of good candidates because some officers won't want to live in a city. Because the BPD is a state agency, the state legislature decides where its officers can live, and efforts to pass residency requirements have consistently failed. Whatever the merits of a residency requirement for Baltimore Police Department officers, the lack of one made it easier for us to prove overtime fraud. When we saw the Task Force officers' phones outside of Baltimore, they were most likely at home and not working. Had they lived in the city, they could have claimed they were working, even if they were at home.

Erika painstakingly analyzed the Task Force officers' overtime claims. We obtained electronic records from ADP, the department's payroll service, which showed how many hours the Task Force officers were paid for, broken down by regular shifts and overtime. Officers had to submit paper slips to claim overtime, and that was useful for a number of reasons. First and foremost, the officers themselves had to prepare and sign the slips, so no one could blame some faceless computer system for awarding them overtime they hadn't earned. Second, because they had to fill out the slips, there were three potential lies in every one: the officers had to certify having worked their regular shift, had to describe what they were doing while working overtime, and had to certify how many hours of overtime they actually worked.

Focusing on the summer of 2016, Erika looked for the days for which Task Force officers claimed overtime but we had evidence that they weren't working. She found multiple examples for each officer. One week in July stood out in particular.

On July 18, Jenkins submitted overtime slips for the previous week. One slip claimed eight hours of overtime, from 6:00 p.m. to 2:00 a.m., for "Proactive Enforcement WD [West District] /ED [Eastern District] /NED [Northeastern District]." On the slips for the rest of the week, he submitted similar justifications, slightly adjusting the times he claimed to have worked. The problem was that Jenkins was on vacation in Myrtle Beach that entire week, not in Baltimore doing police work.

While Jenkins was gone, Gondo, Hersl, and Rayam submitted time sheets that showed them working hard, but they, too, were hardly working. On a call we intercepted the morning of July 11, 2016, Rayam told Gondo that he had just dropped his kids off, was running a few errands, and needed to get some sleep. No work that day, but Rayam was still on the clock. Later that evening, a friend of Gondo's called him.

"I didn't know you wuz home, man," said his friend. "I thought you was workin' or something."

"Naw, whatchucallhim off for a week," Gondo said, referring to Jenkins. "So you know, everybody just takin' it easy."

"Enjoy your day off," the friend said, at the end of the call. Gondo's timesheet showed him at work all day.

On July 14, Rayam called Gondo at 1:25 p.m., and Gondo said he was at home. Around 8:00 p.m., Gondo called Rayam and boasted that his paycheck for the previous fourteen-day pay period was for $5,700. Gondo had claimed to work 102 hours of overtime in two weeks. Rayam was impressed. "That's where I should be at," he said to Gondo. A casino is where Rayam was at that moment.

For July 14, Gondo submitted an overtime slip claiming an eight-hour day with overtime from 4:15 p.m. to 12:15 a.m., despite having been home at 1:25 p.m. and telling Rayam at 9:45 p.m. that he was headed downtown to have some drinks. Rayam submitted an overtime slip for a sixteen-hour day on July 14 despite not working at all, listing "OIS Crime Suppression HGV 4600 Grindon, 4-160705968," to justify the overtime. In reality, Hendrix, Ward, and Taylor had made the arrest that Rayam claimed on his slip. Rayam wasn't involved, and neither was Hersl, who submitted an overtime slip for the same sixteen hours as Gondo and Rayam, citing the same arrest. According to Gondo, Hersl had left at 7:00 p.m. for the bar.

The next morning, Rayam told Gondo that he had to "take care of shit at home" and wouldn't be in until the next day.

"Easy money, J. Easy money . . . One hour can be eight hours," Gondo replied.

We understood what that meant. One hour of work, if that, could turn into eight hours of overtime pay. Good work if you can get it.

A little later that morning, Gondo told Rayam that Hersl wasn't coming in either.

"I'm goin' home, goin' to sleep," Gondo said. "Fuck that shit yo."

Rayam sympathized, "Yeah, man. I work that overtime slip when Wayne comes back, man."

On July 23, we intercepted a series of calls in which Jenkins and Gondo planned their "work day." Their shift was from 3:00 p.m. to 3:00 a.m. Early in the afternoon, Gondo had told two people he was "going in at 8 tonight." There went five hours. Around 5:30 p.m., Jenkins called Gondo: they'd meet at the Task Force's office at 9:00 p.m. "That way we have time to go out to eat with our families," Jenkins said. There went another hour, shortly followed by some more: "Hey, hey," Jenkins told Gondo. "We don't get off till 3, [but] we aren't staying until fuckin' 3."

Jenkins only worked with Gondo that night, but overtime slips came in from every Task Force member but one. We had cell phone location data putting Gondo in Owings Mills, outside the city, until after 8:00 p.m. Jenkins's phone put him at home for three evening hours—perhaps for dinner. Rayam, Hendrix, and Ward's phones were outside Baltimore City near their homes all day. Hersl spent the day in Harford County and then in Canton, the Baltimore neighborhood where we believed his girlfriend lived, for the rest of the day. Taylor's phone put him in New York City.

On July 29, the Task Force had an 8:00 a.m. shift. Once again, Jenkins planned a 9:00 p.m. start; they'd head out and get "just one" gun arrest so they could get home by 11:00 p.m. Gondo later told Rayam that Taylor couldn't even make the nine o'clock punch in and that Jenkins was furious. Gondo, in apparent disbelief at Taylor for pushing the envelope this far, said, "Your shift is 8 to 3. You six hours late on top of that. So you can't be here at 9 for this man?" Jenkins had wanted to throw Taylor off the squad, but the ever-practical Gondo reminded him that the speedy Taylor often chased down the suspects they sent scrambling: "Who else is gonna run?" he asked.

That same day, Ward flew to Myrtle Beach, returning on August 2. For August 1, he claimed a thirteen-hour shift and forty-five minutes of overtime performing "HGVx4 Proactive Enforcement." A week later, Hendrix, Taylor, and Ward took a week-long vacation in the Dominican Republic. They were on the clock the whole time.

We were astonished when we added up the Task Force's haul: every single member made a six-figure salary, and all but Gondo and Rayam nearly doubled their salaries with overtime. So much for the argument that they were underpaid, and that because they made so little, they couldn't resist taking some of the drug money they encountered.

The overtime fraud was important to us not only because it was a crime, but also in terms of presenting the case to a jury. We worried that there would be jurors who refused to believe someone who sold drugs when they accused a police officer of robbing them. How could we convince those jurors to believe that the defendants had crossed a line and were actually the criminals? The overtime fraud gave us a set of charges that didn't depend on drug dealers.

Hovering above the signature line on a BPD overtime slip was the following: "We certify that the overtime hours reported herein are authorized, were in fact worked, and are correct." The "we" referred to both the officer and his or her supervisor. If the officers testified at the trial, we could point to this line and argue that if they couldn't be trusted to tell the truth then, when all that was at stake was money, then they shouldn't be trusted to tell the truth in court, when they had everything to lose. This was no trivial matter.

In relative terms, our victims would typically walk into the courtroom with a credibility deficit, and the police officers, who would be our defendants, would enjoy a credibility surplus. We, therefore, had to do everything we could to address the disbelief that would meet our victims by corroborating what they said with video and audio recordings, including jail calls, and physical evidence. We also had to weaken the presumption of believability that the defendants would enjoy. We tried to address this imbalance primarily by revealing patterns in the robberies. What is the likelihood that all these victims, none of whom knew any of the others, spontaneously decided to falsely accuse the same group of officers? Exposing the lies on these overtime slips presented another important way to drive home that the Task Force members shouldn't be believed.

The need to offer our likely jurors a pathway to conviction that ran through something other than East and West Baltimore was more than just theoretical. In federal court in Baltimore, members of the jury come from across the state of Maryland. We thought that such a jury would be harder to convince than one drawn solely from Baltimore City. Our jurors wouldn't likely live in hyper-segregated neighborhoods of concentrated poverty and crime, like those where the Task Force operated. They would drive to the courthouse every day from places that experienced none of the conditions that made it easy for the Task Force to take advantage of people. The overtime fraud, however, would speak to these jurors.

We thought that even if jurors didn't believe the cops were robbing drug dealers, they would believe overtime fraud, which was stealing from taxpayers. The divide between the life experiences of our likely jurors and the Task Force's victims was further exacerbated by so few BPD officers actually living in Baltimore. As a result, the people on our jury were more likely to know BPD officers as neighbors, as fellow parents, as people in the community whom they respected, rather than as someone patrolling them. That said, jurors who had never set foot in East or West Baltimore would think it wrong to falsify overtime.

Overtime fraud was the last piece of the puzzle. With it, we were ready to charge.

PART II

THE PROSECUTION

TEN

Indictment

When it came time to charge the case, we had to navigate the limits on federal jurisdiction. States exercise the full range of police powers. Most violent crimes, like murder, and most property crimes, like burglary, are prosecuted at the local level. Federal law enforcement focuses on serious, but more narrow areas, like terrorism, narcotics, firearms offenses, public corruption, and major financial fraud. The Gun Trace Task Force officers were abusing their official positions—a form of corruption, broadly speaking—but theirs wasn't traditional corruption, like taking bribes. The Task Force officers were committing armed robberies, something mostly prosecuted by local authorities.

The federal government can prosecute robbery under the Hobbs Act, but like all other federal criminal statutes, the act relies on a "jurisdictional hook": something that gives the federal government, rather than the states, the power to prosecute. Commercial robberies, like hijacking a tractor trailer full of expensive electronics, can be prosecuted using the Hobbs Act because the federal government regulates interstate commerce. Similarly, federal law enforcement can prosecute robberies involving narcotics because the drug trade is national and international in scope.

The Stevenson robbery involved drugs, so we could prosecute it under the Hobbs Act. The Task Force members' robbery of Ronald Hamilton included proceeds from his used car business, which involved buying and selling cars made all over the United States and even overseas, so it could be charged under the Hobbs Act. Most of the robberies we uncovered, however, involved stealing from individuals, such as Herbert Tate and Sergio Summerville. In those cases, the Hobbs Act did not apply. Instead, these "small" robberies were crimes under Maryland law. The broader pattern of the big robberies and the small ones, more than anything else, showed the victims weren't lying. We needed a way to charge all the robberies. Enter RICO—the Racketeer Influenced Corrupt Organizations Act.

RICO is most often associated with mob prosecutions, but it isn't limited by its text or application just to the Mafia. Broadly speaking, it's meant for prosecuting organized crime and preventing the infiltration or corruption of legitimate entities like businesses and labor unions. Today RICO is used most often in gang cases. Charging it in a police corruption case would be unusual, but not unprecedented. Personally, I had been involved only in RICO cases that didn't involve gangs or drugs. My very first case when I joined the Department of Justice was a RICO case against the tobacco industry. More recently, I had used it to charge prison guards at Maryland's largest state prison for taking bribes to smuggle contraband into the facility.

Various aspects of the RICO statute suited it to the Task Force's crimes. Among them, RICO makes it a crime to "conduct and participate in the conduct of an enterprise through a pattern of racketeering activity." That artful bit of legislative drafting has several distinct parts.

First, the "enterprise" can be a legal entity like a business or a union or even a government agency, or it can be something called an "association in fact," like a gang. The enterprise itself can have a legal purpose, and it doesn't have to exclusively engage in criminal conduct. To "conduct and participate in the conduct of an enterprise" means the statute principally, although not exclusively, targets insiders—such as employees at a company or members of a gang—who used the enterprise to carry out their crimes. The statute doesn't require that the leadership of the enterprise be complicit or even aware that the enterprise is being used to commit crimes.

Second, the statute defines "pattern of racketeering activity" as two or more acts of racketeering within a ten-year period. Racketeering acts include both violations of federal law, like the federal wire fraud statute, which we could use to charge overtime fraud, and importantly in our case, certain state laws, including robbery.

We drafted a racketeering charge naming the Baltimore Police Department as the enterprise. The Task Force members weren't police officers during the day and robbers wearing black masks at night; they were robbers operating under the cover of being police officers. With more than a dozen robberies at hand, we easily met the requirement of two racketeering acts over a ten-year span. We could also include overtime fraud under RICO. The BPD contracted ADP for its payroll processing, run out of a mainframe server in South Dakota. That meant interstate wires, and therefore wire fraud, which we could also charge as racketeering acts.

We were confident about RICO as the right way to charge the Task Force officers, but we remained concerned that the jury might struggle with the unusual nature of the robberies. Under Maryland law, robbery is a crime against a person. In other words, theft from someone's body, like their pockets, or from some area under their control, like their home, if they are present. Indeed, Maryland courts have ruled that it includes taking money from one room in someone's house while the person is restrained in another room in the house, like Hamilton and his wife were. Proving robbery also requires the prosecutor to show that the perpetrator either applied force to the victim to take their property or put the victim "in fear."

Still, the Task Force robberies weren't your average stickups. The detectives stole from people when they arrested them or searched their houses. In most robberies, victims submit and relinquish their property because of the gun pointed at them or pushed into their back. We had force, and the threat of force, in our case, but not like that. The Task Force officers all carried guns, but they were supplied by the BPD, and the victims submitted to the Task Force out of fear, but the force or threat of force flowed from the officers' police powers put to a bad purpose.

Each episode we chose to charge involved a Task Force officer taking money directly from someone, for example: Daniel Hersl taking money from Antonio Santiful's pocket after arresting him, Jemell Rayam taking the Hamiltons' money from their bedroom closet while the couple was detained in their living room. Even in the case of Oreese Stevenson, we had evidence that Marcus Taylor stole some of the seized money when Stevenson was arrested mid–drug deal and that Keona Holloway had stayed just outside the house in her car while the officers were cracking the safe in their basement.

We could prove that force was involved: each episode involved victims who were in handcuffs when their money was taken. We could also establish that victims experienced fear. The law evaluates the idea of "putting in fear" from an objective standard: would a reasonable person be fearful based on the actions of the defendant? We knew victims would testify that they feared the police and thought that any resistance might provoke the officers to beat them or even kill them. The jury could easily digest that testimony in determining whether a "reasonable person" would be put in fear by the police. Even without such testimony, we felt confident that the jurors would conclude that a reasonable person would fear the police might use force against them, even deadly force, if they didn't do what they were told, including handing over their property.

Yet I still worried that a jury might struggle applying Maryland's robbery law to police officers acting as police officers. I worried less about the jury understanding the overtime fraud charges. The federal wire fraud statute we chose to apply was more straightforward and its application in our case rather conventional. Unlike robbery, which relies on force and fear, at the heart of fraud lies deception. Fraud isn't violent because it doesn't need to be. A victim of fraud relinquishes his property in response to the perpetrator's lies. The deception in our case? The Task Force officers' lies to the BPD about how much overtime they worked. The victims? The BPD and the taxpayers funding the BPD, including likely jurors.

As we envisioned the trial, the two sets of charges—robberies and overtime fraud—played important but different roles. The robberies stood at the heart of the case. They represented a profound abuse of police power, a total inversion of what the public expects from the police. Proving them at trial, however, presented challenges.

We realized we would have to rely on the testimony of the victims, some of whom sold drugs or had sold drugs in the past. We knew that jurors might have trouble believing people like that, particularly when they were testifying against police officers. Proving the robberies would require the jury to find our victims credible, as we did. We had evidence to corroborate the victims in every instance—jail calls, wiretaps, the bug in Momodu Gondo's car, bank records, CCTV and CitiWatch camera footage, and more.

The overtime fraud was important because it didn't depend on the jurors believing the victims. The evidence came straight from the officers themselves, via their phones, telling us where they really were, and from their own overtime slips, which were fraudulent because they said they were working when they weren't. The jury would likely find it easy to approach the overtime fraud in a dispassionate, even clinical way. They didn't have to wrestle with their feelings about the police or about people who sold drugs. They just had to look at a map to see that an officer claimed to be working in Baltimore City, when in fact, he was at home miles away in the suburbs.

Even with the overtime fraud charges in the case, we had one more worry: jury nullification, when jurors acquit a defendant based on considerations other than the facts and the law. It can occur, for instance, when the jury blames the victim. The inverse is also true; jury nullification can occur when jurors have positive feelings about defendants and excuse their conduct. Our case posed both risks and a hybrid of the two. On the one hand, the jurors—or a single juror, as it only takes one—might vote to acquit because they didn't like the victims. On the other hand, a juror might refuse to convict a police officer under any circumstances. We had to thread that needle.

With more than one potential motivation for jury nullification, we hoped to use the jury-selection process to identify jurors who held biases, either in favor of police officers or against people like our victims. This was another example of flipping the playbook. Usually, the prosecution tries to choose jurors who are pro–law enforcement, and the defense tries to exclude them. Now, we were on the lookout to strike jurors who might have biases favoring the police, and the defense wanted those who did.

Regardless of what the future held, the time had arrived to bring the case to a head. In late February 2017, we presented an indictment to the grand jury, and it found probable cause existed to charge the defendants and returned the indictment. The court, at our request, sealed the indictment to allow for the defendants' arrest, planned for several days later.

The die was cast. All the decisions we had made up to that point would be tested through the adversarial process. It felt like jumping out of a plane and not knowing if your parachute would open. I hoped we had enough evidence and had chosen the right charges to hold the defendants accountable. In the end, though, it wouldn't be our decision. It would be a jury's.

In the early morning hours of March 1, 2017, I drove to the FBI's building in Woodlawn, in Baltimore County, just outside Baltimore City.

It was still dark. The route from my home takes me west across the northern part of the city, and it took me past the Barn.

A great deal of planning had gone into this day. The defendants, after all, were armed police officers trained in law enforcement techniques, including making arrests; now, those same techniques would be used against them. Would any of these officers barricade themselves in their homes when they realized the FBI was at the front door? Would they come out shooting? Commit suicide? Both?

The FBI devised a ruse to protect the officers conducting the arrests. Instead of arresting the Task Force members at home, BPD internal affairs would call them all in on the same day to explain why one of their vehicles had been badly damaged. Visitors to the internal affairs building have to secure their firearms in small lockers when they arrive. That's what each of the Task Force officers did upon entering the building, arriving at different times as we expected.

One by one, each Task Force officer locked up his gun and got in the elevator to the fourth floor, where he believed internal affairs would interview him about the damaged car. When the elevator doors opened, the FBI stood waiting for them. When they got off the elevator, FBI agents arrested them, putting them in handcuffs. That March 1, they entered the elevator as police officers; they exited as defendants. Their metamorphosis was complete.

Each officer was taken to an interview room wired for sound and video. I watched the feed to see if any of them wanted to talk. None of them did. I left the FBI building late in the morning to drive back to the US Attorney's Office for a press conference with US Attorney Rod Rosenstein, who the White House had announced would be nominated to be deputy attorney general of the United States two months earlier.

"This morning seven Baltimore City police officers were arrested on federal racketeering charges," Rosenstein told reporters. He wore a dark suit and a red tie. Perched on his nose were rimless glasses, which I always thought reflected his personality—unadorned and clear. He chose his words deliberately.

I stood behind Rosenstein, over his right shoulder. Derek Hines, my co-counsel for the case, stood next to me. My goal was to not be noticed: no smiling, no grimacing, no visible signs of emotion. I described it to a colleague as acting like a tin soldier. To the US attorney's right stood BPD commissioner Kevin Davis and the special agent in charge of the FBI's Baltimore Field Office, Gordon Johnson. Davis provided one of the more memorable lines of the press conference, calling the Task Force officers "1930s-style gangsters."

It had been a remarkable journey. In a conference room in the fall of 2015, someone had floated the idea that a police officer might be helping Antonio Shropshire's drug crew. Now a US attorney was announcing charges against an entire unit of the Baltimore Police Department. As I stood there looking back on the investigation, three things truly surprised me. First, the original hypothesis, that Gondo was helping Shropshire evade law enforcement, wasn't the worst thing he was doing; he was robbing people. Second, Gondo wasn't acting alone. Third, Gondo and all the other officers on the Task Force had been robbing people even before they came together in the unit.

With the hard work of the investigation over, the challenge of proving the case in court lay ahead. The FBI took the Task Force members, now charged defendants in handcuffs, straight to the federal courthouse in downtown Baltimore. They didn't enter through the front door like other police officers; they came in through the basement like every other defendant in custody. One at a time, they appeared before a US magistrate judge for an "initial appearance." US Marshals sat behind them all through the proceedings to watch them, even in the courtroom.

The main event at an initial appearance is the judge's decision on whether to release the defendant on bail. Derek and I asked the court to detain each defendant for two reasons. First, they had committed multiple armed robberies, which made them dangerous. For any other defendant, we would ask for detention and get it. Second, to cover up their robberies, they had obstructed justice—filing false police reports and lying to judges. How could they be released on bail and then supervised by the court?

When someone is released on bail, a pretrial services officer monitors them to make sure they comply with the conditions of their release—like not travelling out of state or only leaving their home for specific reasons, like meeting with their lawyer or going to the doctor. Such supervision involves having the person meet with the pretrial services officer or speak to them on the phone every week or so, but the system is largely honor based. What realistic chance would a pretrial services officer have of adequately supervising the Task Force defendants? None, in our estimation.

Each of the Task Force officers was entitled to a detention hearing. At Taylor's hearing, more than twenty of his family members showed up. Derek made the two-part argument that we had developed to use in all the detention hearings.

"Starting with the nature of the offense, if this were a case where a series of robberies were charged against the defendants, the Government would be seeking detention to protect the community," he told Judge Stephanie Gallagher. "What makes this case and these facts far worse, Your Honor, is that in each example of a robbery in this case, the Defendant and his co-defendants engaged in obstruction of justice in order to conceal evidence of the robberies and extortions in which they participated."

Then Derek laid out the facts: the false incident reports, the citizens arrested because of those reports, that the officers had coached each other to lie to internal affairs, something we had heard from the bug in Gondo's car.

"These facts, your Honor, raise a central issue in his case, and that is, whether this Defendant can be trusted," Derek said. "If the Pretrial Services officers cannot trust the Defendant, trust the response they receive to their questions, trust that he will abide by the conditions set on him, then Pretrial Services cannot protect the community by supervising the Defendant."

Taylor's father appeared as a witness for his son. Dressed in a dark suit, he walked slowly to the stand. He seemed like a serious man, betraying no emotion when he first saw his son at the defendant's table.

"How do you know Marcus?" Taylor's lawyer asked.

"Oh, he's my son," said the elder Taylor. "He's my son when he first came into the world."

I found the latter part of his answer touching. It didn't seem coached or inauthentic. He told the court that he had retired after twenty-two years in the US Army, and now he worked at the Port of Baltimore. He told Judge Gallagher that he had a bedroom where Taylor could stay before the trial. He said his son was a good father to his own son, talking to his teacher, taking him to soccer practice.

Taylor's lawyer then asked if he knew whether his son was a violent man.

"No. No. That doesn't sound like my son." This comment also struck me. The man described in the indictment, who robbed and cheated, probably also didn't sound like his son—but it was.

Judge Gallagher ordered Taylor detained, based on two findings. First, the court found there to be "strong evidence" that Taylor had participated in a series of armed robberies. Judge Gallagher reasoned, "[In] cases involving armed robbers, detention is quite customary and it has nothing to do with the Defendant being a police officer or not being a police officer. Armed robbery poses a serious risk to the community's safety."

But that wasn't all. Judge Gallagher added, "The Defendant was a sworn law enforcement officer on a very serious task force investigating gun crime in a city with a serious problem of gun crime." In that capacity, he had submitted false reports regarding his duty to enforce the law. It all added up to "an extremely egregious breach of public trust that I think inhibits my ability to find that he could be trusted to comply with conditions of release."

Taylor was, she found, a danger to the community—a police officer, a danger to the community.

It was remarkable to hear a federal judge reach that conclusion. Standing in the courtroom at that moment, I thought I had just witnessed the judge make the same journey that I had made, through belief and disbelief, to arrive at the truth.

Would the jury do the same?

ELEVEN

Legacy Task Force Members

By the summer of 2017, the investigation had evolved from one into whether a drug dealer named Antonio Shropshire had a cop helping him to an investigation into whether an entire plainclothes unit of the Baltimore Police Department was robbing civilians, stealing their money and even drugs. Our first big break had come when Shropshire found a GPS tracker stuck to the bottom of his car and called a cop, Momodu Gondo, and asked him what to do. When that happened, we had a wire on Shropshire's phone, and his call to Gondo enabled us to spin to a wire on Gondo's phone. From there we discovered, unexpectedly, that Gondo, Daniel Hersl, and Jemell Rayam, three of the five members of the Task Force at that time, had robbed a civilian they'd stopped. If they did it once, would they do it again? Had they done it before? Those were the questions we faced as the investigation expanded.

We pulled their arrest records and found the answer in phone calls made from jail. Again and again, when arrestees tried to make bail, they discovered their money was missing. And it wasn't just people who were arrested. We also learned the officers had robbed people when searching their homes.

Unexpectedly, in the summer of 2016, the Task Force got a new sergeant, Wayne Jenkins, and he brought three detectives with him—Evodio Hendrix, Marcus Taylor, and Maurice Ward. The new sergeant and the three new detectives were robbers, too, before joining the Task

Force. The confluence in one unit of the "legacy" Task Force members—Gondo, Rayam and Hersl—and the newcomers—Jenkins, Hendrix, Taylor, and Ward—created a perfect storm of corrupt cops.

From the start of the investigation to the day we charged the case, our team saw the truth about the Task Force from the outside. We had never spoken to any of its members. Their own thoughts, intentions, and interior worlds were beyond our reach, at least in the beginning, but not their actions.

The grand jury returned the indictment on February 29, 2017, under seal, which meant it was kept secret, by order of a US magistrate judge, and didn't appear on the court's docket, the public listing of all the documents filed in a particular case. The Task Force members wouldn't see it until the next day, when they came to court after being arrested. At that time, we asked the magistrate judge before whom they appeared to unseal the indictment.

Indictments tell defendants the charges they face. Some indictments function as simple lists: the defendant is charged with violating this or that part of the criminal code on such and such a date. We had gone further, presenting a "speaking indictment," which told the defendants not just which laws they had broken, but presented a narrative of what they had done. We hoped it would trigger an opening, giving us our first look at the truth from the inside; the idea was that by telling the defendants what we could prove at trial, they might decide to cooperate.

Defendants plead guilty and cooperate all the time. In fact, "cooperator" testimony is central to most fraud and corruption cases. White-collar cases turn on questions of intent, and insiders supply crucial evidence of that. They can describe what they observed and, more importantly, what a defendant told them when they thought no one was listening or looking. This offers a window into a defendant's thinking and, therefore, his or her intent. We had charged the case without any insiders. Even if none of the defendants cooperated, or flipped, we were confident a jury would convict based on the evidence presented. In other words, we would go to war with the army we had, not the army we wanted. If any of the defendants decided to cooperate, it would only make the case stronger.

The victims' testimony stood at the heart of the case, supported by their jail calls. We also had non-testimonial evidence to corroborate their testimony: recordings from Gondo's phone and car; surveillance footage of the Danziger robbery on North Longwood Street; CCTV footage of Sergio Summerville being robbed at the U-Store; location data from the Task Force officers' phones to prove overtime fraud; Gondo's and Rayam's suspicious bank deposits following the robbery of the Hamiltons; and more. We also had the testimony of the good cops in this story of bad cops, like the state trooper who had seized the $50,000 at the Westminster search and whom Ronald Hamilton called to complain about his missing $20,000 and other evidence.

Still, testimony from the Task Force officers themselves would be devastating at any trial. We could also learn about other crimes the officers had committed, and, indeed, we expected there were more. We had considered approaching one of them before the arrests were made and the charges unsealed. A cooperator at that point could have acted proactively, for example, recording conversations with other Task Force members. We ultimately decided it was too dangerous. We assumed they were loyal to one another and would follow the maxim that they would either hang together or hang separately. Still, we hoped that once the case went public, some of the officers would decide it was in their best interest to cooperate.

As we were getting ready to charge, my co-counsel, Derek Hines, found news reports of a police corruption case in Philadelphia. Six officers in a narcotics unit had been accused of robbing drug dealers and acquitted at trial. The "backbone" of the government's case, according to one newspaper article, was a corrupt police officer who had agreed to cooperate. The government also called nineteen drug dealers to the stand to testify that the defendants had robbed them and beaten them up. The article reported an alternate juror saying, "These guys have a tough job . . . The prosecutors were just nitpicking on paperwork." Of the government's cooperating witness, he remarked, "It was hard to believe a word he said, because of all the lying."

That was our fear. We needed to avoid both of these outcomes: one where the jury thought we were "just nitpicking" the police officer defendants' paperwork, and one where the witnesses would be dismissed by the jurors because the witnesses had sold drugs. We hoped our case was different, that we had enough evidence—the wiretap, the bug, the overtime fraud—that didn't rely on anyone's credibility.

We decided to wait to see if any of the defendants came to us after the charges were unsealed. We didn't have to wait very long. One at a time, four of the seven came forward—Rayam, Gondo, Ward, and finally Hendrix. Although defendants cooperate to get less jail time, there's no guarantee that they actually will receive a lighter sentence because judges, not prosecutors, impose the sentence.

When I work with a cooperator, my biggest concern is whether they are telling the truth. These are people who were involved in the same crimes as the defendant they're testifying against. Specifically, I worry about two things: the cooperator trying to shift blame from themselves to the defendant and trying to minimize their role, regardless of whether they try to shift the blame to someone else. Having said that, a cooperating defendant has a real incentive to tell the truth.

Prosecutors can decide not to recommend a reduced sentence if a cooperator lies, and they can even recommend a longer sentence. A cooperator doesn't know the full extent of a prosecutor's knowledge about their conduct, so hopefully, they will tell the prosecutor things the prosecutor doesn't know. A cooperator revealing things the prosecutor already knows is also valuable. The prosecutor can compare what she knows with what the cooperator is telling her to help gauge how honest the cooperator is being and to hear how the cooperator describes those facts.

Our indictment told the defendants that we knew about certain robberies. In our interviews with the cooperators, we first wanted to know whether what we thought had happened during those episodes had actually happened. Had we been justified in believing the victims? Were our interpretations of the wiretap and bug recordings accurate? In other words, had we gotten it right? We also wanted the cooperators to tell us about robberies we didn't know about, being confident that there were likely more.

In confirming details of the robberies we knew about and to learn about ones we didn't, our interview approach was to just let the cooperators speak, telling us what they had done. We didn't start with detailed questions about specific incidents, but instead asked open-ended questions. We began at the beginning: when was the first time they broke the law or saw someone else breaking the law? We didn't limit it to just taking money or seeing someone else taking money. We then moved chronologically through their various assignments and asked about the times they'd broken the law, episode by episode; if it was easier for them, we'd proceed by category of misconduct: stealing money, going into houses without warrants, lying on police reports, whatever they told us they had done. We only turned to specific episodes we knew about after we were satisfied that we'd gotten out of them everything that they were willing to volunteer.

The lawyers for each cooperator asked for immunity for their client. We gave each of them a limited form of immunity—colloquially "queen for a day" immunity—to get them to talk to us. Being queen for a day means whatever the defendant tells the government in an interview can't be used against him or her directly—"directly" being the operative word. The government can make "derivative" use of the information to acquire additional evidence, which *can* be used against a defendant. For instance, if a defendant admits that he shot someone and tells us he buried the gun in the woods, we can't use his confession against him, but we can go dig up the gun. If it has his fingerprints on it, we can use that evidence against him in building the case for that shooting. We tell cooperating defendants that we can use their testimony in such a way. In fact, I use the example of the buried gun when I explain it to them. Importantly, queen for a day immunity also doesn't mean that a defendant won't be prosecuted for the crimes he tells us about. That's a different kind of immunity—transactional immunity. No one was getting that.

I want cooperating defendants to know exactly what the deal is: We're not friends. They're not recipients of a Get Out of Jail Free card. They have to tell the truth—and they can help themselves by doing so—but there are still consequences for what they've done. If a defendant doesn't tell the truth, then even his admissions can be used against him. To "tell the truth" means not only answering our questions, but also not holding back. When I sit down to interview a defendant, I use the following example to demonstrate this point: If I ask you who was at a particular meeting and you say, "John and Tom," but you know that Mary was also there, you've left out a key fact that makes what you've told me untrue. The question asked required revealing everyone who was there, but if you deliberately leave someone out, you'll blow up your immunity, and I can use all the statements you made against you.

Rayam and Gondo—who along with Hersl formed the legacy contingent of the Task Force—were the first two cooperators we interviewed. We started with Rayam on March 21, 2017, twenty days after his arrest, spending almost an entire day with him. Then we talked to Gondo a week later, on March 27, 2017. Rayam's memory was good, but Gondo's was better. Rayam didn't volunteer much, but Gondo did.

Gondo told us what he and Rayam had been doing, stuff we hadn't known about. Then we went back to Rayam, and he confirmed what

Gondo had told us. That became the pattern. We ping-ponged, back and forth, between the two of them, with Gondo providing information new to us, and Rayam admitting his role when we mentioned what Gondo had told us.

We conducted the first of several sessions with Rayam in the middle of March 2017. Before that, I had only seen him in pictures and on grainy videos. When we met him in person, he had lost all his hair; he didn't even have eyebrows. I wondered if it was stress-induced. He was the most emotional of all the Task Force members by far. As we went through the incidents he participated in, he would put his head in his hands, sometimes lowering it all the way to the table, sometimes looking up at the ceiling. At times it looked like he was in physical pain recounting what he had done.

Gondo and Rayam had worked together on the Task Force for six years. In many respects, they were quite different. Rayam was emotional, Gondo was not. Rayam's recall of events jumped from episode to episode, detail to detail. Gondo's recall was chronological and precise.

Rayam had grown up in Newark, New Jersey. He graduated from DeSales University, in Pennsylvania, and moved to Maryland in 2005 to join the BPD. Two years later, he became a detective. He joined the Task Force in 2011. Gondo had grown up in Baltimore, on the Alameda. He finished high school and had "some college." He joined the BPD in 2005. His first assignment was patrol in the Northwest District. He became a detective a year or so before joining the Task Force in 2010.

Gondo's lack of emotion and precise, methodical recall came across most strikingly when he told us how he had been shot in 2006. Gondo had just driven up to his parents' house and was finishing a call to his girlfriend when two men approached his car. He described what happened next: "I proceeded to walk in front of my vehicle to go inside my parents' house. At that time something told me to turn around. Once I turned around, the guy rushing me with a .357. I hit the gun, reached for my gun, 'cause I had it in—in my waist area, tried to shoot back. He shot me three times in the back." Gondo described it in a matter-of-fact way and didn't even know why they had shot him.

Gondo admitted to helping Shropshire and Glenn Wells "by giving them information about police officers' whereabouts when they were committing their own crimes of selling drugs in the northeast area." He also remembered Shropshire finding the GPS device and calling him for help, so with him, we went back to the beginning of the investigation.

Both Rayam and Gondo admitted to robbing people, telling us that it had started when they left patrol and joined specialized, plainclothes units focusing on drugs and guns. Gondo explained that sometimes they only took some of the money, but other times they took it all. He also admitted to creating false police reports describing what they had done, to "cover our tracks."

Rayam said he robbed people "in a law enforcement capacity," during car stops and when executing search warrants. This was important information, as it confirmed our prosecution theory: the police powers of the officers facilitated their crimes. They could stop people like Ronald Hamilton on the street and then take money out of their pockets or go into their homes precisely because they were police officers.

Gondo told us that he and Rayam also robbed people while off duty, what Gondo referred to as "black ops." The first one he told us about, the only one he directly participated in, was the robbery at Aaron Anderson's apartment on Marnat Road. We had suspected from the beginning that Rayam and Gondo had played a role, and as it turned out, they had. Gondo was a lookout, standing by to respond as a police officer in case someone called the police. Had an officer shown up, Gondo would've pretended that he had also responded to the service call.

This was a trick I had heard about in a case I prosecuted against a defendant named Mario Wair, who went by the memorable nickname "Unda." In that case, Wair claimed that he was a BPD informant, which was true, and that he had been authorized to sell drugs by his BPD handler, which we knew wasn't. The BPD authorizes informants to buy drugs from other drug dealers, not sell them. That's one of the cardinal rules of undercover drug operations. If his BPD handler had indeed authorized Wair to sell drugs, then he would have had a "public authority defense." In other words, he would not be guilty because a police officer, who had the authority to authorize Wair to engage in criminal conduct—which is what happens in nearly all undercover operations—had given him permission to do so. The twist was that Wair's police handler had a horrendous internal affairs record. Specifically, he had beaten up his girlfriend, and when she called the police and they showed up, he claimed to be responding to the call and swore them off. I had assumed that that's why Wair went to trial: if Wair claimed the handler had authorized him to sell drugs, and the handler denied it, the jury would believe Wair, because the handler had so blatantly abused his police powers when he beat his girlfriend. In the end, the jury didn't believe Wair and convicted him.

In the Marnat Road robbery, Rayam's role differed from Gondo's. He wasn't a cop, but a robber. Gondo explained how it all began: Wells told Gondo that "an individual"—he didn't know Anderson—had $100,000 in his home that they could steal. Gondo then reached out to Rayam. Gondo wanted Rayam and Wells to "run in there and get it." Rayam's response was, "Yeah, I'll do it." That's all it took.

They placed a GPS device on Anderson's car. This was the other one we found when we arrested Anderson, the one that BPD detective Jonathan Crawford had bought. Gondo and Rayam had borrowed it from Crawford, who, Gondo explained, wasn't involved in the Anderson robbery. Gondo and Rayam used the GPS tracker to make sure Anderson was away from home when they "made entry," a law enforcement term that becomes an odd turn of phrase when describing kicking in someone's door while wearing a black mask.

Rayam told us that once he and Wells got inside, he went into the bedroom and discovered a woman lying on the bed. They weren't expecting anyone to be there. Rayam said she startled him. He pointed his gun at her. Rayam had trouble admitting that he threatened her. He told us he "could" have told her that he would kill her if she didn't tell him where the money was. We took that to mean that he did. She told him it was in a chest of drawers. Rayam found some money, a Rolex watch, a gold chain, and a gun. Meanwhile, Wells found about 800 grams of heroin. Rayam and Wells later met up with Gondo to split up what they had stolen. Wells sold the drugs, the gun, and the watch, giving some of the proceeds to Gondo and Rayam. They also shared the money that Rayam had found.

One of the things we asked Gondo and Rayam was how they came to be comfortable enough with Hersl to rob people with him so soon after he joined the Task Force. That had puzzled us. Gondo explained that Jenkins had vouched for Hersl when he became the Task Force's sergeant. Hersl was someone Gondo could trust to "have his back" when they were on the streets, going after "some of the worst people in Baltimore," and with internal affairs, when there were complaints. Gondo also understood that "if money was taken, they'll be with it basically." I asked Gondo what he meant by "if money was taken, they'll be with it." Was it turning a blind eye or lying to cover a colleague if internal affairs asked questions, or was it something more than that? He explained, "Basically that they have taken money before, and if money comes up, you can basically split the money with them, and they'll keep their mouth shut." It was all of the above.

On top of Jenkins vouching for Hersl to Gondo, Rayam had had an experience with Hersl taking money. It happened on the day Jenkins took over, June 13, 2016, when Rayam and Hersl were sent to secure a house while another officer went to a get the search warrant. The purpose of securing a location is to make sure evidence isn't destroyed or removed while a search warrant is being sworn out. The police can sit outside a house to stop anyone from going inside. The police can even go inside if there's any indication of evidence being destroyed. These are so-called exigent circumstances. Thus, for example, if the police are outside an apartment door and hear a toilet flushing repeatedly, they can enter the apartment on the prospect of preventing drugs from being flushed.

As Rayam and Hersl sat on the porch, the two had what Rayam described as a "normal" conversation, which he said was, "Hey, if there's any money, you know, we'll split it." What struck me was how abnormal a conversation that should be for two police officers to be having. It also suggested that it wasn't such a big deal for Gondo and Rayam to start robbing people with Hersl. Rayam and Hersl had already tried once. Ultimately, they didn't find any money when they searched the house, so there was nothing to split. After this episode, as Rayam put it, Hersl was "part of the team." Rayam explained that being "on the team" meant "he was okay with taking money." All this helped explain what happened during the search at the Hamiltons' house in Westminster.

Rayam said an informant had told him that Hamilton owned a handgun, something he wasn't allowed to have as a convicted felon. Rayam could seize the gun. Second, Rayam also believed that Hamilton had large sums of money at the house, which he and Jenkins could steal. Gondo told us something similar when we asked what had motivated him to go to Westminster: "For the curiosity of money. Also to see if he had a gun at the house, or drugs," Gondo said. Ultimately, all the Task Force officers would mention this duality: on the one hand, they would engage in some legitimate law enforcement action, like seizing an illegal handgun, and on the other hand, if they could steal money in the course of the same law enforcement operation, they would.

We asked Rayam if the search warrant affidavit he had written for Westminster was accurate. "Some," he responded. Was "some" truth better than none? I wasn't sure. Among other lies, Rayam claimed to be conducting physical surveillance of Hamilton, but we knew from the wiretap that Rayam was, in fact, looking at the illegal tracker app on his phone at exactly the time he claimed to be tailing Hamilton. That's how he knew where Hamilton was, not because he had eyes on him.

We also knew from the wire and from Hamilton himself some of what happened on July 8, 2016, the night of the robbery, and Rayam and Gondo filled in the rest. They both described how they had found money in the bedroom, taking the $20,000 that Hamilton said was missing and leaving the $50,000 for Carroll County officers to find. Before they left the bedroom, Gondo counted the money they would take. That's how they knew it was $20,000. But we also learned from both Gondo and Rayam that Hersl had been left alone in the room with the cash while Rayam went to talk to Jenkins.

That Hersl had been left alone with the money before they left Westminster explained, one, why $3,000 was missing when Rayam counted the money on the way to the casino later that night and, two, the source of the argument between him and Gondo heard that on the wiretap. We knew from calls that Gondo and Rayam eventually went to a bar where they met Jenkins and Hersl. When they got there, Rayam said, Gondo told Jenkins that $3,000 was missing and that Hersl had taken it. Jenkins didn't want any problems. They split the remaining money four ways.

We asked Rayam about the robbery of Sergio Summerville at the U-Store. His version of events tracked with what Summerville told us and what we had seen on the CCTV footage. Rayam admitted taking money from Summerville's sock and said he gave Marcus Taylor $60 of it.

To our surprise, Rayam told us that he hadn't given Jenkins a $100 like he'd told Gondo, and as we had heard him say on the bug. Instead, he kept it for himself. This was another indication that he was being truthful. We had no way of knowing that Rayam hadn't given Jenkins any money, but there he was, admitting to not only robbing Summerville, but to also lying about having shared money with Jenkins.

Rayam told us this wasn't the only robbery of a storage unit he'd participated in. This was new. On August 8, 2016, the Task Force members had chased a man driving a minivan from a different storage facility. When the man, Dennis Armstrong, bailed from his car, the officers pursued him on foot and ultimately arrested him. They found a bag of cash inside the minivan. While Rayam, Hersl, and Jenkins were waiting for Gondo and Crawford to return with the search warrant for Armstrong's storage unit, Hersl approached Rayam, who described Hersl's proposition this way: "Hey, Rayam, let's go to 7-Eleven. We going to get something to drink. We going to split some of the cash up." It sounded an awful lot like what they had discussed on the porch of the house they were waiting to search on Jenkins's first day with the squad.

Rayam was game. He saw Hersl grab the bag of cash. They did, in fact, go to 7-Eleven and then wound up in the parking lot of Archbishop Curley, the school next door. Hersl counted the cash, handing Rayam $500 and keeping $500 for himself.

"We're not going to tell anybody this," Hersl told Rayam.

"Okay, no problem," Rayam told us he said in response.

When Rayam and Hersl drove to the 7-Eleven, they had been in an unmarked BPD Chevrolet Impala. Rayam told us that while they were all detained together after being arrested on March 1, 2017, Hersl had approached him about this episode. Hersl was worried.

"Hey, you know, Rayam, did they have a microphone in the Impala?" Hersl asked. Rayam told him he didn't know.

"Well, what are you going to do?" Hersl asked. Rayam told him he was going to do the right thing. He was going to be honest and come forward with it. And he did.

There was, however, part of this story that Rayam couldn't explain. After he and Hersl split the money, they went back to the storage unit to wait for the warrant. When Crawford finally arrived, and they went to execute it, they discovered that someone had already broken into the storage unit. Rayam said they were all surprised and that Jenkins stated the obvious: Someone had gotten there before them. As we would later learn, Jenkins knew more than he was letting on.

TWELVE

Task Force Newcomers

After interviewing Jemell Rayam and Momodu Gondo, who had agreed to cooperate with us, we met next with Maurice Ward. He together with Evodio Hendrix and Marcus Taylor were newcomers to the Gun Trace Task Force. The three had previously served together under Jenkins in another squad. Jenkins, himself the other newcomer, had brought them with him to the Task Force when he took it over.

Jenkins was the common denominator between the two groups constituting the Task Force. Jenkins robbed people with Gondo, Daniel Hersl, and Rayam—the legacy members of the Task Force—almost as soon as he arrived, specifically the Hamiltons in Westminster. He also robbed people with Hendrix, Taylor, and Ward—the newcomers to the Task Force along with Jenkins—before they all got to the Task Force. When Ward asked to meet with us, we knew we'd get an insider account of the newcomers. We'd also find out what they'd done before they joined the Task Force.

Ward didn't project strength like Gondo or emotion like Rayam. He was smaller than both those men. His voice was quieter, and he didn't smile or find lighter moments as we spoke with him. He seemed profoundly sad. We next met with Hendrix, who was more like Ward than Gondo or Rayam. He was almost without emotion, other than exhibiting a kind of quiet respectfulness that seemed to reflect his midwestern roots. Hendrix's hair was longer than the others and looked like it needed a cut. He spoke slowly and deliberately.

Ward had grown up in Baltimore. He graduated from high school, took some college courses, and joined the Baltimore Police Department in 2003. He remembered the exact date: October 8. Hendrix had grown up in Cleveland and moved to Maryland in 2006 for his wife, who was in the military. They had five children. We knew from the wiretap on Gondo's phone and the bug in his car that Hendrix spent a lot of time with his kids. He seemed like a good father. Hendrix joined the Baltimore Police Department a couple of years after moving to Maryland. He met Taylor at the police academy. After the academy, both Ward and Hendrix worked in patrol. Hendrix started robbing people when he went to work for Jenkins on the Special Enforcement Section (SES) unit years before they all joined the Task Force. Ward couldn't remember exactly when he first stole money, just that it had begun when he went to an operational unit but before he went to work for Jenkins in the same SES unit as Hendrix. He didn't steal while on patrol. It surprised me that Ward had robbed people before he joined up with Jenkins; he seemed so meek. Ward told us that he had robbed people by himself and also with other police officers. When I asked him how often he did it by himself, he replied, "Pretty often." In those instances, he took $200 to $300. Gondo had called it "pocket surfing."

The first incident that Ward distinctly remembered was a robbery during a raid at the home of a man named Shawn Whiting in 2015. Taylor had found some money in a closet. Later, when they were alone, Taylor asked Ward to "look out for him." Ward understood it to mean that Taylor wanted in on any money that Ward stole. I asked Ward who got to decide if money was going to be stolen during the execution of a search warrant, and he explained: "It's usually the person who's in charge of that case, because ultimately they're the one who have to answer for it. So they will determine if money is taken and how much money you should get." Ward had been in charge of the Whiting search and arrest, so it was his call. That's why Taylor asked him to "look out for him."

After searching Whiting's house, the officers packed up the evidence and brought it to BPD's Western District. Taylor was left alone with it for a while. Afterwards, Ward noticed that the amount of money seized looked like less than when they'd arrived at the office. He assumed that Taylor had helped himself. Even so, Ward took $3,000 out of what was left, kept half of it and gave the other half to Taylor.

In early 2015, Ward got a call out of the blue from Jenkins. He asked Ward if he wanted to join a new unit he was standing up. It was going to be a Special Enforcement Section, or SES unit. "All daywork, no weekends, unlimited overtime" is how Ward described Jenkins's pitch. Its focus would be seizing guns and making gun arrests. At around the same time, Jenkins also asked Hendrix to join him. Taylor would join later.

Hendrix explained that once he got to Jenkins's squad, he started getting overtime pay for hours he didn't work. The key was seizing guns: "Because the more guns we got, the more money we would get due to overtime" was how Hendrix described it. Guns were the metric the BPD used to measure success. So, if detectives were seizing guns, no one would question how much overtime they claimed to be working. The higher-ups would just assume that they were working long hours to get all those guns. They assumed wrong. Instead, to seize guns, officers engaged in dubious and abusive police practices on the Jenkins-led SES squad and later on the Task Force under Jenkins. Hendrix described several of them to us, including one involving book bags: "We actually targeted adults with book bags, because the thought was if you're an adult, you know, and you're walking the streets, why do you have a book bag? It could possibly be something within the book bag that was illegal." That's all it took. A book bag.

Ward similarly told us that he'd started committing overtime fraud as soon as he went to work for Jenkins on the SES unit and continued it when he went to the Task Force with Jenkins. And like Hendrix,

Ward also told us about the connection between overtime and questionable tactics. We asked him to explain how it worked, and he responded, "Well, overtime, like I said, was never actually based off how many hours we worked. It was what we did." Apparently, "what we did" meant gun seizures. Ward elaborated:

There were nights where we could come in like a Sunday, 6 o'clock, 7 o'clock, and we would get a gun in 30 minutes. We would go home in two hours, and we'd get eight hours' worth of overtime for things like that.

So the overtime was always based off how many guns we got or what was the quality of the arrest. But then it also always depended on Jenkins, how much he was going to give us. So he was always the one would tell us the amount that we was going to get.

In other words, "overtime" really wasn't overtime. It was a bonus system that Jenkins controlled. We asked Ward if they ever discussed with Jenkins what would happen if someone at BPD questioned why they were submitting so much overtime.

"That's the thing," Ward said. "He would always say about [how] your work speaks for itself . . . If you go out and get three, four guns, he said we could vouch for getting eight, nine, ten, twelve hours' overtime."

But they weren't actually working that much overtime.

Ward explained, "Well, the way our overtime worked, it wasn't based off how many hours. It was what we did. So if we got two, three, or four guns, depending on how many guns we got that night, that's how much overtime. We might could only work four or five hours of overtime that night. If we got three or four guns, we might have got 12 hours of overtime that night because we got so many guns."

The Task Force members were seen as so successful because of the number of guns they seized that Jenkins also let them slack off during their regular shifts. Ward told us that while their shift was 8:00 a.m. to 4:00 p.m., no one ever worked those hours: "The earliest I would say we probably got in might have been 10:00 a.m. at the earliest, typically around noon." That's also what Gondo had told us.

We asked Ward how they knew when to start, and he explained that they would receive a group text from Jenkins using a simple code.

"It was pretty much: 'Break off your investigation and meet me at headquarters,' and he would say a time," Ward explained. "So when he said that, I mean, we all knew what it meant. We were all home. We weren't working on an investigation. So when he said, 'Break off your investigation. Meet me at headquarters at 3 o'clock,' that would mean leave your house, be at work by 3:00."

Ward estimated that he typically worked half his regular shift, but there were also a "lot of times" when they didn't work any of their shifts.

We'd uncovered a vicious cycle: guns meant overtime. Thus incentivized, and lacking integrity, the officers used illegal police tactics to get the guns. For that, they got paid more. The scheme demonstrated how important it is to choose the right metric for measuring the effectiveness of the police. Like Hendrix, Ward described various abusive police tactics that they'd use to seize guns so they could claim more overtime:

Well, it was kind of chaotic. It was the wild way. Jenkins was always the driver because he said he was the slower—he didn't like to run. Taylor, typically, he always rode in the passenger seat because he was the fastest . . . Jenkins had this technique he called a "door pop."

It's pretty much he would pull up to—if he seen a large crowd on a corner, he would pull up to them aggressively speeding and slam on his brakes. And then Taylor would be the passenger. And he would pop his door open real quick and act like he was going to like run out and grab somebody, and it would startle 'em. It would scare 'em. And usually he believed if someone had like drugs or guns, they knew we were coming to get them, and they would take off running. So typically the person who ran from the door pops, that is the person we would chase.

I asked Ward whether they ever had any reason to drive up fast at a crowd of people the way he described. He said they hadn't. When asked how often they did the door pops, he replied, "On a slow night, 15 to 20, a slow night. On a fast night, anywhere 50-plus, easy."

In short, they terrorized the neighborhoods they were supposed to be protecting. The door pop relied on fear. The Task Force officers scared people into running and then ran them down. On average, the door pop tactic yielded two guns a night, so doing the math, if they chased fifteen to twenty people on a slow night or fifty on a fast night, out of those chases, on average, two men would be carrying guns.

I asked Ward whether there was any reason to target the people they surprised with door pops. He told me there wasn't. They were just groups of mostly African American men hanging out on street corners or in other public places in East and West Baltimore. The Task Force's law enforcement strategy, if you could call it that, was that if you scared enough of them, and enough of them ran, they would eventually catch someone with a gun. Most of our jurors—living across the state—would have never experienced anything like this. In their communities, the idea of the police driving at high speeds toward people walking on the street to see if anyone ran would be unthinkable. Where you live determines a lot.

Ward also described how Jenkins did car stops. I started by asking him what kind of circumstances justified one.

"Really none," he said. "It was just, depending on a car, Jenkins liked to profile a lot. So he had his thing he called 'dope boy cars.' A Honda Accord, an Acura TL, any type of Acura, a Honda Odyssey—he claims those are typically cars that drug dealers in Baltimore would drive. And those were the cars that he liked to pull over."

The inclusion of Honda Odysseys, which are minivans, and Honda Accords, fairly nondescript sedans, struck me as odd. They didn't seem like the kinds of cars drug dealers would drive. Having said that, both Oreese Stevenson and Dennis Armstrong were driving minivans when they were arrested. I asked Ward what justification Jenkins used for pulling over these kinds of cars.

"None," he said. "I mean, he would always say seat belts or a tint violation, but those wasn't true. It was just the type of car. That's the reason why we stopped it."

Stevenson had said he was told he had a tint violation when the Task Force officers arrested him, but his windows weren't tinted.

When we charged the case, we knew the Task Force had stolen money. We also knew some victims, like Stevenson, had reported drugs missing. We didn't, however, know if the Task Force was also in the business of stealing drugs. This we would learn from Ward, who told us that when they seized drugs, Jenkins took them. Jenkins claimed he was going to submit them to the BPD's evidence control unit. Ward said he never saw Jenkins do any such thing. He and Hendrix suspected Jenkins was selling them.

Ward described overhearing a conversation that confirmed his suspicions. One evening, Ward, sitting in a cubicle across the hall from Jenkins's office, heard Jenkins talking to someone on the phone. The person they'd arrested that evening had had a couple of ounces of marijuana on him. They weren't turned in, which Ward told us was Jenkins's way; they never saw him turn drugs in to the evidence control unit. Ward heard Jenkins tell the person on the phone that he had "some good weed" and that "it's going to be same price as last time," if the person wanted it. That's where the drugs went.

When it came to money, Ward told us that he usually wanted to turn some of it in when he stole it. Gondo and Rayam had said the same thing, and they all gave the same explanation—to cover themselves.

Ward described a spring 2015 incident that departed from his usual approach.

Ward was in Jenkins's SES squad at the time, along with Hendrix and Taylor; Hendrix was off the day in question. Jenkins, Taylor, and Ward went to a large apartment building, Belvedere Towers, which sits at the intersection of Falls Road and Northern Parkway in Baltimore City. I knew the building—I drove by it on the way to the pool where I take my kids swimming—but I had no idea that it was, according to Ward, the site of a lot of drug deals. As a result, Jenkins liked to frequent it.

In the parking lot that day, the Task Force came across two men standing outside their cars. Jenkins told Ward and Taylor to handcuff them, which they did. Jenkins then informed them that he was a federal agent and had been listening to them on a wiretap. That's how he knew they were about to meet and do a drug deal.

None of that was true, of course. Jenkins wasn't a federal agent; there was no wiretap. Identifying himself as a federal agent though obscured who the officers really were. If the men in handcuffs wanted to complain, it would make no sense to call the BPD, so who could they call? There are dozens of federal law enforcement agencies—the FBI, DEA, ATF, just to name a few. Jenkins didn't tell them for which one he worked.

With the men handcuffed, Jenkins went into their cars and popped the trunks. He found a duffel bag full of cash in one of the trunks, and in the other he found a duffel bag full of marijuana. The Task Force had interrupted a drug deal. Regardless, Jenkins didn't have a warrant for either car, and neither man had given him consent to search their vehicles. Jenkins hadn't even asked. He put both duffel bags in the back of his unmarked BPD car.

Jenkins repeated that he was a federal agent and told them that they weren't the main targets of his wiretap investigation, which is why he wasn't going to arrest them. He told them they would receive documentation from the US Attorney's Office about the seizure. Ward said they took down their names because Jenkins thought the guy with the drugs in his car probably had more marijuana, and he wanted to do a "follow up" on him. Ward didn't, however, remember the men's names. No police report was written about this encounter, and nothing was turned in to BPD, so we had nothing with which to refresh his memory.

After taking the handcuffs off the men, the detectives told them they were free to go. After leaving Belvedere Towers, Jenkins told Taylor and Ward that he knew a spot where they could go to split the money. Jenkins drove to a wooded area in Baltimore County and parked. All three took off their vests, the only thing that would have identified them as police. Jenkins told Ward and Taylor to leave their cell phones in the car. I asked Ward if he knew why Jenkins had done that.

Ward responded, "He said if anybody ever tried to track or trace us, they wouldn't be able to pinpoint us directly back in the woods. You know, we could just say we just pulled over to use the bathroom, went into the woods, use the bathroom or something real quick."

While in the woods, Jenkins gave each of them $5,000. He kept the rest for himself. Before they left, Jenkins gave them a little speech:

> Don't deposit this money into a bank account. Don't pay off no credit card bills and things like that. Just use it for small—like pay for cash or buy small things. Don't go out and buy no big purchase.

Ever their sergeant, this for Jenkins was a teachable moment, a bad-cop training session, if you will.

Gondo had told us how Jenkins had given him and Rayam and Hersl a similar speech after the robbery of Ronald Hamilton at Westminster. That we heard such stories from two different officers in relation to two different robberies increased our confidence that both were telling us the truth. It was a small detail, but details mattered.

With money in their pockets from the Belvedere Towers robbery, Jenkins had wanted to celebrate. "We went to a strip club," Ward told us. "We ate. We had a couple of drinks. Jenkins eventually even got a lap dance."

After that, they went home for the day. Ward said he left his $5,000 in the trunk of the car they'd been using. I asked him why:

I was kind of paranoid, kind of scared. We just took $20,000, 20 pounds of marijuana. There was no documentation. It's a possibility that it might have been on camera.

And I was afraid that—you never know who those guys are. They might have been working with federal agents. They might have been informants. They could have called in a complaint.

And if we're on camera, the next thing I know, I might be getting my door kicked in or something like that and still had the evidence, because $5,000 is a lot of money. I don't just spend $5,000 in one day. There was nowhere I could hide the money, put it anywhere.

That was the most money he had ever taken, Ward told us. Jenkins never mentioned the incident again.

We questioned Ward and Hendrix at length about the robbery of Oreese Stevenson, the theft on Heathfield Road involving a safe with hundreds of thousands of dollars in it. It turned out to be the biggest theft committed by any of the Task Force members. Both Ward and Hendrix told us the same basic story.

Ward remembered that Jenkins had interrogated Stevenson after they'd arrested him. When Jenkins was finished, he told them, "This was a big one." Hendrix told us that this meant someone with a lot of drugs and money. Ward explained that when they got to Stevenson's house on Heathfield Road, Jenkins wanted to do a "sneak and peek."

Both Ward and Hendrix used that phrase to describe what they were up to.

There is such a thing as a "sneak and peek" warrant. When law enforcement executes a search warrant, they have to leave a copy of the warrant with the homeowner and an inventory of what was taken. A "sneak and peek" warrant authorizes law enforcement to go into a location without doing that, in other words, without telling the homeowner that law enforcement had searched their home. Sneak and peek warrants are usually executed in the middle of the night, and typically, nothing is seized because that would tip off the target that someone had been in the house. They're uncommon; judges will only authorize them under special circumstances.

I suspected that Ward and Hendrix weren't talking about a lawful sneak and peek warrant. We asked Ward what he meant. He said, "If we're trying to go in somebody's house, and he might think it was more money or drugs or guns in there, you would go in there without nobody knowing and sneak around the house and take a peek and search through the house without a search warrant."

It was the exact opposite of standard procedure. They were illegally searching a house, in violation of the Fourth Amendment, to see if there was anything inside worth seizing. If they found anything, then they would write a warrant to go back and get it. It was completely backwards.

Once inside the house on Heathfield Road, all four officers fanned out and began their search. At some point Jenkins called them to the basement. When Ward got downstairs, he found Jenkins standing with a kilo of cocaine in his hand.

"When was the last time one of y'all seen one of these?" Jenkins asked.

As Ward looked around the basement, he saw drugs and guns. And then he saw a safe. Jenkins, Taylor, and Hendrix left to get a search warrant. When they came back, hours later, Jenkins had brought a pry bar and battering ram with him. A pry bar, as the name suggests, is used to pry things open. It is a long metal pole, beveled at the end. A ram is the heavy metal tube that the police use to smash open locked doors when executing warrants.

After putting the safe on its back, the officers went to work on it. Jenkins took the lead with the pry bar, sticking it in the seam around the door. Taylor and Hendrix took turns hitting the pry bar with the ram. Eventually they broke it open. I asked Ward what was inside: "A lot of money."

Jenkins asked Hendrix how much money Stevenson had told them was in his house, information they would have learned after they arrested him. "Was it a hundred grand?" Jenkins asked. Hendrix agreed that Stevenson had said a hundred grand even though there was no evidence that Stevenson had actually said such a thing. Stevenson had told us it was $200,000. This dialogue seemed staged so that Jenkins could claim, if the search was ever questioned, that Stevenson had said there was $100,000 in the safe, and Hendrix would back him up.

Jenkins started taking money out of the safe. Once he had emptied it, he put $100,000 back in. But, Ward told us, there had been "a lot more than that" in the safe when they first opened it.

Jenkins placed the cash he hadn't put back in the safe in a black bag, then he came up with another idea: they would close the safe and then, using one of their phones, record themselves opening it as if it were for the first time.

I asked Ward why they had done this. He replied, "Just in case Mr. Stevenson had made a complaint saying that money was taken, we would say like, 'No. Look, we have a video of us opening the safe. This was the first time the safe was opened and the only time the safe was opened.'"

This was the third time we had heard about the officers making phony videos. Sergio Summerville, the man they robbed at the U-Store in South Baltimore, had told us that they recorded him saying he hadn't been hurt. Keona Holloway, Stevenson's wife, who had been at Heathfield Road, told us that they had recorded Jenkins turning his key in the lock after they returned with the search warrant, even though she had been inside with Ward for hours at that point. And now this.

Jenkins went upstairs and told the others to call him once they'd opened the safe again. He would come downstairs, recorded on video, to "make it seem like it was the first time he had knew anything about the safe," Ward explained.

So that's what they did. They closed the safe and it relocked, after which Ward and Hendrix went to work on it, again. The second time was easier, Ward told us. Despite having been forced open once, the safe still made a loud pop the second time they pried it open.

According to Ward, they left with money but not drugs. Stevenson had told us that he had ten kilos stashed in the house, two more than the eight kilos that were seized. We specifically asked Ward whether drugs were taken at Heathfield, and he denied knowing anything about it. Ward had already told us that Jenkins had taken a duffel bag full of marijuana at Belvedere Towers and that he had overheard Jenkins on the phone selling stolen drugs. Ward therefore had no reason to hold back if he knew drugs had been taken. We suspected Jenkins of taking the missing two kilos, but that's a lot of drugs. How had he done it, and what had he done with it?

After robbing Stevenson, they all went to Taylor's house because he lived alone. They divvied up the money, each getting $20,000, so Ward, Hendrix, and Taylor got $60,000 between them. That's the number, "20 gs," that Jenkins had mentioned in a call to Rayam during which this particular robbery had come up. This was the same call that had so enticed Rayam that he told Gondo about it. Rayam, claiming to be in need of "50 gs," thought that Jenkins wanted to do another big robbery, but this time with him and Gondo, not with Hendrix, Taylor, and Ward. That call corroborated what Ward was telling us. He hadn't known about it.

At Taylor's house, Jenkins delivered the same speech he'd given at Westminster and at Belvedere Towers. "Don't go out and buy no cars,"

Jenkins said, according to Ward. "Don't spend the money. Don't deposit it into a bank. Don't spend large sums of money." Then Jenkins added something new.

Ward told us that Jenkins had counseled, "If anybody needed work on your house or anything like that, he had a buddy who fixed homes. And you could pay him and he could like finagle the receipts to make the price show something different to get work done on your house so it wouldn't come back on you." Ward told us that after the Stevenson robbery, Taylor had gotten a new deck, and Taylor told Ward that he had used Jenkins's guy to "finagle the receipts."

On the way home, Ward had time to think about what had just happened. "Should I keep it or not keep it?" was the question he struggled with. He decided not to. It was the same conclusion he had reached after the Belvedere Towers robbery, except that time he didn't have to do anything. He just left the money in Jenkins's trunk. Now he had the money. What to do with it?

When Ward got home, he walked into a wooded area separating his housing development from another one. He tossed the bundle of money into the woods. We asked him why—why didn't he keep the money after having gone through all that trouble to get it?

Well, for one, you don't want to be the one in the squad to be like, you know, I'm not with that. Like, you want not to make them feel that you would tell on them. You don't want to get blackballed.

And I don't have, like—I think I was the only one still renting my house. I couldn't take $20,000 and get my whole house redone, countertops and all that stuff, 'cause I'm renting. So I didn't have the means to put the money to anything.

I wasn't going to put that money and the family in my house, jeopardize and get them in trouble. So it's just too much. The bad outweighed the good.

We asked Ward if he only wanted to take small amounts. Was that what made him toss the money?

He replied, "No, I would have loved to keep the $20,000 if it was a means that I could keep it and not get caught."

That was an honest answer if I ever heard one. He didn't try to minimize his conduct or blame someone else. Jenkins didn't make him do it. He didn't say he *wasn't* greedy. He said he would have "loved" to keep the $20,000. He was just afraid of getting caught. It was self-preservation and nothing else.

After Ward and Hendrix told us about the video, we went back to the Task Force's computers, which we had seized the day of their arrest. We found the video there, and it showed just what Hendrix and Ward had described.

"Do not nobody touch this. Do you understand me right now?" Jenkins is heard shouting. He was huddled with Hendrix, Ward, and Taylor around a safe in a dark basement. The door to the safe had just popped, pried open with a metal bar by Hendrix and Ward. Taylor was recording the grainy video on his cell phone. Someone flooded the open safe compartment with light. When the image focused, stacks of money became visible in the safe, but the safe was only half full.

Like the other videos they had made, but perhaps more vividly, this one revealed another dimension of the Task Force's distortion of the truth: they manufactured false evidence. It was in many ways a perfect piece of evidence because videos, unlike a drug dealer, don't lie. They "produced" the video to cover their tracks, to "document" that they had only found $100,000 in the safe. In the unlikely event that Stevenson complained to internal affairs or anyone else, the Task Force members could present the video to prove that he wasn't to be believed. Now we would turn it against them.

This video and the others demonstrated that body cameras alone can't solve the problem of bad policing. It was made after the death of

Freddie Gray Jr. but before body cameras became widely used in the BPD. Gray's death supported the growing perception that body cameras could help the public monitor the police. The phony safe-popping video demonstrated that although cameras can be used to reveal the truth if they capture what actually happens, they can also obscure the truth by preserving a false record. The larger point is that technology alone can't fix the problem. The integrity of individual officers still matters most.

One of the things that Ward told us, without prompting, was that Jenkins had a habit of asking a particular question when they arrested certain kinds of suspects: "Typically, anytime we ever stopped anybody with any type of like quantity of drugs on them, the big question that Jenkins would always ask them was like: 'If you could put your own crew together and rob the biggest drug dealer you know, who would that drug dealer be?'"

This was what Hamilton had told us Jenkins had asked him. Ward wasn't present when the Task Force officers robbed Hamilton. There was nothing connecting the two of them except the truth. Hamilton was telling the truth when he told us that Jenkins had asked him this remarkable question. Hamilton had told Jenkins he would rob President Obama, but to Jenkins the question wasn't a joke.

On the day we arrested the Task Force officers, we also searched their cars. Among the things we found were BB guns. We asked Ward about them. He told us he kept a BB gun in his trunk because Jenkins had told him to: "Jenkins explained to us it was something that he did just in case we ever, like, accidentally hit somebody or got into a shootout and they didn't have a gun on 'em, so we could plant that BB gun or air pistol on 'em to make it seem like we thought they had a gun; that's why we shot 'em."

Ward said they always kept BB guns in the car they "did their rips in," but that he'd never planted one on anybody. Later we would learn that Jenkins had.

We also asked Hendrix whether Jenkins had ever told him or other members of the Task Force to carry BB guns. According to him, "He said just in case something happens and you need to get yourself out of a situation, like—'cause basically we have wife and kids, you know, that need us, so basically to protect yourself if something was to occur."

We asked what that meant, if something "was to occur," to which Hendrix responded, "Something that happens where you hurt someone and you need to cover yourself, it's easy to put the BB gun down as if they had a handgun."

BB guns. Bad cop insurance.

THIRTEEN

New Charges, New Defendants

As we debriefed the Gun Trace Task Force cooperators in the spring and summer of 2017, we began preparing additional charges against Daniel Hersl, Wayne Jenkins, and Marcus Taylor, the Task Force members who chose not to cooperate and who were heading to trial. First, we decided to bring a superseding indictment, which as the name suggests, replaced the original one that the grand jury had returned in February 2017. A superseding indictment can be used to add defendants to a case, to add charges, or both. In this case, the new indictment against Hersl, Jenkins, and Taylor would include the robberies charged in the original indictment plus the additional robberies we had learned about since then. We also decided to bring charges in separate indictments against new defendants, whom we had learned about while debriefing the cooperators. Finally, we decided to bring a free-standing indictment against Jenkins alone for violating two defendants' civil rights, a charge we hadn't earlier considered.

Processing the additional events we had learned about differed from how we'd previously proceeded. On the one hand, we had the obvious advantage of four insiders telling us what had happened. Before, when we brought the original charges, we had been outsiders looking in. We had various pieces of evidence—the testimony of victims, recordings, video, for example—but we didn't know the whole story. We filled in the gaps by drawing inferences. As we did that, I always worried that we might be getting it wrong and felt we had no margin for error. It would be devastating to go to trial and learn that we had made a mistake, that we had relied on a victim who was wrong or, worse, actually had lied to us. If that happened, I thought we would lose. Our whole argument to the jury was going to be that they should trust the victims, that they should believe them and not the police officer defendants. If that belief was misplaced in one instance, why not in others? That's what the defense would argue in any event.

We mitigated the possibility that the cooperators might coordinate their stories by holding them in four different jails around the state. That they implicated themselves in nearly all the additional crimes they told us about alleviated our fear that they had concocted them to try to get lower sentencing recommendations out of us. If obtaining shorter sentences was their goal, that wasn't the way to do it.

While we now had the advantage of having access to insiders, we had lost the ability to operate in secret. Before we unsealed the indictment, the investigation had been covert. That had allowed us to use techniques like tapping phones and planting the bug in Gondo's Baltimore Police Department car. Nothing rivals that kind of evidence. The statements the defendants made on the phone or near the bug came from their own mouths, so the jury wouldn't need to weigh anyone's credibility or memory to believe the statements. The wiretap and the bug acted like time machines, taking the jury back to the scene of the crime as if they were there. We had no recorded conversations involving the robberies we learned about in the summer of 2017, so without the revelations from the cooperators, it would have taken an actual time machine to take us back to them.

We presented the superseding indictment against Hersl, Jenkins, and Taylor to the grand jury in June 2017, charging three additional robberies on top of the ones in the original indictment. We learned about two of the new ones, the robberies of Shawn Whiting and Dennis Armstrong, from the cooperators themselves, and the third one, the robbery of Jimmie Griffin, was brought to us after the charges became public.

Maurice Ward had volunteered during his debriefings that the first robbery he remembered committing had taken place during the search of a house owned by a man named Shawn Whiting. After Ward told us this, the FBI located him.

Born in Baltimore, Whiting had lived his whole life in the city; his schooling ended in the tenth grade. At 54, Whiting was one of the oldest victims we encountered. He also had one of the biggest personalities and didn't hold anything back. For example, early on during our first interview, we asked him what he did for a living in 2014. "I paint and sell drugs," he told us without missing a beat.

On January 24, 2014, the police had searched Whiting's house on North Gilmor Street, in West Baltimore, and arrested him. He told us he had had $15,970 in a bag in his closet at the time of the search. He'd made the money selling drugs. Whiting showed us a photo he had taken of the money. That's how he remembered how much he had; you could see the bills in the photo, time stamped January 17, 2014, six days before the raid and robbery. Whiting also told us that he had had $5,500 in a jacket in a closet and $2,500 in his bedroom nightstand. That money had come from painting houses. That made a total of $23,970 in his house, nearly all of it in $100 bills.

Whiting told us he awoke to the sound of his daughter screaming on the morning of January 24, 2014. As he got out of bed, the police were already at his bedroom door. Guns drawn, the officers handcuffed him and took him downstairs.

Taylor and a sergeant named David Tusk brought down the bag from the closet containing money, Whiting said. When asked how much was in the bag, he told them $15,970. Then they asked him to count the money in front of them so they wouldn't have to use the money counter at BPD.

"I told 'em I ain't going to do their job," Whiting said. "They do their job theirself." This flash of personality was consistent with how he spoke with us in general.

At the time of the raid, Whiting also had four and a half kilos of heroin in his house. Whiting was booked after his arrest, but his charging documents said the police had recovered three kilos of heroin. We asked why he hadn't complained that some of the drugs were missing.

"Who going to complain about more, extra drugs?" an incredulous Whiting responded.

Exactly. It didn't surprise us that someone who sold drugs wasn't going to complain that he had more drugs than what the police turned in. He told us he worried that saying something would lead to more significant charges. Whiting's charge papers also listed an "undisclosed amount of money" as having been recovered.

Released on bail, Whiting went home. All the money and drugs were gone, but so were other things: a black Gucci belt; Dolce & Gabbana cologne; his brand-new black Nike Air Jordans (a limited edition for which he'd needed a ticket to buy them); a pair of glow-in-the-dark Nike Airs; and two sets of PlayStation game controllers that he had just bought for his kids. Whiting said he still had the receipts for the controllers.

When asked what he thought when he got home and found all these things missing, he told us, "They robbed me and took 'em."

A month later, in February, the DEA sent Whiting a letter telling him how much money had been turned in: $7,650, not the $23,970 that had actually been in his house before the police arrived. Whiting called internal affairs and told them the police had robbed him and taken his money: "I said, 'You can lie-detector me.' I said they only submitted $7,650 in the letter, according to the DEA. But I had way more money than that. And I told them about the other items that was tooken from me."

Whiting not only complained to internal affairs, in 2015 he also wrote a letter to the US Department of Justice. In February 2017—right before we charged the Task Force officers—he wrote to the FBI. We asked him why he wrote those letters. He responded, " 'Cause I knew possibly if they doing it to me, that it's [also] other people. Just like if you going stealing candy from the candy store and getting away with it, you going to keep doing it. And I knew possibly that they were going to get caught."

He was right.

We also interviewed Dennis Armstrong, who rented another storage unit that the Task Force robbed—the one Jemell Rayam told us about when he said that he and Hersl had gone to the Archbishop Curley parking lot to split up some of the money. Armstrong answered our questions about himself and the day of his arrest by the Task Force without any apparent agenda. By the time I met Armstrong, this had been my experience with nearly all the victims, and I developed a theory about why they spoke to us: None of the men, and they were almost all men, had ever been questioned by law enforcement about other law enforcement officers. They had been questioned about their own drug dealing or the drug dealing of others. They had developed strategies for that. Some of them refused to cooperate at all, adhering to a principle that held snitching as something to be avoided at all costs. Others would only talk about their own conduct, not others.

Their approaches made a certain amount of intuitive sense: If no one talked to the police, then it would be that much harder for the police to do their jobs. But there were obvious exceptions. Plenty of arrestees did talk, hoping for a reduced sentence. Others agreed to "take the charge," falsely claiming the drugs belonged only to them when the police found them in their family's home or cars. What we were doing stood the experience of people like Armstrong on its head. We were the police as far as the victims knew, but we were asking them about other police officers in situations where the victims knew the police had done something wrong. The victims, therefore, trusted us and shared with us what they knew.

Armstrong, a life-long Baltimorean, was 37 when we met him, but he looked older. He had a criminal record. In 2011, in state court, he was sentenced to fifteen years in prison, with ten years suspended, for drug distribution. This was a common kind of sentence in Maryland state courts; a seemingly long sentence was actually a much shorter one, but with the possibility of going back to jail hanging over the defendant's head. The logic was that a suspended sentence would keep a former inmate from offending again, at least while they were "backing up time."

When we met Armstrong in 2017, he had been working as a maintenance man for the Baltimore City Housing Authority for four years. What most distinguished him from other victims was how he spoke, in short bursts, like he was spitting words out as fast as he could. He admitted that he had been selling drugs that he kept in his storage locker. Armstrong had $8,000 in his glove compartment when he watched Hersl pry it open. Not long after that, a transport van pulled up to take Armstrong to Central Booking.

After some twenty hours, Armstrong was released on bail. His charging papers indicated that only $2,800 had been recovered from his van, not $8,000. The paperwork also stated that only a few grams of cocaine had been recovered from his storage unit.

Armstrong didn't complain. He only got a month in jail for the few grams of cocaine the police turned in. He would have done a lot more time if he'd admitted to having more cocaine, plus he had the ten years suspended from his 2011 sentence still hanging over his head.

After being released, Armstrong went to his storage unit and took pictures, which he showed us. They showed the unit had been torn apart. The question was by whom?

While our team debriefed the Task Force cooperators and investigated the additional robberies they'd recounted in spring 2017, a lawyer contacted us. His client, Jimmie Griffin, claimed to have been robbed by Hersl when Hersl arrested him on drug charges. Figuring out what happened in this episode required us to rely on what Griffin told us, reinforced by whatever corroboration we could find. It was like the robberies in the original indictment. We had no inside view.

Griffin was in federal prison, which made him different from all the other victims. Griffin's case had been "adopted" federally, meaning that although he was arrested on state drug charges, the BPD had presented his case to federal law enforcement, who then decided to charge him in federal court. Griffin ultimately pled guilty in federal court to possession with intent to distribute a hundred grams or more of heroin. The charge carried a significant sentence. Griffin hoped that if he cooperated with our investigation, we would ask the court to reduce his sentence. So, unlike the other victims in our case, Griffin would get something in return for his cooperation. That meant we had to be extra careful to make sure we could rely on what he had to say.

When we met Griffin, he was in his late twenties. He had grown up in Northeast Baltimore. He graduated high school but had never held a job. He admitted that he sold drugs for a living. His other source of income had been from lead paint settlements.

Many of Baltimore's rowhouses contain lead in the layers of paint on the walls; in addition, old pipes carry more lead into the houses through the drinking water. In 1950, Baltimore became the first US city to ban the use of lead in residential construction, but it didn't remove the lead already in homes across the city. Children exposed to lead experience cognitive delays and learning disabilities. Among the more insidious aspects of lead paint is its sweet taste. As a result, young children, always putting things in their mouth, would eat the paint chips that fall off things like windows as they age or are moved up and down.

Lead poisoning negatively correlates with income, meaning the poorest neighborhoods have the highest incidence of it. Rowhouses in poor neighborhoods are less likely than homes in more affluent neighborhoods to have undergone remodeling that included lead remediation. Lead poisoning became the subject of thousands of lawsuits in Baltimore, and lawyers representing victims like Griffin negotiated settlements with landlords. The victims received payouts in a lump sum or spread over time.

Griffin told us that he had received a little more than $200,000 for a lead paint settlement in 2010. Griffin's sister, aunt, and cousins had received settlements as well. Griffin explained that each time someone in the family received a settlement, they shared it with the others. Griffin used some of his settlement money to purchase a house on Pinewood Avenue. He lived there with his mother, his two sisters, his brother, and a cousin.

On November 5, 2014, BPD police executed a search warrant at Griffin's home and found drugs. At the time, Griffin was in a friend's backyard smoking some of the marijuana he had bought that day. The police, including Hersl, went to the house where Griffin was smoking. Hersl recognized Griffin.

Griffin told us that Hersl grabbed him and said, "Yeah, you didn't think I was going to get you, did you? You didn't think I was going to get you, did you? Don't you know who I am? Like I'm Hersl."

According to Griffin, Hersl then walked him from the backyard into the ground floor of the house. Another officer was with them. Once inside, Hersl went into Griffin's pockets and found $6,000. The money was from Samantha Irby, his aunt, who had received it in a lead paint settlement for her son, Tyrone. Griffin told us he had another $6,000 in a safe at his house. That money had come from selling drugs.

After Hersl found the money in Griffin's pocket, he started counting it in front of the other officer.

"Geez," Hersl said, "this guy making more money than us."

Next, Hersl took some gold chains from around Griffin's neck. With the money and the chains in hand, he turned to leave. As Hersl walked out of the door, he told the other officer, "Check his rectum. He's known to keep stuff in his rectum."

The other officer began pulling down Griffin's pants, but then stopped.

"You ain't got anything else on you, do you?" the officer asked.

"Naw," Griffin said, "I don't keep anything in my rectum."

The officer pulled Griffin's pants back up. Hersl evidently didn't want to do his own dirty work, which in this instance can only be described as sadistic. On this occasion, the basic humanity of the other officer spared Hersl's intended victim.

Griffin's charging papers stated that only $900 had been seized from him, not the $6,000 Hersl had actually taken. The report also said that only $4,003 had been recovered from the safe, not the $6,000 that was actually in it. We knew Hersl had taken the money from Griffin's pocket, but we never found out who stole the $2,000 from the safe.

We interviewed Griffin's aunt, Samantha Irby. An HIV counselor, she was wearing hospital scrubs the day we met her. She had no criminal record and had never been arrested. Irby confirmed that Jimmie Griffin was her nephew, and she told us that both Griffin and her son, Tyrone Creighton, had suffered from lead poisoning.

Creighton filed his lawsuit in 2012, which we confirmed using a Maryland courts database. Irby told us Creighton received his settlement and then shared it with her. We obtained bank records from M&T Bank, where Irby and Creighton had accounts. The records bore out what she told us. We saw a deposit in the amount of $266,801.13 into Creighton's account in 2014. That was the settlement. Creighton then withdrew $120,000 and gave the money to Irby, who deposited it into her bank account.

Irby told us Creighton also shared the settlement proceeds with his cousin Jimmie. In fact, she said that she had given Griffin money from Creighton the day before Jimmie was arrested. She had met Griffin in Northeast Baltimore, she recalled, at a mechanic's shop. She gave him $6,500, a little more than Griffin had told us he had had on him by the time Hersl arrested him. Her testimony was powerful corroboration for what Griffin had told us. She would be a strong witness at trial because she wasn't someone who sold drugs or even had a criminal record. She also told us that Creighton had been killed in August 2015. He was found shot to death sitting in a car near her home. He was 23.

In August 2017, two months after the Irby interview, we charged two more defendants, Thomas Finnegan and David Rahim, who weren't members of the Task Force or even police officers. They were friends of Rayam who had posed as police officers to commit a robbery with him. Rayam told us what had happened when we debriefed him. The people they robbed had owned a pigeon store.

I remember thinking when I heard him say "pigeon store," why would anyone sell pigeons? Pigeons are everywhere. Steve Schenning, the acting US attorney at the time and my boss, laughed when I expressed my bafflement to him.

Pigeon racing, he explained, had been a popular sport when he was growing up in 1950s Baltimore. His next-door neighbor in Locust Point, a peninsula on the harbor that was now home to Under Armour's headquarters, kept pigeons. He had a coop in his backyard. The man lived in a seventeen-foot-wide rowhouse, and the birds gave him a chance to escape from his kids.

Rayam and Gondo received a tip about an illegal gun at the pigeon store, but they didn't find a gun. While in the store, Rayam "noticed"— his word—that they had a lot of cash. It turned out to be $20,000. Rayam wanted to steal it, Gondo didn't. Gondo's concern was that the owners were "legit" and would complain. He'd had the same concern when they'd robbed Ronald Hamilton and his wife in Westminster.

With Gondo resisting, that same day Rayam rounded up two friends: Thomas Finnegan and David Rahim. Finnegan, a Caucasian, was nicknamed "White Tom." Rahim, Rayam's cousin, worked in the Baltimore City medical examiner's office.

Rayam used a police database to find the home address of the pigeon store owners, and later that night, he gave Finnegan and Rahim tactical vests marked "POLICE" before they headed to the owners' house.

According to Rayam, "I just told them to go inside and just knock on the door and, you know, act like police and see if you can find the money."

This they did, with the owners inside. Rayam served as lookout like Gondo did when Rayam and Wells robbed the Marnat Road apartment of Aaron Anderson. Finnegan and Rahim came out with $12,000, which they all split. Rayam said he didn't know what happened to the remaining $8,000. This wasn't the first time that money had gone missing from a robbery, as we knew from Westminster.

We found a police report that showed that on June 27, 2014, officers with the Task Force, including Gondo and Rayam, executed a search and seizure warrant at a store with "feed and supply" in its name. This was the pigeon store. The two owners, Donna Curry and Jeffrey Shore, were the people Finnegan and Rahim had robbed while posing as police officers while Rayam waited in his car. Because Rayam had stayed outside the house during the robbery he didn't know what had happened from the time Finnegan and Rahim went inside until they came out, but the victims could tell us. The FBI found them, and we interviewed them.

They confirmed that they owned a store that sold birds and birdseed in Brooklyn, the southernmost neighborhood in Baltimore, directly across the bay from the city's redeveloped Inner Harbor. The store sold pigeons, as Rayam had remembered.

Curry remembered June 27, 2014, vividly.

Rayam had come into her store claiming to have a search warrant. He asked, among other things, whether she had any large amounts of money. Curry told Rayam that she had $20,000 in her "pocketbook." It was from sales from the store, their federal tax refund, income from her husband's side business selling used cars for scrap, and loans from friends and family.

Curry had been carrying such a large amount of money so she could pay property taxes on a rental home they owned. She'd planned to go to the Municipal Building and pay the taxes the very next day. She had cash instead of a cashier's check because they couldn't figure out the exact amount they owed.

Later in the evening, two different "officers" came to their home. Curry let them in because they said they had a warrant. She assumed it was related to the earlier visit at the store. Her young granddaughter was sleeping upstairs, and the officers made Curry bring her down to the living room. One of the officers watched her and her husband and their granddaughter, while the other one searched the house. The police left abruptly when one of the officers seemed to get a call on his radio.

Almost immediately after they left, Curry discovered her pocketbook was empty, but it was too late. She and Shore called the Baltimore County Police Department, their home was in Baltimore County, not Baltimore City, and reported the robbery. She was told that someone from internal affairs would contact them. No one ever did—because the robbers weren't actually police officers.

With the information that Rayam provided, and Curry and Shore corroborated, we indicted Finnegan and Rahim. Both of them eventually pled guilty, admitting what they had done. Their version of events matched what Rayam and Curry had told us.

As with Marnat Road, we layered facts upon facts to create a full picture of what had happened at the home of the owners of Baltimore's last pigeon store. We started with what Rayam had told us. Then we spoke to the victims. Finally, Finnegan and Rahim confessed when they decided to plead guilty. All of the participants in the drama that unfolded that day told us the same story. That's how we knew it to be true.

Curry came to Finnegan's sentencing hearing. She told the judge that she'd lost the rental house that she was trying to pay the taxes on when she was robbed. She also lost her business, which meant that Baltimore lost its last pigeon store. Curry told the court that her six-year-old granddaughter suffered lingering effects from that night. "I have [taken] her to a courthouse to pay a parking fine, and as soon as she sees a police officer, she clings so tight to my legs," she said. "She's really scared of police."

The judge sentenced Finnegan, who held the gun during the robbery, to eight and a half years in prison. Rahim got a few years less.

From Finnegan and Rahim, we moved on to the Task Force's other sergeant, Thomas Allers. In debriefing sessions in the summer of 2017, Gondo and Rayam admitted to committing a dozen robberies with Allers, who had been in charge of the Task Force before Jenkins. For each robbery they told us about, we were able to find and ultimately interview the victim. In all twelve cases, the victim told us they had more money in their home than the police turned in. In other words, there were no false positives.

None of the victims knew that Gondo and Rayam were talking to us, but all of the victims confirmed what the two had told us. Gondo and Rayam hadn't made anything up to try and win a better sentencing recommendation. They hadn't falsely accused Allers, and they didn't try to shift the blame onto him. They didn't claim to have seen only Allers taking money alone; they implicated themselves in most of the robberies.

Unlike the robberies that Gondo and Rayam committed with Hersl and Jenkins, all the robberies with Allers took place inside people's homes during the execution of a search warrant. Allers casually encouraged them each time, saying things like, "Just do this here," as they split up cash and the homeowner "wouldn't miss a stack." He even referred to what they took as "lunch money," to minimize the significance of their actions.

In some ways, Allers's robberies seemed less risky than the ones committed on the street. The officers weren't going to be caught on CCTV like they'd been outside Sergio Summerville's storage unit, and the search warrant gave them court authorization to be where they were. Allers also turned in most of the money recovered during the searches.

Among Allers's robberies one stood out in demonstrating the awful consequences that can come from robbing someone who sells drugs. In April 2016, Allers, Gondo, Hersl, and Rayam arrested a man and then went to the house he shared with his girlfriend and their two small children. His girlfriend gave the officers consent to search the house. I imagine she never would have if she had known what was going to happen next.

The man they arrested had $10,000 in the house at the time of the search. Allers found it and stole it. Following the search, the man was shot and killed because he couldn't pay a drug-related debt.

In August 2017, five months after we brought the initial charges in the case, we presented an indictment to the grand jury charging Allers with racketeering, the same charges we brought against the rest of the Task Force in March 2017, for the robberies he committed with Gondo and Rayam. On December 1, 2017, Allers signed a plea agreement. He confessed to all twelve robberies.

All the cooperating defendants had told us about Jenkins's admonition that they carry BB guns in their cars. The cooperators all also told us fragments of a story that Jenkins told them about a deadly car crash where evidence had been planted. In that incident, it was drugs, not a BB gun, but the lesson Jenkins took from it was to always have a BB gun around in case you needed it. We took what we learned from the cooperators and identified the incident. The two men Jenkins chased and planted evidence on were Umar Burley and Brent Matthews.

On April 28, 2010, Umar Burley was sitting in his car in the 3800 block of Parkview Avenue, in Northwest Baltimore. Matthews, his friend, exited a nearby apartment building and got into the vehicle. They were going to the courthouse in Towson, Maryland, to show their support for a friend who was going to be sentenced.

In Jenkins's mind, according to what the cooperators told us, the situation looked like a drug deal. The neighborhood had a high incidence of drug arrests, and Jenkins came to it apparently looking to make one. He saw a Black man sitting in a parked car, and then another Black man get in the car. The passenger had a backpack. Jenkins believed that men only carried backpacks if they were selling drugs. That's all he needed.

Jenkins pulled in front of Burley in his unmarked BPD vehicle to cut him off and ordered an officer driving another unmarked BPD car to pull up behind Burley. He'd used this box-in maneuver countless times. Dressed in street clothes, Jenkins jumped out and approached Burley's car. The situation went downhill from there.

Burley thought he was being robbed. After Matthews got into the car, Burley had seen men in black clothes, he claimed wearing face masks, approaching his car with guns drawn. The second BPD car hadn't pulled up close enough, so Burley backed up and took off. What happened next didn't depend on anyone's perception.

Burley sped through several intersections in a residential neighborhood. Jenkins followed. At the intersection of Belle Avenue and Gwynn Oak Avenue, Burley struck another car. The force of the impact was so great that it threw the car Burley hit onto the porch of a corner rowhouse. Burley's car ended up on top of a fire hydrant. Water spouted in a plume, adding to the chaos of the scene.

Burley and Matthews got out of the car and ran. Jenkins, driving his BPD car, and the other BPD car that had tried to box Burley in, were right behind them. Jenkins jumped out and chased and ultimately caught Burley. The officer driving the other unmarked car chased and caught Matthews. It was only while walking Matthews back to his BPD car that the other officer noticed the crumpled vehicle on the porch of the corner rowhouse. Inside was an elderly man, Elbert Davis, and his wife. Mr. Davis was taken to a nearby hospital, where he died. Ms. Davis survived.

Jenkins searched Burley's car for the drugs he thought Burley was going to sell to Matthews but found nothing. The decision to approach Burley's car had set off the chain of events that led to Davis's death.

Panicked when he couldn't find any drugs to justify the chase, Jenkins called another officer, who brought heroin to the scene. The heroin was then planted in Burley's car.

Faced with the prospect of a state vehicular manslaughter charge and a federal drug charge, Burley pleaded guilty. When Burley pleaded guilty, Matthews decided he had to plead guilty, too. Both men served years in jail before we learned what Jenkins had done. By the time we did, Matthews had completed his sentence and been released. Burley was still in jail.

In a closed proceeding, we asked the court to release Burley while we assembled the case against Jenkins. The court agreed. At the end of November 2017, we brought separate civil rights charges against Jenkins for planting the drugs. Now we'd have two opportunities to hold him accountable.

Once we brought the new civil rights charges, we moved to wipe out the convictions of Burley and Matthews. At the hearing to vacate the convictions, the US district court judge, Richard D. Bennett, the same judge who had overseen the wiretap of Gondo's phone, came down off the bench to apologize to them on behalf of the United States.

I had never seen anything like it and hoped I never would again.

FOURTEEN

Middle River

By the end of 2017, the Gun Trace Task Force partners of Wayne Jenkins, Daniel Hersl, and Marcus Taylor—the three noncooperating defendants—had told us a great deal about their unit's illegal activities, but one major question remained unanswered. Both Maurice Ward and Evodio Hendrix said that Jenkins, the Task Force leader, had routinely taken drugs off of arrestees, but the drugs were never turned in to the Baltimore Police Department. What was Jenkins doing with all those drugs?

The answer: Donald Stepp.

Their connection: Middle River.

Stepp first appeared on our team's radar in the fall of 2016 when Jenkins brought Stepp to a house that was being searched. A Baltimore County detective recognized Stepp, not as a cop but as a drug dealer, and asked why he was there. Jenkins lied, telling the detective that Stepp was law enforcement. This was another example of how everything about this case seemed upside down. A cop bringing a drug dealer to execute a search warrant? Luckily, the detective complained to the FBI, and we found out about the incident. We asked the Baltimore County Police Department to keep an eye on Stepp and to let us know if he did anything that would allow us to charge him and then try to flip him against Jenkins.

On December 14, 2017, Baltimore County police arrested a woman coming out of Stepp's house. She had half an ounce of cocaine on her and admitted that she had just bought it from Stepp for $650. With that information, the Baltimore County police officers who arrested the woman were able to get a search warrant for Stepp's house. During the search, they recovered large quantities of crack, cocaine, heroin, MDMA, digital scales, packaging materials, $20,000 in cash, five Rolexes, and a Breitling. Baltimore County police, based on what they'd found, arrested Stepp and called us that day.

My partner, Derek Hines, quickly prepared an indictment, which the grand jury returned a few days later. Stepp was arrested on the federal charges and decided to cooperate almost immediately. Derek and I met Stepp for the first time in the federal courthouse office of the US Attorney's Office. Oddly, like Jemell Rayam, he had no hair, not even eyelashes. What he did have was a big personality, the biggest of all our witnesses.

Stepp was a bail bondsman. When someone gets arrested in Maryland, they go before a district court commissioner who determines whether they should be detained pending trial. If the commissioner releases an arrestee on bail but the arrestee or his family doesn't have the money to post bail, they can approach a professional bail bondsman like Stepp, who for a fee, provides the required bail. If the arrestee shows up for court when they're supposed to, the court returns the money to the bondsman at the end of the proceeding. When arrestees don't show up, the court keeps the money. If a defendant flees, the bondsman can try to track him down and bring him to court.

Stepp had grown up in Middle River, a blue-collar town east of Baltimore City also home to the Jenkins family. Middle River and the neighboring community of Essex expanded rapidly during World War II. At that time, many residents of Middle River worked at the Glenn L. Martin Company, an airplane manufacturer that later became part of Lockheed Martin. During the war, Martin employed 53,000 people. After the area's industrial jobs moved out in the 1960s, Middle River and Essex remained majority white. The massive Martin Company manufacturing facility sits largely vacant now, with a small Lockheed Martin office building on the site. The other major employer in the area was a steel mill at the end of Back River. It shut down in the late 1990s.

Stepp, 51 when we met him, estimated that he had known the Jenkins family for close to forty years. Jenkins's older brother, Bobby, had been a schoolmate of Stepp's. As an adult, Stepp attended card games at a friend's house in Middle River, and a lot of the players were police officers. That's how he met Bobby Jenkins's brother Wayne. He told us he got to know Wayne "real good."

A little before Christmas in 2012, Stepp and Jenkins took a ride to the Delaware State Park Casino. On the way, Jenkins told Stepp that he was making some of the biggest drug busts in Baltimore City. He then asked Stepp if he could sell the drugs that he seized. Stepp said he could. We asked Stepp why he agreed to do it.

"I felt comfortable with it because all the police officers that I met—which were many during the card games—in my opinion, they owned the city," he said.

"To me it was just a mathematical equation, and I felt good," Stepp continued. "After knowing the family for 40 years and knowing what I knew about [Jenkins], I felt as though it was a good gamble and a good risk.

"I evaluate risk every day, what I do with my job," he said. "I thought it was a winner."

Stepp remembered the precise date of Jenkins's proposition because he had a picture on his phone of himself and Jenkins at the roulette table. Some of the other pictures on Stepp's phone evinced just how close they were, including Jenkins and Stepp smiling in the stands at the Super Bowl and Stepp beaming inside BPD headquarters wearing a tactical vest and holding a BPD service weapon Jenkins had given him for the picture.

Right after the trip to the Delaware casino, Jenkins started bringing drugs to Stepp's house. We asked what kinds and in what quantities.

"Phew," Stepp said. "It was just over the top. Everything and anything that could be imagined."

Stepp further explained that at the time that Jenkins asked him to sell the stolen drugs, Stepp had been selling cocaine to professionals in and around Baltimore. He could sell a gram to them for $100 to $125, and since the drugs didn't cost Jenkins anything, he would sell them to Stepp at a steep discount compared to what Stepp had been paying his supplier. A kilo from Jenkins cost $15,000, a much better deal than the $34,000 to $39,000 Stepp had been paying. The math was simple; the profits were enormous. Stepp could make more than $100,000 off a kilo from Jenkins.

Jenkins delivered the cocaine in different ways. Sometimes he and Stepp met for breakfast or lunch. Sometimes they simply met for an exchange. Other times, Jenkins called him late at night and told him to open his garage and meet him there. Often, Jenkins just left the drugs in Stepp's shed, which Stepp would leave unlocked. If the shed door was locked when Stepp woke up, he knew Jenkins had made a drop-off. This happened almost every day. Stepp estimated he made more than $1 million off the drugs Jenkins brought him and that Jenkins made between $250,000 and $500,000.

Stepp knew all about Jenkins's progression through the BPD, including his various assignments. We asked Stepp if Jenkins had told him anything about his last assignment, as leader of the Task Force. "There's umpteen conversations that I've had with him about it," Stepp said. "It gave him the pick of the cream-of-the-crop officers in what he was doing, and it gave him the ability to be able to have the entire city at his disposal."

Stepp told us that Jenkins liked the Task Force because other units had confined him to "special areas." Most tellingly, Stepp said that Jenkins had called the Task Force "a front for a criminal enterprise." That's exactly what we would say in the RICO charge.

Stepp also shared information that explained a surprising find. The FBI had searched Jenkins's van on the day of the Task Force members' arrest. Before I could even ask about the search, our lead FBI case agent, Erika Jensen, called.

"You're not going to believe what we found," she said, before going on to tell me that there were two enormous bags of burglary tools and related clothing and accessories in the back of Jenkins's minivan. Stepp volunteered to us that Jenkins had given him lists of the tools he wanted and that he had bought them for Jenkins. We showed Stepp the contents of one of the bags from Jenkins's BPD take home vehicle: ski masks, black gloves, shoes, wire cutters, binoculars, pry bars, sledgehammers, machetes, a grappling hook, a slim jim. Stepp called these "quick bags" and said he'd bought the contents himself so they couldn't be traced back to Jenkins. Stepp had cover for the purchases; as a bail bondsman, he could claim that he'd bought the equipment to use in apprehending fugitives who'd skipped bail. He'd ordered the stuff on Amazon. We got his account records. It was all listed there.

Jenkins told Stepp about the robberies he was committing with other members of the Task Force, including some we had not charged. Stepp remembered, among others, the robbery that Jenkins, Taylor, and Ward committed at Belvedere Towers. Jenkins had called Stepp late that night, waking him up and telling him to open his garage door. Jenkins pulled his car in, popped the trunk, and then looked around to make sure no one was tailing him.

Stepp asked him why he was so nervous. Jenkins took out a duffel bag, the one he'd taken from the seller in the Belvedere Towers parking lot deal. "What do you got?" Stepp asked. Jenkins told him the bag was full of cocaine. "And I'm like, 'Oh, my God,'" Stepp told us. "So I'm thinking he's got, you know, a hundred pounds of cocaine." But Jenkins then said, "Just kidding. Thirty pounds of weed."

Stepp's recounting struck us for two reasons. First, this episode wasn't public knowledge. No one had been charged with it in our indictment. We had only learned about it when Ward started cooperating. There was no way Stepp could be making this up. Second, Stepp still had the duffel bag, which he handed over to us.

A few weeks after that delivery, Stepp went to a strip club with Jenkins and some other BPD officers, including Taylor. It wasn't a social occasion. Stepp explained to us that the BPD officers had been hired to provide private security that night at the club for a New York drug dealer. While there, Stepp heard another officer ask Jenkins how Taylor was doing as one of the "newbies" in the unit. Stepp told us, "Sergeant Jenkins replied that he's doing great, that he was part of the 30 pounds that come from the Belvedere Tower." Indeed, he had been.

To our surprise, Stepp had been involved in the Oreese Stevenson robbery, too.

"I was home," Stepp said. "The phone rings. It's Sergeant Jenkins. Says, 'Donnie, I need you to come to this address as quick as you can. I got a monster.'" Jenkins told Stepp he was debriefing a "drug lord" at his office. He gave Stepp an address—Stevenson's house on Heathfield Road. Jenkins told Stepp that he would find ten kilos of cocaine and a stash of money on top of a safe. Jenkins wanted Stepp to get there quickly, before the other officers arrived. Jenkins said the house would be empty and that his squad didn't yet know what was happening. Stepp plugged the address into his GPS and took off. Jenkins had told him to go in through the back door, but when Stepp arrived someone, Stevenson's son, was on the back porch. The boy was waiting for his mother to come home and let him in.

Stepp told us he was a burglar, not a robber. Burglars take things from empty houses; robbers steal from people, threatening to hurt or even kill them if they refuse to part ways with their property. Stepp parked a block or so away, and through a pair of binoculars, watched what transpired from his truck. Later, on Stepp's phone, we saw a picture he'd taken from that spot. It showed Jenkins in front of the house, in the center of the photo, with Ward, Hendrix, and Taylor in the background.

Stepp said Jenkins and Taylor had gone in first, and then Jenkins came out a few minutes later looking like Santa Claus with his police tactical vest puffed out. Stepp watched Jenkins throw a bag in the back seat of his unmarked BPD car. Then Jenkins called Stepp and asked him where he was. "Don't come to the house," he warned Stepp. Jenkins wanted to meet him nearby, without the other officers seeing him.

"I started driving down the street," Stepp told us. "He come flying behind me with the police car. I stopped. He jumps [out]. He opens the passenger door to my truck, throws two kilograms of cocaine in it and says, 'Donnie, can you get me $5,000 within this week? I'm leaving for vacation.'" Jenkins was planning to go to Myrtle Beach. Stepp added, "And he told me if I got pulled over, to give him a call, that he would come and fix it." Stepp ultimately gave Jenkins $30,000 for the two kilos, which Stepp then sold to his "professional clientele."

Stepp also filled in some of the missing details from the Dennis Armstrong storage unit robbery. It had started like the Stevenson robbery: Jenkins called Stepp and told him he was at a storage unit and that he "had the guy." As Stepp recalled, "He said, 'Donnie, there's $220,000 in cash. There's eight kilos of cocaine. I have the codes to the door. I need you to head this way and bring something to get through the door.'" That's all Stepp needed to hear, even though, he acknowledged, Jenkins sometimes "embellished" things.

Stepp approached the storage facility from behind, as Jenkins had told him to do; there were no cameras in the back. It required climbing a fence, which didn't go so well. Stepp rolled his ankle as he jumped off. He thought he had broken it, and the next day he took a photo of his grotesquely swollen ankle. We found the photo on his phone. The date stamp, August 9, 2016, was the day after the Armstrong incident.

We asked Stepp why he hadn't given up and gone home after he hurt himself. "Well, I was driven by the $220,000 and eight kilos," he said. "I went ahead and sucked it up and started heading in to get into this storage unit."

Stepp limped along until he found the unit. Then he pried the door open with a crowbar. Inside, he found empty kilo wrappers stuffed in a bag. One of them did contain about three-quarters of a kilo of cocaine, much less than the eight kilos Jenkins had said. Stepp smashed holes in the walls looking for hidden drugs and money but didn't find any. He went back over the fence with his busted ankle and the three-quarters of a kilo.

Back in his truck, he called Jenkins to tell him about what little he'd found. Stepp told us he was anxious: would Jenkins think he'd actually stolen the money and the drugs, a sort of triple cross? We never learned what happened to the drugs in Armstrong's storage unit or who got there before Stepp. Like the missing money from Jimmie Griffin's safe, it remained a mystery. The search for the truth isn't always complete.

Stepp told us that Jenkins had called him in April 2015 during the unrest following Freddie Gray Jr.'s funeral. Once again, he asked Stepp to open his garage door. This time, he pulled out two trash bags.

"I just got people coming out of these pharmacies," Jenkins said, according to Stepp. "I've got an entire pharmacy. I don't even know what it is." The two garbage bags were full of prescription drugs. They had been taken by rioters who had broken into a pharmacy. Jenkins had robbed the looters.

In this, Stepp revealed to us the most symbolic of the Task Force's crimes. A segregated neighborhood in Baltimore erupted, devastated by forces outside their control, and Jenkins further compounded the damage—stealing drugs from residents who'd stolen them from a pharmacy and then selling them back into the community. People had clamored for police to secure the neighborhood and contain the unrest, but instead, Jenkins sowed the seeds of more distrust and sought to profit from it.

After Stepp's arrest, he mentioned a piece of evidence hidden at his waterfront home in Middle River. Stepp had read in our indictment that the police had allegedly stolen a watch from Stevenson. Jenkins had brought Stepp a watch to sell. Worried that that was the same watch, Stepp sunk it at the bottom of a pylon under his dock. After he told us this, the FBI dive team went to his dock and searched around the pylons. They found a Breitling in a waterproof bag a few feet below the surface. It wasn't the only stolen watch Stepp had, but its location was certainly the most unusual place where we retrieved one.

Stepp admitted that he and Jenkins had broken into a drug dealer's house looking for drugs and found six expensive watches instead. Stepp estimated they were worth a quarter of a million dollars. He had stored them in a fancy case with six separate compartments that Baltimore County police found in the ceiling when they searched his house.

Stepp had given us a lot to work with, but now we faced the recurring question: Will a jury believe Donnie Stepp given all his baggage? If anyone had trouble, well, there was a watch in a waterproof bag under his dock to prove he was telling the truth. On his court date, January 12, 2018, he arrived well dressed, wearing a black, close-fitting short overcoat with the collar upturned against the cold and a scarf around his neck. His suit looked expensive. He wore a stylish pair of glasses. He didn't look like a man who was going to plead guilty, but he did.

The week before Stepp pled guilty in court, Jenkins had done the same. Stepp had signed his plea agreement first, but the timing of their hearings had Jenkins appearing in court before Stepp.

Defendants who plead guilty have to admit to what they've done, but they don't have to explain why they decided to plead guilty. Jenkins availed himself of this and kept quiet in the latter regard. Was it because he thought he'd be convicted? His trial was scheduled for the end of January 2018, and four of the detectives he'd supervised and committed robberies with had already pled guilty. Then Stepp was charged. Jenkins had to know there was a good chance they were all cooperating against him though he couldn't be sure. This he wouldn't know until the eve of trial—that is, the deadline for us to disclose our witness list.

Our offer to Jenkins was not generous. It required him to plead guilty to charges both in the racketeering case, which meant he'd have to admit to robbing arrestees, and in the civil rights case, for planting evidence on Burley and Matthews after they'd struck Elbert Davis's car. The plea agreement also said he couldn't argue for less than twenty years in prison, and we couldn't argue for more than thirty years. Federal plea agreements include a factual statement in which the defendant admits what he did. Jenkins's factual statement ran on for twelve pages. It was so long and detailed that it had subsections. Jenkins admitted to all the robberies we had charged him with in the superseding indictment. That meant that none of the victims who implicated Jenkins in a robbery had lied to us—not a single one.

The first robbery he admitted to was one he'd committed in 2011 with Gondo. Through Gondo's cooperation, we had learned that he and Jenkins had briefly served on the Task Force five years before Jenkins became its sergeant. Back then, they were both detectives, and though only together for a couple of months, it was long enough to feel at ease committing crimes together. This piece of history helped to explain why less than a month after Jenkins took over the Task Force, he felt comfortable robbing the Hamiltons with Gondo.

The first robbery Jenkins admitted to doing with any of the officers who later became members of the Task Force was with Hendrix, in 2014. Hendrix had told us about it: They had attempted a traffic stop in a mall parking lot. The arrestee fled, first in his car and then on foot. As they pursued him, the arrestee jumped over a retaining wall and then fell one story, landing in a parking lot, injuring himself. When he jumped, he let go of a bag full of money, and the wind blew the cash all over the parking lot, like it was snowing. While passersby became distracted trying to grab bills, Jenkins and Hendrix took somewhere between $12,000 and $14,000 from the driver's car.

Jenkins admitted to the robbery at Belvedere Towers. Even though no record of the incident existed, Ward had volunteered the truth.

Jenkins admitted that he took the duffel bag of money and split it with Ward and Taylor and that he also stole the duffel bag of marijuana from the two men they'd stopped in the parking lot. Jenkins confirmed Stepp's role in the episode, which Ward hadn't known about but that Stepp had told us about. Jenkins gave the marijuana to Stepp, who told us he paid $30,000 for it. Jenkins confirmed what Stepp said.

Jenkins admitted to robbing Stevenson with Hendrix, Ward, and Taylor, and he corroborated what Stepp had told us about his running out of the house with two kilograms of cocaine and giving them to Stepp, waiting nearby. Jenkins also confessed that he, Gondo, Hersl, and Rayam had robbed the Hamiltons and that he had stolen Ronald Hamilton's Breitling wristwatch and given it to Stepp to sell. That's the watch the FBI dive team found sunk off the pier at Stepp's home.

The Armstrong robbery found Jenkins running two operations at once, as he had done during the Stevenson robbery. He admitted to sending Stepp ahead to get the drugs out of the unit while the Task Force officers sat outside, waiting for the search warrant to arrive, and confirmed that someone had gotten there before Stepp. He didn't, however, know who that was.

Jenkins admitted to providing Stepp stolen drugs to sell. Stepp told the truth about having given Jenkins a key to his shed so that Jenkins could drop drugs off at all hours of the day and night. It was also true that Jenkins had robbed looters after Gray's death and given Stepp prescription drugs to sell. Jenkins also confessed to breaking into drug dealers' homes to find money and drugs to steal, which is how he got his hands on the watches recovered from Stepp's house. Jenkins admitted to framing Umar Burley and Brent Matthews.

When a defendant pleads guilty, he or she gets a hearing before a federal judge. The judge describes the charges and potential penalties and asks a series of questions to make sure the defendant is voluntarily pleading guilty. Defendants typically say little more than "yes" or "no."

After Jenkins answered the judge's questions at his January 5, 2018, plea hearing, he blurted out, unprompted, that he was ashamed of what he had done.

And then there were two. The trial of Hersl and Taylor would begin in a few weeks.

PART III

THE TRIAL

FIFTEEN

Symbols of Authority

Criminal trials are a uniquely important, but increasingly rare event in the US criminal justice system. More than 90 percent of criminal cases in the federal courts are resolved with a guilty plea. Several factors help produce the high rate of guilty pleas in the fraud and corruption cases I typically prosecute.

First, prosecutors can choose which cases to pursue, which often isn't the situation with other kinds of crime. For example, when someone is murdered, there is enormous pressure on the police and prosecutors to hold the perpetrator accountable, regardless of whether the evidence is particularly strong or compelling. By contrast, prosecutors can choose to prosecute fraud and public corruption cases that have the strongest evidence and can decline to bring ones where the evidence is relatively weak. Most of the time, there aren't public demands that charges be brought against a particular executive or politician. Unlike a brutal murder, fraud and corruption is typically only known to the public because it gets exposed through a criminal prosecution or investigative journalism or both. There are, of course, exceptions. For example, when Enron collapsed, politicians, journalists, and various commentators publicly demanded that the executives responsible be held accountable.

In a prison corruption case I prosecuted in 2016, we indicted eighty people and got seventy-five guilty pleas. A number of lawyers told me that when their clients saw how strong the evidence was, they decided not to go to trial. We had tapped fourteen different phones; subpoenaed thousands of financial records from prepaid debit card companies like PayPal to show how the inmates bribed the guards; recovered smuggled drugs, tobacco, and cell phones during searches of inmates' cells; seized packages of contraband from guards pulled over in traffic stops on their way to work; and discovered text messages on seized cell phones with details about meetings to pay bribes or to give drugs to guards to smuggle. We had also interviewed more than two dozen inmates who described in great and overlapping detail the various smuggling rings operating within the jail. Given the overwhelming nature of the evidence, only four defendants went to trial. Two were convicted, and two were acquitted. The eightieth defendant was given a deferred prosecution agreement, a kind of pretrial diversion reserved for very rare cases.

The second major reason white-collar defendants plead guilty is because they believe they have a better chance at getting a lower sentence if they avoid a trial by accepting responsibility. A guilty plea hearing is a fairly unemotional event. The facts supporting the defendant's guilty plea are summarized in a plea agreement, which the judge reads before the hearing and is then summarized aloud either by the judge or by the prosecutor, depending on the judge's preference, at the hearing, where the defendant pleads guilty. That part of the hearing takes only a few minutes.

By contrast, a trial establishing a defendant's guilt can take weeks, sometimes even months. While the jury ultimately decides whether a defendant is guilty or not guilty, the trial plays out in front of the judge who will sentence the defendant if the jury finds him guilty. So, on the one hand, the judge can spend weeks or even months hearing about the defendant's bad conduct, sometimes in quite dramatic testimony, or the judge can read about it and hear it summarized in a matter of minutes. That's one of the choices a defendant has to consider.

Furthermore, white-collar defendants usually have done things in their lives that they can argue mitigate their crimes, like giving to charity or community service or even their professional accomplish-ments at their sentencing hearing. At every sentencing, the defendant is given the chance to speak directly to the judge. In drug cases and cases involving violent crimes, the defendant often chooses to say nothing. In white-collar cases, the defendant almost always makes a statement, and these can be compelling.

Whatever the reason, most defendants don't exercise their right to a public trial. The downside of the paucity of trials is that much of the work of the criminal justice system rolls along with little or no public notice. In addition, public reporting on the criminal justice system di-minished as local newspapers across the United States folded or dra-matically cut their newsrooms in the face of various economic pressures and trends. One of the senior prosecutors in my office described to me how back in the day when Baltimore had two daily newspapers, the *Baltimore Sun* and the *Evening Sun*, each kept reporters posted at offices in the federal courthouse. Those days are long gone. Most of the guilty pleas that do occur, particularly in fraud cases, don't get covered in the press at all. Trials, on the other hand, are a different story, and they open a large window through which the public can see the criminal justice system in operation.

Gun Trace Task Force members Daniel Hersl and Marcus Taylor wanted a public trial. It was scheduled to begin January 23, 2018. Their trial would focus on the racketeering charges in the superseding indictment.

The case had attracted a lot of publicity up to that point, and the ex-cruciating details of what the Task Force had done still awaited expo-sure at the trial. My hope was that the experience would be cathartic for the victims and for the community. My fear was that if we lost, it would further erode the public's confidence in the criminal justice sys-tem, particularly within the African American communities in East and West Baltimore, where the Task Force had operated.

Our team worked around the clock in the weeks leading up to the trial. Co-counsel Derek Hines and I divided up the witnesses. We drafted separate outlines of questions to ask each witness and then swapped them to review, to make sure we had everything covered. The goal with any witness is to elicit the information needed to prove the case in as clear and efficient a way as possible. Each witness thinks and speaks differently and therefore should be questioned with that in mind. For me, an outline is not a script to follow at trial, but a way to organize my thoughts and develop a plan for getting the key testimony before the jury. Once the witness is on the stand, a good trial lawyer needs to actually listen to what the witness says and react accordingly. You can always tell inexperienced or, frankly, ineffective trial lawyers by the degree to which they are wedded to their outline. They just read the questions, regardless of the answers they get.

We had to decide the order in which to call our witnesses, an important issue because they would be telling the jury for the first time what had happened. In fact, we select jurors precisely because of their unfamiliarity with what we're going to present to them. It matters who says what to them and when. Witnesses help frame the story for the jury, provide details, corroborate one another, and above all communicate why the facts matter. A criminal trial is a morality play, not a dry recitation of facts.

The government is asking the jury to find that someone did something wrong, and even though the jury doesn't decide a guilty defendant's sentence, every juror knows that a vote to convict may lead to prison. In the run-up to the trial, we marked the exhibits to present to the jury. We had photographs, recordings, overtime slips, videos, and other evidence. These exhibits would be presented with our witnesses and would corroborate them in important ways.

Picking the jury is the first step in any trial. The United States is one of the few countries that uses juries of regular people, drawn from the community, to decide criminal cases. In many legal systems, professional judges decide a defendant's guilt or innocence. Even the United Kingdom, where our legal system originated, has largely abandoned the practice. The use of juries persists in the United States and probably always will because the US Constitution requires that nearly all criminal cases be tried before a jury.

Juries are, as the judge tells them, the judges of the facts; they decide what happened and ultimately whether the law was broken. The judge in the black robe is the judge of the law, a gatekeeper who decides what evidence the jury can hear or see by applying the rules of evidence. The judge also instructs the jury on the law they must apply in deciding whether the defendant is guilty or not guilty.

In federal court, the trial judge runs the process of picking jurors. He or she asks the jurors questions and then, if the lawyers have follow-up questions, they will be allowed to pose them. The judge, however, usually keeps the lawyers on a pretty tight leash because lawyers sometimes try to use their questions to influence jurors even before the trial begins.

On the morning of the first day of trial, a group of potential jurors are assembled in the courtroom. Every federal criminal case must be tried before twelve jurors, no fewer. Those jurors are chosen from a much larger venire, pronounced "vin-ear" in Baltimore, but "vin-eye-ree" in Texas, where I tried the Enron case. At the beginning of the selection process, the prosecution and defense are provided basic information about each member of the venire: names, hometowns, ages, occupations, whether they are married, and, if so, their spouses' occupations. Some information, such as their names and addresses, comes from the court, while some of it comes from a questionnaire mailed to state residents with their jury summons. If a juror doesn't fill out the questionnaire in full, it is risky to pick them because you might not know what they or their spouse, if they have one, do for a living. Each side is keenly interested in these facts.

Typically, defendants don't want police officers or their spouses—or anyone associated in any way with law enforcement—on the jury. Such jurors might be more inclined to believe police officers who testify for the prosecution. Meanwhile, prosecutors tend to want to have law enforcement, or their spouses, on juries. Similarly, in a typical case, the defense prefers jurors potentially sympathetic to their client, charged with the crime at hand. So, for example, the defense typically favors jurors who have incarcerated family members. By contrast, prosecutors look for jurors who do not have family members with criminal records because these jurors might be more sympathetic to someone charged with a crime.

In our case, the logic of jury selection was flipped. We assumed that the defense would want jurors connected to law enforcement on the theory that they might be less likely to convict police officers, and we wouldn't want them because we needed jurors willing to convict police officers. Similarly, we assumed the defense would want jurors who did not have family members who were incarcerated since the prosecution's witnesses against them would largely be people who sold drugs or were associated with people who sold drugs. We, on the other hand, looked for jurors who would be sympathetic to people with criminal records for the very reason that our witnesses had records. Both sides were also concerned about jurors with overexposure to the publicity the case had received. The *Baltimore Sun* and local TV stations had been covering developments in it since the Task Force members' arrest, on March 1, 2017.

On the morning of the first day of the Task Force trial, courtroom deputy Karen Moye led potential jurors into the courtroom and arranged them by their juror number in the rows of the gallery. This was the first time I'd seen them and the first time they'd seen me. The federal courthouse in Baltimore draws jurors from the entire state of Maryland except for Montgomery and Prince George's Counties, which ring Washington, DC, to the east, and some of the counties on Maryland's Eastern Shore; jurors from those areas report to a separate federal courthouse in Greenbelt, Maryland. As a result, federal juries in Baltimore City often have more members from other parts of Maryland than city residents and are usually overwhelmingly white. White suburban jurors haven't usually experienced what life is like in East and West Baltimore, the neighborhoods where the Task Force found their victims, and I assumed them more likely to believe authority figures like the police. The challenge we faced in this script-flipping case was to lead them on the same journey to the truth that Derek and I had made. That included putting aside preconceived notions about the police and drug dealers and whether to believe the former over the latter. Doing so would undoubtedly be difficult for some, and those were the jurors we tried to identify and strike.

It had been my experience in more than a decade in courtrooms that due to a variety of structural factors, there are often only a few young Black men in the venire in Baltimore. In Maryland, a person is disqualified from jury service if they've been convicted of a crime punishable by more than one year in prison, have been sentenced to more than one year in prison, or have pending criminal charges punishable by more than one year in prison. That means that both felony and misdemeanor convictions can result in exclusion from jury service and makes Maryland's juror qualification law one of the most restrictive in the United States. In Maryland, more than 70 percent of the prison population in 2018 was Black, compared with 31 of the state population. In Maryland, as in other states, white, suburban residents are more likely to own homes and are less likely to move frequently, which makes them easier to reach with a juror summons, which is sent by mail.

The process that Judge Catherine Blake used in our case to select jurors was the same one I had seen her use in other trials. She asked the venire a series of questions suggested by us and the defense in advance. The jurors raised their hand if they had an affirmative answer. The judge went down the row and listened to each of their answers. For example, the judge asked the venire if any of them or a close family member or friend worked for law enforcement or in an attorney's office. The jurors stood up and answered, for instance saying that their father had been a police officer, their wife was a lawyer, and so on. If a question called for an answer that might be embarrassing or quite personal, the judge asked the potential juror to come up to the bench. For example, the jurors were asked whether they or any close family members or friends had ever been arrested or charged with a crime. The answers to that question were taken privately at the bench. As a follow-up to that question, the potential jurors were asked, while at the bench, whether they thought they or their family member or close friend had been treated fairly by law enforcement, regardless of the outcome. If a potential juror said no, the judge would ask whether they could put that experience aside and only consider the evidence presented in court when deciding the defendant's guilt or innocence. An affirmative answer allowed them to continue to the next round in the selection process; those who said no were typically struck from the panel "for cause," in other words, for a specific reason, in this example, for bias.

I was surprised by the jurors' responses about pretrial publicity. Several indicated that they had seen press coverage of the investigation, but the number was lower than I expected. Most of the potential jurors had only a passing familiarity with the case. My takeaway was that people didn't read the *Baltimore Sun* or watch local TV news as much as I thought they did. While that might be troubling for many other reasons, it meant that pretrial publicity wouldn't be a problem in picking the jury.

After the questioning, both sides were given the opportunity to exercise a certain number of peremptory challenges—rejecting a person as a juror for any reason other than the venire member's race or gender. For example, in our case, the defense might strike someone who had been arrested or had a criminal record, which by itself wouldn't have been enough to strike them for cause. Sometimes peremptory challenges are used not because of anything a potential juror says, but because he or she hadn't answered any questions affirmatively, and one side or the other is uncomfortable not knowing more about the potential juror. To record peremptory challenges, each side is given a list of the venire members and a colored pencil—red for the government, blue for the defense—to "X" out jurors they want to strike.

We made our strikes and then handed the marked-up lists back to Karen Moye, the courtroom deputy, who then handed them to Judge Blake, to review. Judge Blake then returned the forms to Moye to read out the numbers of the jurors. Once she read off fifteen numbers—twelve jurors and three alternates—we had our jury. It was mostly white and mostly from the suburbs. We would have liked a more diverse jury with more Baltimore City residents, but it didn't work out that way.

The law says that a jury *panel* must represent a cross-section of the community, in other words, the sixty or so people summoned for jury service for the venire from whom the twelve trial jurors are selected. That doesn't mean the jury ultimately selected in any given case represents a cross-section of the community because jurors are disqualified for a variety of reasons that have nothing to do with whether they represent the community. For example, jurors who say they are more likely to believe police officers over other witnesses are often struck. Similarly, jurors for whom service would be a hardship, if their job won't pay them or if they are self-employed, are often released. By way of example, I once tried a case where the jury had nine women on it, out of the twelve. So while the jury was two-thirds women, and the community was not, the panel the jury was drawn from, of more than sixty people, had a gender makeup that was closer to the gender makeup of the broader community.

While there were several African Americans on our jury, only one of them was a young man—the only juror who looked like most of our victims. I had seen research indicating that disproportionately white and suburban juries were more likely to convict Black defendants. Our case, however, scrambled the pattern. We had two defendants on trial, one white and one Black, and their victims were all African Americans.

Our jury was not unlike most of the juries I had presented cases to, and those juries typically convicted the defendant. Nonetheless, I was acutely aware of the unique risks involved with bringing this case. While I thought we had identified everyone biased in favor of law enforcement, there's always the risk of the "sleeper," in other words, the juror who harbors a bias that they haven't disclosed and that the selection process hasn't been able to suss out. Such jurors can sabotage a case from inside the jury. Did we have a sleeper on our jury? Would we ever even know?

After jury selection, we reconvened the next morning for the second day of the trial. Moye swore in the jury, which isn't just a formality. It's what gives jurors their power. One day earlier, the jury had been a collection of individual citizens. Now they were entrusted with deciding whether the law had been broken. In that regard, they were the most important and powerful people in the courtroom, more than the judge or the prosecutors or the defense attorneys. Entrusting a civilian jury with this responsibility is an important check on the power of our government. It's also a remarkable vote of confidence in the good judgment of ordinary citizens.

Next, Judge Blake gave the jury a series of preliminary legal instructions. Later, she would provide more detailed instructions. For now, however, she set out some signposts for the jurors to follow. Judge Blake told them that they would decide, based on evidence presented in the courtroom, whether the defendants had broken the law. This transformed the courtroom, as in every case, into a kind of alternate reality—that is, the determination of whether Hersl and Taylor robbed people would not depend on whether they had actually done it, but on the evidence we, the prosecutors, presented in the courtroom and what evidence Judge Blake allowed the jury to see.

Reality outside the courtroom can diverge from reality inside the courtroom, so a complicated set of rules acts as a filter between the two, determining what facts from outside the courtroom can enter it. These rules serve two at times contradictory ends. On the one hand, a trial is supposed to be a search for the truth. On the other hand, the defendant enjoys important rights meant to protect the individual against the power of the state, and many of these rights frustrate the truth-seeking process—by design. The most obvious right is the Fifth Amendment's privilege against self-incrimination. A straightforward way to determine what happened in a given case would be to ask the defendant, but that's the one thing the prosecutors cannot do. Relatedly, the judge instructs the jury that they can't infer anything from the fact that a defendant declines to testify.

Putting aside any particular rule of evidence or criminal procedure, the very notion that a trial is a truth-seeking exercise is debatable. The US criminal justice system relies on an adversarial process. It is based on the idea that the truth will emerge from the clash between two sides, the government and the defendant, with the judge acting like an umpire. In other fields, for example, the sciences, the truth is sought through objective proof, not the product of two sides having an argument.

It has always struck me that the adversarial system is better at safeguarding a defendant's rights than it is at ensuring that the jury hears the truth. I go into the courtroom with what I believe is the truth, and my job is to present it to the jury. On the other side, the role of the defense lawyer is to convince the jury to acquit his or her client, regardless of whether the defendant actually did what he or she has been charged with doing.

As a result of legal rules and the competing interests of the criminal justice system, there are times when a jury acquits a defendant who did in fact commit the crime in question. There are also instances when juries convict the innocent. In striking a balance between convicting the innocent and acquitting the guilty, we are taught in law school that our system skews towards acquitting the guilty. I have no idea if that is true in practice.

We also learned during our investigation that there are even times when innocent defendants plead guilty because they calculate that a jury will believe police officers over them and that they will face longer prison sentences if they go to trial. This isn't supposed to happen. When a defendant pleads guilty, they are put under oath and asked by the judge if they have committed the crime to which they're pleading guilty. There is a type of plea—called an Alford plea, after the court case from which it arose—allowing a defendant to maintain their innocence but to nonetheless plead guilty because they acknowledge the government could prove the case against them. These kinds of pleas are highly disfavored in the federal system and almost never happen. What our investigation uncovered is that there are backdoor Alford pleas happening in federal courts, without the government or the judge or even the defense attorney knowing it.

My fear in this case was that the guilty might indeed be acquitted because of how upside down everything about this trial was likely to be. We were going to ask the jury to believe drug dealers and to convict police officers—the opposite of what goes on in nearly every other criminal trial. We'd come to see the truth through the eyes of our victims. Could the jury? Would they?

Judge Blake in her preliminary instructions specifically identified the two kinds of evidence the jury would hear: direct and circumstantial. She explained that direct evidence is evidence like eyewitness testimony, such as from a person on a street corner who saw something. By contrast, circumstantial evidence, she said, is "proof of certain facts, and based on those facts you can conclude, using your common sense, that other facts exist." She then gave an example of circumstantial evidence that I had heard other judges give:

Simple example of this is you go off to work in the morning. It's a bright, sunny day. You happen to work in an office where there's no windows. A couple of hours later, one of your co-workers comes in, taking off a wet raincoat, folding up a dripping umbrella.

You didn't see it rain because you couldn't see outside. But based on what you did see, you can conclude that it was probably raining outside. That's what we mean by circumstantial evidence. You may consider both kinds, direct and circumstantial, that you find helpful in this case.

It was the part about applying common sense that worried me the most. Would the jurors consider it common sense that police officers told the truth and that people who sold drugs for a living lied? I hoped not, because in this case it simply wasn't true.

Although Judge Blake told the jury that both kinds of evidence deserve equal consideration, I've always thought that jurors tend to discount circumstantial evidence. That makes white-collar cases, including this one, particularly difficult to prove because they turn on questions of intent, which is almost always proven through circumstantial evidence. Judge Blake also told the jurors that when they began their deliberations, choosing a foreperson should be one of the first things they did. Many see this as a formality, but in our case, I had no idea what a strong message that choice would ultimately send. After Judge Blake finished her preliminary instructions, both sides gave opening statements. As is customary, the government, bearing the burden of proof, went first. I would deliver ours.

I spend a lot of time drafting my opening statements. It's the government's first opportunity to frame the case for the jury. I try to do so using a narrative. By the end of my opening, I don't want the jury to be wondering what the case is all about. I pick my words carefully. With an audience of twelve people, some with very different backgrounds and life experiences, I am mindful of the potential of some words to mean different things to different people.

I also use the opening to try and connect with the jurors and to get them engaged in the case. Sitting through a trial can be physically and intellectually demanding. If the jurors are invested in it, they are more likely to pay attention and not get confused or sidetracked. I decided to use an approach that I had seen in the Enron trial. The senior prosecutor on our team delivered an outstanding opening statement for the government, telling the jurors that over the course of the trial, they would go "inside Enron." I thought something like that would be effective with the Task Force jury.

"In the course of this trial," I said, "you will go inside the Baltimore Police Department, inside the operations division, and into special elite units, including one called the Gun Trace Task Force, where detectives and other senior officers operate, including these men, Defendant Daniel Hersl and Defendant Marcus Taylor." I gestured at each defendant with an open palm as I said their names and paused so the jury could look at them. I then continued:

> They stole money from people that they stopped and detained. They stole money from houses that they had gone into to search. And they stole money from taxpayers when they claimed overtime they did not work.

That was the whole case in three sentences.

> They did this on all these occasions that you will learn about. And be clear, if they had done it once, we would be in this courtroom trying this case. Once would be one time too many.
>
> But they did it again and again and again. And what this shows is a pattern of criminal conduct, a pattern of racketeering activity, as Her Honor referred to, over a number of years.

We thought that highlighting this pattern would prove compelling.

Taking direct aim at Hersl and Taylor, respectively, I remarked, "And a police officer who has served a long career doesn't get to rob people a couple of times in that long career. And a police officer who hasn't served for a long time doesn't get to rob people because it's what everyone around him is doing." Hersl had been on the BPD far longer than Taylor.

Appealing to a bigger idea for the first time, I told the jury, "And what these defendants did at its base was to abuse the trust placed in them as police officers, as senior officers assigned to elite units, to enrich themselves." What made these defendants unique was how they had violated the trust the community had placed in them to enforce the law. As a society, we expect everyone to obey the law, but we expect the police to do so more than any others. Echoing what US Attorney Rod Rosenstein had said at the press conference announcing the charges, and to appeal to all the jurors, regardless of their views on policing, I told them,

> In the course of this trial, you will learn about the criminal conduct of these men, and that's what this case is about, criminal conduct.
>
> This isn't a case about police tactics or aggressive policing. It's a case about greed.
>
> This case isn't an indictment of all police officers. The indictment in this case was brought against these two officers and their co-defendants for criminal conduct that isn't subject to debate. Regardless of one's views on crime, the role of the police in our community, the appropriateness of various police tactics, the law is clear: the police can't commit robbery and extortion and fraud.

Later, as I summarized the defendants' backgrounds and the units they'd served in, I called the Gun Trace Task Force a "perfect storm of officers who took advantage of their position to enrich themselves," which it was: "The Gun Trace Task Force wasn't a unit that went rogue. It was a unit made up of detectives that had already gone rogue, men that had crossed over from the side of those who uphold the law to the side of those who break it."

I then introduced the duality the jurors would hear the cooperating defendants describe—that the Task Force officers did legitimate police work on the one hand and, in the course of doing that police work, also robbed people and committed overtime fraud on the other: "The evidence will show that these defendants and the other members of the Gun Trace Task Force had both purposes: to seize guns in the exercise of their powers as law enforcement, and using or abusing those same powers to steal money. They were, simply put, both cops and robbers at the same time."

I also tried to get ahead of one of the main lines of cross-examination that the defense would use with our witnesses: that they were lying and would say anything prosecutors wanted to hear in order to get a lower sentence. In my experience, nearly every defense attorney makes this argument. The extraordinary thing is that it is totally wrong, to the point of being fantastical. If what they said really happened, the cooperating witnesses would be committing perjury, and I would be suborning perjury in every trial. I warned the jurors, "The defense attorneys may argue that the truth is whatever the United States says it is, but it's not, ladies and gentlemen. It's not. The truth is the truth."

I also wanted to address the fact that the victims would in some cases be people who sold drugs:

Now, you will also hear from victims, victims who had money and property stolen from them.

Some of these victims were drug dealers, and they will admit that to you. They will tell you they were selling drugs, and that's how they made the money these defendants stole.

But some of the victims were not drug dealers. They were just in the wrong place at the wrong time and got into the sights of these two men and their co-defendants.

But to be clear, it doesn't matter if the victims in this case were or weren't drug dealers. The police can't rob drug dealers just like they can't rob people who aren't drug dealers.

The law applies to the police just like it applies to anyone else and it doesn't depend on the status of the victims.

What I had in mind as I spoke those words was the statue of Justice found in many courthouses across the United States. They invariably portray Justice as blindfolded and using one hand to hold the scales with which to weigh evidence. The blindfold communicates that Justice is blind to a defendant's race, gender, class, and any other characteristic of the person standing before court. Instead, Justice weighs only facts to determine the defendant's fate. That's what I hoped would happen here. The image of the blindfolded Justice was therefore particularly symbolic in our case.

In concluding, I returned to one of the main themes of the trial: how the defendants had violated the trust that the public had placed in them. I held up each officer's gun in one hand and their badge in the other.

The police officers in this case were entrusted with these: . . . This is Detective Taylor's badge; this is Detective Hersl's badge.

And these: this is Detective Taylor's gun; and this is Detective Hersl's gun.

These badges are symbols of authority. And these guns are weapons.

And before these badges and these guns, people yield. They give up their liberty. They give up their property. And they submit.

So these are powerful, powerful things, these badges and these guns. And they can be used for good to protect the community from those who break the law, but they can be used for evil by those who are entrusted with them but choose to break the law instead.

After my opening statement, Hersl's main lawyer, William Purpura, delivered the opening on his client's behalf. His arguments were unconventional.

Purpura pointed out that Hersl had violated not one but two oaths he had taken: the pledge of allegiance, which Hersl evidently recited when he first graduated from the police academy in 1999, and an oath to uphold Maryland and federal law and the US Constitution, which Hersl also took when he graduated from the academy.

The evidence will show—and it will show—that Daniel Hersl did breach that oath, that his actions embarrassed the city, the Baltimore Police Department, his family, and himself.

The evidence will show—and it will show—that on several occasions in a 17-year history of work for the Baltimore City Police that Daniel Hersl either took money and/or received money which was taken.

The evidence will show—and it will show—that Daniel Hersl committed the crime of theft. That's not a crime of violence. That's not a crime of use of violence. That's a crime of dishonesty and a crime of stealth. Nothing to be proud of. That's what he did.

What he didn't do is commit the crime of robbery and/or extortion by force. Those are oversimplifications, but you know the difference.

Purpura next asserted that Hersl had been "lumped together" with the real robbers—our witnesses Momodu Gondo and Jemell Rayam—and described the home invasion at Aaron Anderson's apartment as an example of the "real" robberies they'd committed. And that was Hersl's defense: he was a thief, not a robber. Purpura had previewed it in pretrial motions that he filed with the court so it came as no surprise.

Purpura told the jury, "We are here in a United States District Court before a United States District Court judge, appointed by the President, confirmed by Congress, rather than down a few blocks to the north on Calvert Street in state court where the theft case would be and should be tried." In this regard, the defendants' destiny depended in part on geography.

Purpura was asserting, in short, that had his clients been charged in state court—located "a few blocks to the north" of the federal courthouse in downtown Baltimore—then they would have been convicted. But because they had been charged in US District Court, they should be acquitted. His point was that state criminal laws are broader than federal laws, something we confronted when we were drafting the charges. Notably, while theft is a crime at the state level, there is no general theft statute in federal court; also, theft isn't a state law that can be charged federally under the RICO statute as can others. This defense was largely a legal one, although he would dispute certain facts during trial. His basic argument was that we had charged the defendants with a crime they hadn't committed—robbery—so we could bring a federal case because the crime Hersl did commit—theft—could only be prosecuted at the state level.

I had heard this argument before. I once tried a case with a colleague in the US Attorney's Office involving the Baltimore City landfill. Commercial junk haulers were bribing city employees to dump their garbage without paying the required fees. The scheme cost the city millions. Because it involved bribing city employees it was, at its heart, a corruption case. One of the haulers decided to go to trial. Perhaps this shouldn't have come as a surprise when I heard how he behaved when the FBI went to arrest him at his home. He was completely naked and refused to put on his clothes. Instead, he clasped his hands between his legs and asked the FBI agents, "Who's gonna cuff me?" He also called out to his wife, "Bring me my wallet so I can bribe these FBI agents." At trial, his attorney argued that this was a state theft case and not a federal corruption case. After two weeks of trial, he was convicted.

Purpura next addressed the overtime fraud charges and did so in a way that tried to connect them to Freddie Gray Jr., the young Black man whose death from injuries sustained in police custody almost three years earlier had unleashed protests and violence in the city.

"As to the overtime fraud," Purpura began, "the year 2015 is an important year. The year 2015, the city of Baltimore was gripped with riots." His use of the word "riots" was risky. Language divides us in Baltimore like everywhere else. One part of our community refers to the protests and the violence that occurred after Gray died as "riots"; another part refers to it as an "uprising." Which word one uses telegraphs which camp you're in and is seen by some as signaling your views on politics and race. Purpura was casting his lot with the "riot" community. This segment of the community was more likely to support the police.

"In 2015, we had at that point a record number of homicides by handguns in Baltimore City that shocked not Baltimore City but shocked the country," Purpura said. "The mandate of the GTTF was to get guns off the street. Quite frankly, we don't care how you do it, but do it." This introduced another dimension of the defense—that the defendants' bad police tactics were sanctioned by the BPD. As the trial unfolded, the defense never offered any evidence that this was, in fact, the case. Neither Hersl nor Taylor testified, and no witnesses were called who said that higher-ups at BPD "didn't care" how the Task Force operated.

Making another strategic concession—telling the jurors they were going to hear about bad police tactics used by his clients, but then claiming they were in the service of good ends—Purpura said, "In return, they got guns off the street. And what they did, they have violated the Fourth Amendment on a few occasions, but they got guns off the street." As this case demonstrated, however, this is a false dichotomy. Bad policing doesn't result in good cases. Hendrix, Jenkins, Taylor, and Ward interrupted a drug deal when they approached Oreese Stevenson, who was about to sell half a kilo of cocaine. Jenkins, however, violated Stevenson's rights when he lunged into his car and grabbed his passenger's book bag. Because of Jenkins's illegal search, Stevenson's lawyer was able to get the drugs in the backpack suppressed. Without the drugs, the case had to be dropped.

Hersl's lawyer then explained that the Task Force members were given days off, so-called slash days, and overtime as a reward for the guns they seized. The defense embraced the vicious cycle we had learned about during the course of the investigation: the Task Force members used unconstitutional and illegal police tactics to seize guns in order to get overtime. Purpura claimed, the whole thing had been blessed by BPD, so the Task Force officers lacked criminal intent.

In an attempt at a second explanation for the overtime fraud, Purpura floated the idea that Hersl may have been visiting his mother when he put in for overtime he didn't work: "And, you know, it is a fact: the Government has surveillance on this. They even have his phone showing where he is in Little Italy a couple of times, maybe—maybe more than a couple times, because he does go there while he's working and on overtime. And he loves to visit his mom. He might bring her coffee and doughnuts, so he's done that. There's no question. We're not hiding that." On the days for which we charged Hersl with overtime fraud, his phone did not, in fact, show him in Little Italy.

Then Purpura returned to his argument that Hersl was a thief and not a robber. He asserted, "The evidence will show—and it will show—that on each and every one of these instances [of robbery] in a 17-year career, that it was Daniel Hersl's intent as he was making the arrest and seizing guns or drugs or money to do everything properly." Purpura briefly went through each of the robberies in the indictment that involved Hersl. Previewing how he would cross-examine Antonio Santiful and Herbert Tate, he referred to both as having been arrested in "open-air drug markets." He called Ronald Hamilton a criminal and twice said that the government would "vouch" for his credibility despite the fact that he was a liar.

Describing the Hamilton robbery, Purpura told the jury, "Rayam took $20,000, put it in the back of the police car. Maryland State Police came in. Only thing they got was that $50,000." This was the version of events that the jury would hear from us, so to that point, the prosecution and the defense agreed as to what had happened. Purpura continued, "When they got back to Baltimore City, Gondo and Rayam split the money. Jenkins got a share of the money. Jenkins then gave Dan Hersl approximately $3,000 of stolen money." He added, "Not extortion. Not a robbery." In other words, Hersl hadn't participated in the robbery of the Hamiltons at their home in Westminster. He just got a cut of the proceeds after the fact.

Finally, Purpura addressed the Dennis Armstrong incident. After colorfully describing what had happened, telling the jury that Armstrong had been "tossing snowball-sized chunks of cocaine outside of the car window" as he fled from the Task Force, Purpura made a second admission. He told the jury that Hersl had searched Armstrong's car and found money. "And there was money placed in a bag. It was placed in an evidence bag along with the rest of the evidence seized," he said. "And the evidence will show—and it will show—that, again, this is another time that before the evidence gets to the evidence storage locker, Dan Hersl takes maybe $500 out of the bag. There's multiple thousands in there. He gave 500 to Rayam and perhaps 500 to Gondo. The rest is turned in."

What's interesting about the latter comment, "perhaps 500 to Gondo," was that it meant Hersl evidently didn't remember whether he had given Gondo any of the money. Gondo told us that Hersl hadn't given him any of it. This was another instance where Gondo could have gone farther if he were making up a story; he could have told us that

Hersl had given him cash. Hersl, apparently, wouldn't have contradicted him.

Wrapping up Purpura offered, "The crime of the moment, the crime of theft. No one's proud of it. Shouldn't be a police officer. He's not a police officer. But it's not, as all these incidents will show, what the Government's charged. That's really your duty in this case. You take one wrong versus another wrong. Just make the right decision which one it is."

With that, Purpura sat down. That was Hersl's defense: he was a thief not a robber. Would the jury see it that way?

Jennifer Wicks, one of Taylor's lawyers, followed Purpura with her opening statement. Taylor's defense was more conventional than Hersl's. There would be no admissions. It boiled down to the argument that Taylor was a good cop surrounded by bad cops.

Wicks's main line of attack held that the witnesses against Taylor had been incentivized by the promise of reduced sentences to get them to lie and implicate him in crimes that he hadn't commited.

Wicks told the jury, "But the Government has the key to help these people get out of prison, to get out of jail eventually, and that's a considerably compelling reason for people to be saying what they're saying now, to be turning the finger, and to be pointing it at Marcus Taylor: what they want, what they need for themselves." The defense was that the truth was on Taylor's side. "The evidence in this case will be people from the stand saying, 'Well, Marcus Taylor did that,' or 'Marcus Taylor did this,' or 'I heard Marcus Taylor say this,' or 'So-and-so told me this is what they did or this is what he said.'"

The problem with that argument was that none of the victims who testified against Taylor were in jail. So none of them had an incentive to lie and falsely implicate Taylor in crimes he didn't commit. In fact, the incentives ran the other way. It would have been far easier for the victims to say that they didn't know anything about Marcus Taylor; then they wouldn't have to be witnesses. All they got out of telling the truth was a trip to federal court and a grilling by Hersl and Taylor's lawyers. Hardly a reason to make things up.

Wicks continued, "But at the end of the day, you have to believe the source of information. You have to be able to put your trust in that person." In other words, both the government and Taylor agreed that this case came down to whether the victims and the cooperating defendants were telling the truth. The ultimate question posed to the jury was one of belief and disbelief.

Wicks further argued that not only did all the witnesses have an incentive to lie, but that the cooperating police officer defendants were particularly unreliable because they had lied in court many times before: "But they have lied. They have lied to other officers. They have lied to prosecutors. They have lied to juries. They have lied to judges. And this is all before they are caught and arrested in March of 2017." She added, "They have a career of lying, according to them."

She was right, but at the end of the day who else but a bunch of rotten and corrupt cops would be able to describe how their rotten, corrupt police squad operated? It brought to mind an expression I've used in closing arguments and have heard other prosecutors in my office use: if you want to know what's going on in Hell, you don't call a bunch of Angels.

Wicks then made a related argument about the ability of the witnesses to tell the truth. It was subtler than the argument that the witnesses were lying to get out of jail.

> Some of these witnesses, as [Purpura] talked about, are drug dealers. They're people out there with guns and drugs that have gotten stopped and detained for guns and drugs, and evidence is seized. And they have an incentive at that very moment to be pointing the finger at Mr. Taylor and other officers saying they did something wrong.

And, ladies and gentlemen, what I'm just talking about is someone's personal bias. Bias is what comes between that person and really their ability to tell the truth or even perhaps their ability to even see the truth. It's like a coloring of their lenses in the view of the world. It's colored by what is motivating them, by what they want to be true.

So, Wicks argued, some witnesses were incapable of telling the truth. It seemed designed to address instances where a witness might seem credible to the jury. Despite an outward manifestation of reliability, the witness should nonetheless not be believed; their biases made them incapable of telling the truth. It was an interesting argument. But is anyone incapable of telling the truth?

With opening arguments over, we turned to the presentation of the evidence. By the time a trial starts, the facts are known. The government doesn't call witnesses they haven't already interviewed or called to testify before the grand jury. A trial is a presentation of the evidence amassed during the investigation. At its most basic level, it is meant to answer the question of whether that evidence proves beyond a reasonable doubt that the defendant or defendants broke the law. That question is for the jury.

While the truth is known before the trial starts, it unspools over the course of the proceeding, sometimes in ways that you expect and sometimes in ways you don't. In this way, a trial is like a play but without rehearsals. The first and only time the evidence is presented from start to finish is when the case is being tried before the jury. Witnesses say things they hadn't said before; even things you've heard a witness say before sometimes take on new meaning because of the different context or because you've since learned something else that gives it a deeper or different understanding. The order of witnesses also affects how the truth unfolds. Sometimes hearing a particular witness testify right after another one puts things they both say in a new light. All this plays out with defense lawyers objecting to the evidence and the trial judge ruling on their objections. Those three factors—the jury, the defense, and the judge—are all variables that manifest themselves only when the trial actually begins.

What all this means, among other things, is that by the time a trial begins, there shouldn't be significant unresolved factual questions. That doesn't, however, ensure against assorted surprises and dramatic moments.

We would have our share of those.

SIXTEEN

Cops versus Cops

"Government is calling a witness?" Judge Catherine C. Blake asked matter-of-factly after the opening statements.

"The United States calls Maurice Ward," I responded.

And so the trial of Gun Trace Task Force members Marcus Taylor and Daniel Hersl began. We had chosen Ward as our first witness for a variety of reasons: he was smart, thoughtful, and had a good memory, particularly for details. He was also disciplined in his answers; he listened to questions, answered them, and didn't go off on tangents. We thought he could tell the story of the Special Enforcement Section squad Wayne Jenkins had led and describe what happened when Jenkins took over the Task Force. He had also committed a robbery with Taylor before they both went to work for Jenkins when they searched Shawn Whiting's house. That robbery was the chronological beginning of our case against Taylor and Hersl.

Ward's testimony during direct examination tracked with what he had told us when we debriefed him over the summer. It also provided our first dramatic moment at trial, this one involving duffel bags.

Ward testified that before all the Gun Trace Task Force members were arrested, Jenkins had proposed robbing a drug dealer who supplied cocaine to a friend of Jenkins. Part of the plan was to wear masks. When Ward mentioned masks, I recognized I had an opening to have him show the jury something jaw-dropping.

"Now, you said that he wanted to wear masks," I reiterated. "At some point, did Jenkins show you that he actually had masks like that to wear?"

"Yes, sir," Ward responded.

"And I'm going to show you what's been marked as Government Exhibit 19A."

Government Exhibit FBI-19A was the first of the two black duffel bags recovered from Jenkins's van, both of them filled with the burglary tools that Stepp had ordered for Jenkins on Amazon. We had marked them as exhibits and put them on the floor behind the prosecution table in the courtroom.

At that point, I moved toward the table. My co-counsel, Derek Hines, got up to help me drag the bags to the middle of the courtroom. I then asked Ward to come down from the stand, look into the bags, and take out the things that he remembered Jenkins showing him. Afterwards, Derek told me that when I did this, the marshals had looked alarmed. I was so focused on the witness and the bags that I hadn't noticed. Ward was in custody. A magistrate judge had declared Ward a danger to the community. Now I was asking him to come off the witness stand and start handling machetes and sledgehammers in the middle of a courtroom. And that's exactly what he did.

Ward started with the duffel bag containing clothes and shoes and masks. He picked out the ski masks Jenkins showed him that day. Then a pair of shoes Ward remembered Jenkins having. If they wore those shoes and then got rid of them, any footprints found couldn't be traced back to them. Ward also remembered the dark-colored clothing in the bag.

"And it was actually—it was tools in there also. There were some tools," he said.

Tools? I asked him to look in the other bag.

Ward recognized a grappling hook on a long length of rope, a pry bar, an enormous pair of metal cutting shears that could be used to cut padlocks off fences or doors, a crowbar, a tool to open car door locks, and an enormous yellow sledgehammer. I asked Ward if any of this equipment had been provided by the Baltimore Police Department.

"None of it, no."

The contents of the bags weren't for enforcing the law. They were for breaking it.

When Evodio Hendrix took the witness stand, Derek questioned him about the duffel bags full of burglary tools. This time, to avoid the uncomfortable situation we'd had with Ward, Derek showed Hendrix pictures of the bags' contents. Hendrix started by explaining how one day Jenkins had called him to the back of his van.

"He actually opened up the back of the van," said Hendrix. "There were two black duffel bags. Opened one. He had all black clothing, like ski masks, other kind of masks. And another one was multiple tools, like construction-type tools."

Derek showed Hendrix the picture of the bag containing black clothes and ski masks. Hendrix recognized it and testified that it was one of the bags from the back of Jenkins's van. Derek then asked Hendrix whether Jenkins had told him the purpose of the black ski masks.

Hendrix replied, "He said he had all this stuff just in case he ran into a monster or a big hit."

"Monster" was the word Jenkins had used to describe Oreese Stevenson to Donald Stepp. Indeed, Stevenson was their biggest hit.

"And what is a monster?" Derek asked. "What did you understand that to mean?"

"Someone with a lot of money or drugs," Hendrix answered.

"And did you understand him to be saying that he had these masks if he ran into a monster so that he could arrest him?"

"No. Once I seen all that, I came to the conclusion he was talking about robbing 'em."

Derek next showed Hendrix a photograph of the bag with all the tools. Hendrix confirmed that he had seen the bag of tools depicted in the photograph. He particularly remembered the grappling hook, "as if [Jenkins] was going to climb a building or some type of situation," Hendrix shook his head as he said it, in apparent disbelief at the lengths that Jenkins would go to rob people, a kind of bad guy Spiderman.

Derek asked him if the grappling hook had been given to the Task Force by the Baltimore Police Department?

"Definitely not," Hendrix said.

"Did you have any reason to use this tool in your duties as a detective in the Gun Task Force?" Derek continued.

"Definitely not, no."

"Weren't scaling any tall buildings or anything?"

"No, sir."

Derek next showed Hendrix a picture of a machete and a sledgehammer and asked the same series of questions. Hendrix testified that no, these hadn't been issued by the BPD, and no, they weren't used in any kind of police work.

They were used for robbing people.

Ward also testified about another duffel bag, the one full of marijuana that they had stolen at Belvedere Towers. Although less dramatic in presentation, that duffel bag demonstrated to the jury that both he and Donald Stepp were telling the truth.

Ward told the jury how Jenkins had taken the duffel bag full of cash into the woods to split up the money from the Belvedere Towers robbery and how Jenkins had left the duffel bag full of drugs in the trunk of the car that the Task Force members had used when they committed the robbery. After Ward first told us about the Belvedere Towers robbery, the FBI went to the spot where Ward said they had divvied up the money to see if the money bag was still there. It wasn't, which was hardly surprising since several years had passed since the incident. Ward didn't know what had happened to the other duffel bag, the one full of drugs.

The person who did know what had happened to it was Donald Stepp. Jenkins had given him a duffel bag full of marijuana to sell, and Stepp had kept the bag. When Stepp started cooperating, he gave us the bag.

After Ward told the jury that Jenkins had left the duffel bag full of marijuana in his trunk, I said, "All right. I'm showing you what's been marked Government Exhibit FBI-24. Do you recognize this?"

"Yes," Ward answered.

"What is it?" I asked him.

"That's the duffel bag that was in the trunk full of marijuana."

Ward didn't know how we got the bag, and we never told him. He didn't know Stepp, who would only later testify that Jenkins had given him the bag, at that time full of marijuana. Since Ward and Stepp had never met, they couldn't be making up what they told the jury. Their only connection was the truth.

The main thrust of the defense's cross-examination of Ward was that he was a liar. One of Taylor's defense lawyers, Christopher Nieto, went first. He asked Ward if he had ever lied on the witness stand.

"Yes, sir," Ward answered.

"How many times?"

Ward didn't know how many times, but after further back and forth with the defense lawyer, he said it was somewhere between five and ten. Nieto asked Ward whether on those occasions he had taken an oath like the one he had taken in this trial. He had. I wondered what the jury would make of this.

Before prosecutors call a witness to testify, they have to give the defense any statements the witness previously made and any information in the government's possession that could be used to impeach the witness. That includes any prior testimony under oath, notes of interviews with them when they weren't under oath, and emails and anything else they have written about the case. Also covered is any information that establishes that the witness wasn't truthful in a different proceeding, such as a finding by a judge that they weren't credible, no matter the topic, even in a divorce proceeding.

This obligation arises from the Supreme Court's decision in *Giglio v. United States* (1972). As a result, impeachment information is referred to as *Giglio*. Federal prosecutors are required by Department of Justice policy to interview a law enforcement officer before they take the stand to determine if there is any *Giglio* material that the prosecutor needs to turn over. The prosecutor has to ask the law enforcement officer whether they have ever lied on the stand or whether a judge has ever found that they had lied. *Giglio* also includes information that would indicate bias or motive or prior inconsistent statements. Individual law enforcement agencies also maintain files on their officers, including *Giglio* information, that prosecutors can request. Typically, when a police officer has significant *Giglio*, they are no longer called as a witness.

In previous cases I had tried, none of the federal law enforcement officers I called had significant *Giglio* issues. I don't think I would have called an officer, whether local or federal, who did. Ward and the other cooperators were obviously the exception. They probably had more *Giglio* than any law enforcement witness ever called in the courthouse.

While our cooperating defendants were unique in that regard, I had called plenty of others who had lied before they took the witness stand. Politicians and executives at big companies aren't used to having their actions questioned. Sometimes they lie because they think they're smarter than whoever is questioning them. They deny they did anything wrong or try to explain away, falsely, the evidence against them. Some of these targets stick to their story and wind up going to trial. Most don't. Instead, they eventually admit what they did and that they had lied when first confronted about it and agree to cooperate and testify against their now-former partners in crime.

When a cooperator who previously denied doing anything wrong testifies, their having lied in the past is used against them during cross-examination. To draw the sting, I always bring out that fact in the witness's direct examination before they are cross-examined. My fear, among other things, is that the jury will think that I tried to deceive them by presenting a witness who lied and not telling them that up front. A jury hearing from any witness has a couple of tools to help them determine whether to believe a cooperating witness.

First and foremost, the jurors draw on their own experiences. We have all told the truth and have experienced someone else telling us the truth, and we have all lied and have experienced someone lying to us. Juries can put that life experience to work to figure out whether to believe a witness. Is the witness evasive? Do they seem uncomfortable answering certain questions but not others? Do they make eye contact? Does their volume or tone change in response to certain questions? Are there "tells" that suggest that they are lying, like a nervous cough or clearing their throat at certain times but not at others? As in everyday life outside the courtroom, all these factors come into play in evaluating whether someone is telling the truth.

Sometimes telling the difference between the truth and a lie is easy. Sometimes it's not. In every case involving cooperating defendants, I worry about being duped. To reduce that risk, I never call a cooperating defendant unless I can corroborate their testimony with other forms of evidence. This can include physical evidence, recordings, documents, emails, financial records, surveillance photographs or video, and the testimony of other witnesses, just to name a few. That's what we did in this case.

All of the cooperators in the Task Force trial—Ward, Hendrix, Jemell Rayam, and Momodu Gondo—admitted that they had previously lied in police reports and in some cases even in court. Now we were asking the jury to believe them in this trial. Unlike other cooperating defendants I had called, many of whom had lied when first confronted by law enforcement, these witnesses had actually previously lied in court, under oath.

In a role reversal, and another example of how this case flipped the playbook, Nieto asked Ward about some of the police tactics that Ward had described during his direct examination. Nieto seemed to pursue this line of questioning in an attempt to demonstrate that Taylor was actually a good cop. Usually it's the other way around: the defense lawyer criticizes how a police officer conducted himself in making an arrest or undertaking a search. Nieto returned to the topic of "door pops" and asked Ward to explain the technique. Ward repeated what he had testified to earlier—that the Task Force would sometimes approach young men on a street corner, pretend to identify a suspect for whom they had a warrant, and then jump out to see if anybody ran. Then Nieto added, "And so if somebody ran, and if they looked like they were holding something in their waist that could be a gun, you guys would give chase, correct?"

Ward answered in the affirmative. But Ward had told us, when we debriefed him, and had earlier testified, that they didn't just go after young men who "looked like they were holding something in their waist that could be a gun." They chased whoever ran, regardless of whether they exhibited characteristics that might legitimately give rise to what is referred to as a "*Terry* stop."

Terry stops, named after *Terry v. Ohio* (1968), the Supreme Court case that blessed them, are also referred to as a "stop and frisk." They are "brief, investigative encounters" in which the police temporarily detain someone in order to pat down their outer clothing. *Terry* stops must be based on "a reasonable suspicion" that an individual is armed *and* engaged—or about to be engaged—in criminal conduct.

This line of questioning tried to reframe Ward's earlier testimony that the Task Force went after people because they were young Black men hanging out on a street corner and instead suggest that they chased these men because the officers noticed they had a bulge in their waistband. Ward had testified that the Task Force chose targets not because of any specialized training or experience of its members, but because of their victims' skin color and where the arrestees were—on street corners in certain neighborhoods in East and West Baltimore—when the Task Force came across them.

But defense lawyers often try and defend against the case they want to defend against, not the one actually confronting them. Thus, Nieto tried to make bad policing sound better than it was, which was another example of the upside-down nature of this case.

Later, while winding up, Nieto returned to the theme of truth and lies.

"So for the past 13 or 14 years, how many years would you say that you were a professional liar?"

I objected to the question, and the court sustained my objection, but this was the argument—that Ward was a liar. And that was how the cross-examination of Ward ended, with a series of questions about all the ways and times Ward had lied.

"So for the better part of a decade, professionally, you've been lying; right?" Nieto asked.

"Yes, sir," Ward replied.

"But you lied on statements of probable cause—"

"Yes, sir."

"You lied to prosecutors?"

"Yes, sir."

"And you lied to the citizens who you arrested about what was going on?"

"Yes, sir."

"And you lied to your family?"

"Yes, sir."

And then Nieto passed Ward to Bill Purpura, Hersl's lead defense lawyer.

Before my team's first interview with Ward, we had offered him an immunity letter, also called a proffer agreement. Sticking with the theme of the witness's credibility, Purpura questioned Ward about the agreement.

Purpura asked, "And that proffer agreement says: We're not going to use any of this against you so long as you tell us the truth?"

Ward answered, "Yes, sir."

"Okay. And they also say that if you are not 100 percent truthful, if you withhold information, if you minimize your role or try to protect anyone, deal's off; right? That was your understanding of the agreement?"

"Yes, sir."

So far, this was an accurate summary of the agreement.

"Now, the definition of 'truth,' right, as to if you are not truthful with us, that's the Government who makes that determination; isn't that right."

This wasn't what the agreement said. Unfortunately, Ward agreed with him, responding, "Yes, sir."

"Okay," Purpura continued. "So if you say something that you believe to be the truth and the Government or the agents disagree with you, you're the one who's out of luck; right?"

This also wasn't accurate but Ward, again, agreed.

This line of questioning demonstrated that a lay witness doesn't always fully understand the legal documents he or she signs. The proffer letter actually said that a court would determine whether the witness receiving immunity had lied and, therefore, breached the agreement, and that the government has to prove it to the court by a "preponderance of the evidence," which is an evidentiary standard in between probable cause and beyond a reasonable doubt. Preponderance of the evidence roughly translates to a greater than 50 percent chance.

I had seen this line of cross-examination before and, unfortunately, I had seen witnesses make the same mistake that Ward made. I had also tried cases where defense attorneys tried more broadly to argue that there was more than one version of the truth.

I have always pushed back on this argument because, fundamentally, I don't think there is more than one version of the truth. The truth exists independently of any witness. Hersl either took Santiful's money or he didn't. Taylor got some of the money stolen from Stevenson's safe or he didn't. These weren't arguments. There is no "government truth." The truth is the truth.

Purpura tried to weave Freddie Gray's death into the narrative, asking Ward whether the murder rate "blew up" after Gray's death. Ward said it had. Next, Purpura asked whether there was "pressure on you and your fellow officers to do something." Ward said there was, and Purpura followed with, "But what really happened during that time? Is it fair to say that a lot of officers on the west side, on the east side after the Freddie Gray incident said, 'I don't want to get involved'? Is that fair to say?"

"Yes, sir," Ward said.

"So there was a lot fewer arrests by a lot of officers out there, isn't that correct, sir, during that time period?"

"Yes, sir."

"And the mandate of your SES, Special Enforcement Section, back in 2015 and the GTTF starting in 2016 was to get guns off the street, right?"

"Yes, sir."

After more questions like this, Purpura addressed the police tactics Ward had testified about. Like Nieto, he seemed to be trying to reframe these tactics as effective.

"But you were out there doing like what you said, 20 to 25 or more attempted stops every night, day in and day out when you were working; is that correct, sir?"

"Yes."

"And you were ripping and roaring; right?"

"Yes, sir."

"And that's what Jenkins liked to do. He never got tired; right?"

"Absolutely."

It appeared to me that Hersl's defense would be that in the aftermath of Gray's death, with homicide rates soaring, Jenkins was driving them hard to seize guns, all in the service of fighting crime.

Next Purpura tied the aftermath of Gray's death to the overtime fraud, the other part of the charges, asking Ward, "But because during this time period when the murder rate was blowing up and there was havoc, you had a gun or two guns, you get a reward and that's a slash day, correct?"

"Yes, sir," Ward said.

"And that's because your group was out there proactively doing what they should have been doing at that point, getting guns off the street during a time of crisis; is that correct, sir?"

"Yes, sir."

This was the defense's counter-narrative. The Task Force members were heroes not villains.

Would the jury buy it?

To challenge the charge that the defendants were in a conspiracy, Purpura ended by drawing out one of the odd features of the case. He noted that there were essentially two subgroups in the alleged conspiracy. On the one side was Gondo, Rayam, and Hersl, who all committed robberies together. On the other side, was Hendrix, Taylor, and Ward, who all committed robberies together. The common link was Wayne Jenkins. He committed robberies with both cliques. Jenkins was the linchpin in the conspiracy, but Jenkins wasn't on trial. The two defendants who were on trial—Hersl and Taylor—had never, at least directly, participated in any robberies together.

Despite Purpura's statements, the law of conspiracy, as the judge would instruct the jury at the end of the presentation of evidence, doesn't require every co-conspirator to commit crimes with every other co-conspirator. They don't even have to know one another. The crime of conspiracy is a criminal agreement. It can be among some members who know one another and some who don't, provided there are members in common, like Jenkins, and that all the conspirators agree to the same thing. It can be a difficult concept and, as a practical matter, I worried that the jury might struggle with it.

Purpura's question elicited the fact that Ward had no direct evidence that Hersl had committed any crimes, even though they were both charged with being members of the same conspiracy. As a legal question, it didn't matter, but as a practical matter, the jury might get hung up on it. Purpura brought it out with a series of pointed questions.

"Now, in your testimony on Tuesday and in your proffer sessions, you never said that you gave Daniel Hersl any money which was stolen; is that correct, sir?"

"Yes, sir," Ward responded.

"And you never saw Daniel Hersl steal or take money unlawfully; isn't that correct, sir?"

"Yes, sir."

"You never saw Daniel Hersl steal or take drugs unlawfully; is that correct, sir?"

"Yes, sir."

"And you never saw Daniel Hersl steal or take anything of value, such as a watch or jewelry, unlawfully; is that correct, sir?"

"Yes, sir."

"I have no further questions. Thank you."

Then the US marshals approached the witness stand and escorted Ward back to the lockup.

Ward wasn't the only cooperator who was called a liar. When Rayam took the stand, Purpura took a similar tack with him on cross-examination. To make the point that the jury shouldn't believe Rayam, Purpura asked him a series of questions about his having lied in police reports, in search warrants, to judges, to other juries. Rayam confirmed all of it.

In the first criminal trial I worked on, the Enron case, I closely watched one of the senior prosecutors prep Andy Fastow, the company's CFO, who agreed to cooperate with the government. The prosecutor, who also promised the jury in his opening statement that they would be going "inside Enron" over the course of the trial, told Fastow that when he took the stand he needed to "put on his shit hat" and "get out his rubber neck," explaining to Fastow that the defense attorneys were going to dump on him everything that he had done wrong. Then the prosecutor explained his colorful metaphor this way: the shit was going to rain down on him, hence the need for the "shit hat"; he needed a rubber neck because he would be asked to agree that he had done all the bad things he would be accused of, and that he should agree, if he had done them, taking the punches, and not try to resist.

Ever since, I had used the prosecutor's same two phrases with most cooperators, including Rayam. The shit had rained down on him, and he had agreed with all of it. But then Purpura asked an open-ended question that we had never asked Rayam: "Despite all those lies to judges, District Court, Circuit Court, to internal affairs, to juries, despite all those lies, why should this jury believe you today?" I held my breath as Rayam thought about it. Then he ran with it:

> Like I said, it's never too late to do the right thing, and I have a clean conscience. I go to sleep knowing that what I did was wrong, and I'm ready for my consequences and my punishment.
>
> The judge could give me more time than what the plea deal is. I took an oath; I broke it. I'm not looking for any sympathy.
>
> I know what I did. I'm not blaming Wayne for being the supervisor. I blame myself because at the end of the day, we all had that badge, the Baltimore City Police Department. So whether you were a sergeant, a lieutenant, or a captain, we still had a badge. I broke it, and I'm saying what I did was wrong.

Purpura interrupted him, trying to regain control.

"And you did wrong, and you did lie over and over again; correct? And you don't want to spend one extra day in jail than you have to, do you sir?"

"I have a clean conscience," Rayam reiterated.

"Do you want to spend one extra day than you have to, sir, in jail?" Purpura tried again. But Rayam wasn't backing down.

"I'll spend as much time as the judge gives me," he said.

"You will," was Purpura's response. Then he sat down.

Gondo was the last of the cooperating defendants we called. He projected strength when he testified. He didn't display emotion, like Rayam had, or seem defeated, like Ward. He spoke loudly and clearly and answered every question exactly as he wanted. He didn't tell me what I wanted to hear, and he wasn't intimidated by the defense lawyers' persistence. His answers were emphatic. He didn't just respond "Yeah" or even just "Yes" or "No" when answering questions. He said things like "Absolutely" and "100 percent."

During direct examination, Gondo accepted responsibility for everything: robberies, overtime fraud, and helping and protecting his friend Glenn Wells and, by extension, Shropshire and his drug crew. In all important respects, Gondo's testimony about the Task Force matched Rayam's, who had testified before him. He described robbing the Hamiltons in great detail and also corroborated Rayam's testimony about the home invasion at Aaron Anderson's apartment on Marnat Road.

Taylor's lawyer Chris Nieto began the cross-examination and came out hot. He called Gondo a drug dealer. Gondo disagreed. They went back and forth for a while, and then Gondo explained why he had helped Glenn Wells. Gondo even referenced how our case against him had begun—with Shropshire discovering the tracking device and afterwards calling Gondo.

"I felt as though they were being targeted by . . . Wayne and the squad," Gondo testified. "I gave them information, which I wasn't supposed to. I broke the law. Even though he was a friend of mine, I shouldn't have told Brill [Shropshire] to remove a tracker. Even though

I believe Wayne [Jenkins] was targeting my friend to rob him, I still shouldn't have told Kyle [Wells] that information, because I was in law enforcement. That's where I broke the law."

Gondo had consistently said that he had given Wells sensitive law enforcement information because Jenkins was trying to rob him. He recognized that by doing so, Wells was able to both avoid getting robbed by Jenkins and also being arrested by Jenkins, and the latter allowed Wells and Shropshire to keep selling drugs. Gondo's motivation revealed a bizarre intersection of Jenkins's wrongdoing and Gondo's loyalty to Wells. Gondo wasn't helping Wells because Jenkins was engaged in legitimate police work. Gondo was helping Wells because Jenkins was trying to rob him. Whether Gondo would have helped Wells evade Jenkins if Jenkins was doing legitimate police work was something we'd never know.

Nieto tried to highlight a contradiction between Rayam's testimony and Gondo's. Gondo testified that he didn't know why he had been shot. Rayam who testified before Gondo, had said that Gondo's 2006 shooting was drug related. Nieto asked Gondo if it was.

"Absolutely not," Gondo answered.

"Absolutely not? That had nothing to do with drugs?"

"100 percent not," Gondo reasserted.

"A hundred percent."

"On my father's grave, 100 percent not."

"Okay," Nieto said. "So if somebody said that that shooting was, in fact, drug-related, they'd be mistaken right?"

The "somebody," of course, was Rayam, and Nieto was trying to use Gondo to discredit Rayam.

"They're entitled to they opinion," Gondo replied. "The government can investigate it. BPD can investigate it. If they come up with anything different, so be it. But my shooting was no way, no how drug-related." Gondo was adamant.

"I mean, you're a hundred percent certain that it had nothing to do with drugs, right? So their investigation wouldn't reveal anything?" Nieto continued.

"I have no idea. They're entitled to their investigation."

They went back-and-forth like this for a while.

Nieto tried again with, "Oh, okay. Okay. So, once again, as I suggested, then, if somebody were to say that that shooting were drug-related, they'd be wrong, right?"

Gondo seemed smart enough to know this was a setup.

"That's their own personal opinion," he said. "I'm just telling you my half, the truth."

"Well, the truth is the truth, right?" Nieto responded.

"Right."

The exchange encapsulated the theme of the trial.

Later, Nieto tried to bring out another inconsistency between Rayam and Gondo, this time over their respective accounts of one of the times when Rayam shot someone.

"But you knew that Rayam had murdered someone, right?" Nieto asked.

"He shot a person on the street, yeah. That's correct," Gondo replied.

"Right. Right. So the Rayam-involved shooting, right, you had learned about that through Detective Edwards and through Rayam himself, right?"

"That's correct."

"All right. And it had occurred over on Spalding Avenue? It was a traffic stop?"

"That's correct."

"And the driver had taken off, and Rayam just shot him at point-blank range, correct?"

"Yeah, that's correct."

"All right. And do you remember what Rayam told you was his rationale for shooting the guy?"

"He just shot him. He had a bulge in his waist, he just shot him."

"Didn't you tell federal agents that Rayam told you, 'Fuck it. I just didn't want to chase him'?"

"Absolutely."

"Right. And that Rayam also told you that Baltimore Police Department Colonel Dean Palmere had arrived at the scene and coached Rayam on how he should sort of explain the shooting, right?"

"He coached everybody who was at the scene: Tariq, Jason. He coached the individual. People in command coached, yeah."

Rayam, during his testimony, had denied that he'd "murdered" this man. But that didn't mean that he hadn't told Gondo he had, maybe to sound tougher than he was. Maybe the jury would draw the same conclusion. In any event, it was an incongruence between their testimony, not the only one, but certainly one of the most dramatic ones.

In a particularly testy exchange, Nieto tried to get Gondo to admit that he wanted to get a reduced sentence and would therefore do anything to make the government "happy." Gondo wasn't having it.

"So it's still very important for you, then, that the Government is happy with the work that you're doing, right?" Nieto began.

"I don't know if it's happy," Gondo answered. "I'm just here to speak the truth."

"Okay."

"That's it. I'm not here to make the Government happy."

Nieto also pressed Gondo on why he didn't report Jenkins to internal affairs after Gondo said he didn't approve of a lot of things Jenkins did.

"Working in law enforcement," Gondo said, "if I would have notified anybody, Wayne knew so many people up in command, I'd have been blackballed. So, no, I didn't—"

Nieto interrupted to ask Gondo why he was talking about it now.

"At this point, I'm not a detective," Gondo said. "I'm not BPD. I'm myself. So as I stand here as a man, I'm going to face everything head on. That's it. I don't have to cover up for anybody. All I have to do is speak my truth, and that's it. So that's what I'm doing."

As Nieto prepared to sit down, he tried to summarize Gondo's two lives, asking him,

"Okay. So in sum, right, you have stolen money as a drug dealer and as a police officer, right?"

Gondo replied, "When I took money, I was a police officer. You're saying I stole drug money as a drug dealer and a police officer. When I took money, when I took drugs, I was a police officer. I broke the law. I was there to enforce the law. I didn't. That's it."

Gondo's recitation of what he did and who he was and when he did it encapsulated the crimes of the Task Force.

SEVENTEEN

Drug Dealers versus the Cops

In the trial of Gun Trace Task Force members Daniel Hersl and Marcus Taylor, the first victim we called to the witness stand was Shawn Whiting, a drug dealer. My co-counsel, Derek Hines, questioned him on the witness stand.

Whiting told the jury about the search at his home on January 24, 2014, describing in detail how much money he had (more than $23,000), how he made it (painting and selling drugs), and how about $15,000 of that money went missing, along with other property, such as expensive shoes and cologne, while the police were there. This was the earliest robbery involving Taylor and Maurice Ward. It happened even before they were both on Jenkins's Special Enforcement Section squad, and it showed that they weren't just sheep following his lead.

During cross-examination, Whiting was ready to fight. That Whiting had been robbed wasn't at issue. Ward had admitted to that. Taylor's other lawyer, Jennifer Wicks, went first. Her goal seemed to be to distance her client from Ward, but Whiting wasn't having any of it. Whiting told the court, "I mean Sergeant Marcus Taylor and Maurice [Ward] be together like peanut butter and jelly every day in the same car."

Wicks also brought out one of the truths that the investigation had laid bare: that victims wouldn't complain that the police had stolen their drugs because it would expose them to more charges and longer sentences. She asked Whiting, "And you didn't want to tell 'em back then that there were four and a half kilos because that's more weight than three kilos?" She was referring to Whiting having been charged with possessing with intent to distribute three kilograms of cocaine in state court.

These charges had been thrown out before we met Whiting. To his credit, Whiting told us that he'd really had four and a half kilos in the house when the police searched it. The obvious conclusion to draw from that discrepancy was that the police had stolen the difference. "If I'm on trial for something, why would I mention more drugs?" Whiting responded to Wicks. It made perfect sense. And that reluctance is exactly what the Task Force officers could count on. Until now.

The next drug dealer we called was Oreese Stevenson, the victim of the biggest robbery the defendants committed.

In the weeks leading up to the trial, we had tried to meet with all the witnesses who were going to testify, which is not unusual. I've done it in every trial; the practice is widespread in the federal system. I meet with witnesses to explain, as best as I can, what it's like to testify in federal court. I do that because being called as a witness can be a strange and uncomfortable experience. It's not like having a conversation with someone in the real world. The rules that govern the taking of testimony have developed over centuries of Anglo-American legal history and have their own logic and eccentricities. I want to help the witnesses navigate the rules so the truth can come out.

The most important thing I tell every witness is that their only job is to tell the truth. They're not a witness for one side or the other. They're just a witness. I tell them not to think about the consequences of their testimony. That's not their job. The jury and the judge decide consequences.

I tell each witness that for them to be able to testify truthfully, they have to hear and understand each question. If they can't, it leaves them guessing. If they can't hear a question or understand it, they should ask the lawyer to repeat it. Courtroom 1A, where the Task Force trial was held, is enormous; it's easy to miss part of what someone says. Also, lawyers often turn to grab a document or look at something on their table, and it's harder to hear them when they do that. In everyday conversations, when a person misses something, they might guess at what someone said. I tell a witness not to do that because guessing might result in answering a question different from the one asked.

Even if a witness can hear the lawyer, they sometimes might start thinking about an answer before the question is finished. There's a natural tendency to do that because sometimes we anticipate where a question is going. That's dangerous in court. A skilled defense attorney can add a twist to the end of a question and take it in a different direction. As a result, I encourage every witness to listen to a question in its entirety before they even begin to think about an answer.

I also convey that it's okay to say you don't understand a question. Some witnesses worry that the jury will think they're stupid. I encourage them to tell the lawyer that they don't understand, rather than trying to figure out what the lawyer is getting at. Sometimes, I explain, lawyers may have to try multiple times before what they're asking becomes clear.

During these meetings, I tell the witness that there are different rules for direct examination and cross-examination. During direct examination, the lawyer has to ask questions like a reporter, establishing basic facts: who, what, when, where, and how. The lawyer cannot, however, ask "leading questions," in other words questions that suggest the answer. The exact opposite is true for cross-examination. Lawyers are taught that on cross-examination they should only ask leading questions.

The example I usually give is that on direct, if the lawyer wants to know who was at a meeting, they will ask, "Who was at the meeting," and the witness should answer with the names of whoever was there.

By contrast, on cross-examination the lawyer will likely ask a string of questions that elicit yes or no answers: "You were at the meeting, right?" Then the lawyer might ask the same question about other people: "John was at the meeting, right? And Thomas, right?" "And Hillary, right?" It continues like that until the lawyer has finished the line of questioning, the lawyer's goal being to get the jury to transfer its attention from the witness to him. These two different questioning styles mean that during direct examination, the witness does most of the talking, while during cross-examination, the lawyer does most of the talking, and the witness is likely to say very little.

I also explain to the witness that they have only one audience: the jury. It is the jury's duty to try to determine what actually happened, based on the evidence presented, and whether it amounts to a violation of the law. I encourage them to speak to the jury when they answer, even though I'm the one asking the questions, and to make eye contact with individual jurors if they're comfortable doing that.

Meeting with a witness just before trial helps me keep their language and manner of speaking fresh in my mind. That's important because I try to elicit the facts as efficiently as possible, and to do so I have to tailor my approach from witness to witness. Some witnesses give long answers, requiring fewer questions; others give answers as short as one word, requiring more questions to extract all the relevant information. Witnesses also differ in their vocabulary, which I also have to learn in order to elicit accurate information. Most importantly, meeting with a witness gives me one last chance to hear the facts I want to elicit when they testify. That's also one last opportunity to make sure the witness is telling the truth. If I find any significant differences from what they've previously told me, I won't call them.

Stevenson had refused to meet with us before the trial began. In my career, he's the only major witness to have done that. I didn't have the chance to talk to him about what it's like to testify or hear him talk about what had happened to him. That meant his testimony could go badly, and he wasn't a trivial witness. The robbery in his basement was the biggest one that Taylor had committed.

While Evodio Hendrix and Ward had both testified to committing the robbery with Taylor and splitting the money with him, they were cooperators who would be attacked as inherently unreliable. Stevenson, by contrast, had nothing to gain by lying. He wasn't in prison looking to reduce his sentence. The charges against him had been dismissed even before we found him. Why would he make up a story that he had hundreds of thousands of dollars more in drug proceeds than he actually had? He wouldn't, but we didn't even know if he would show up.

When a witness is subpoenaed to testify and doesn't come to court, the government can ask the judge to issue an arrest warrant, what's called a material witness warrant. The US Marshals then go out and arrest the witness and bring him to court. The witness is released after he finishes his testimony. I've only requested a warrant like that once in my career. A witness who had participated in a fraud, but hadn't been charged, didn't want to testify against his uncle, who was on trial. The witness had come to court the day he was supposed to testify but left before being called. When we realized he was gone, I asked the judge for a material witness warrant, which he signed, and the US Marshals went looking for the man. They quickly found him, hiding in his basement behind a locked door. They brought him back to court, but by then it was the end of the day. The judge ordered him held in jail overnight. The next morning, he testified and was released. Were we prepared to do that if Stevenson didn't show up? It didn't seem right to arrest a victim, but we needed his testimony. Thankfully, it didn't come to that.

When the witness before Stevenson finished, Judge Catherine Blake asked, "I assume the Government will be calling another witness?"

"We will, your honor. The United States calls Oreese Stevenson," I responded. I then turned to face the main entrance to the courtroom not knowing if he would talk through the door. He did.

Right out of the gate, I wanted the jury to know what a reluctant witness Stevenson was. This would enhance his credibility, so I brought it up in my first question.

"Just to be clear, Mr. Stevenson, you are appearing here today under a subpoena, right?" A subpoena is a court order, not an invitation.

"Yes," he said.

"Is it fair to say that you don't want to be here, sir?"

"Not at all," he replied, his voice loud and strong. Everything about his tone and body language lent credence to his answer.

"And you and I haven't spoken or had any contact, frankly, since February of 2017; right?" That's when he testified in the grand jury.

"No."

"We didn't talk before you just walked out of that door just now; right?"

"No."

"And so I know this is uncomfortable for you and not something you want to do; is that right."

"Absolutely." It was clear Stevenson meant it.

Stevenson's trial testimony matched what he had told us before. He admitted he was caught mid–drug deal by Hendrix, Jenkins, Taylor, and Ward. He admitted that he had had a safe with close to $200,000 in drug proceeds in his basement, but he resisted revealing the amount of cocaine he'd had in his house. I understood his reluctance. He was sitting in a courtroom, in front of a federal judge, a jury, and a gallery full of people, including reporters. He was being asked to admit that he'd had ten kilograms of cocaine in his house. The strangest part was that even if he did so, he would still be able to walk out the front door while one of the police officers who arrested him was going to be taken back to jail. In some respects, that most of the victims freely admitted their own criminal conduct—Dennis Armstrong for instance describing throwing cocaine out of the window as the police chased him—was perhaps more surprising than Stevenson's reluctance to do so.

When I asked Stevenson how much cocaine had been at his house on Heathfield, he said, "I don't recall." When a witness can't remember something, the rules of evidence allow the lawyer to try to refresh the witness's recollection. When I was studying for the bar, a professor in a video lecture who taught this rule of evidence said something I remember to this day: you can refresh a witness's recollection with anything, even a bowl of spaghetti. He was right. You could show a witness whatever might jog their memory—notes they had taken or an email they or someone else had written or a transcript of their testimony before the grand jury. That's what I did with Stevenson.

When Stevenson testified in the grand jury, he admitted to having ten kilograms of cocaine in the house. It was an important point: only eight kilograms were turned in. Donald Stepp would tell the jury later in the trial that Jenkins had come running out of Heathfield like Santa Claus with his vest stuffed—with the missing two kilos.

I showed Stevenson his grand jury transcript. Under the rules, you ask the witness to silently read the document that you are using to refresh their memory. Neither the lawyer nor the witness can read it aloud. When they finish, you have to ask them, "Did that refresh your recollection?" If the witness says yes, then you can repeat the question that prompted the whole exercise. If the witness says no, then you have to move on. But if the witness had previously testified under oath about the fact that they now can't recall, the rules of evidence allow the transcript from that testimony to be read into the record and treated as evidence by the jury.

After I let Stevenson read his grand jury transcript where he had testified, under oath, that he had ten kilograms at Heathfield, I asked him if that transcript "refreshed [his] memory about how much was in the house."

"Maybe," he answered, so I read the transcript into the record.

"All right." I continued. "Well, you were asked, Mr. Stevenson, so was the total more like closer to 10 kilograms? Correct?"

"Yes," he responded.

"And your answer was 'yes,' right?

"Yeah," he acknowledged.

This exchange demonstrates one of the reasons prosecutors call witnesses in the grand jury. It's referred to as "locking them in." A witness who testifies in the grand jury and later becomes reluctant or unable to give the same testimony can still be used at trial because their earlier testimony can be read into the record and considered as evidence by the jury. It's not ideal: on the one hand the prosecutor is calling this witness but must concede that their memory is faulty or that they're being uncooperative. But it's also not fatal, and this time it worked.

On cross-examination, Taylor's lawyer Jennifer Wicks went first. Stevenson clearly wasn't intimidated by the defense lawyers, or for that matter by me either, or the setting. Wicks pointed out that Stevenson didn't know how much money the man in his van had brought to the drug deal before the Task Force arrested them.

Wicks asked, "Sometimes when you're dealing with someone, they don't have the right amount of money; correct?"

"Not correct," Stevenson replied.

"Pardon me?" Wicks said, apparently surprised by the answer.

"Not correct."

"That's not correct?" Wicks reiterated.

"No."

"They always have the correct money?" Wicks again asked.

"Yeah, when you know 'em."

"Okay. So this is someone that you knew?"

"Yeah."

"Mr. Brown; correct?"

"Yeah."

Whether Stevenson knew the correct amount was an important point for our theory of the case. Taylor had turned in $15,000 to the BPD's evidence control unit, but Stevenson had told us that the going rate for half a kilo of cocaine was $22,000 at that time. That's what he expected

"Mr. Brown" had brought with him that day because he knew him. It was our view that Taylor had stolen the difference. That meant Stevenson was robbed twice—when he was arrested, and later, when the Task Force broke open the safe at his house.

Wicks next tried to walk Stevenson through the sequence of events described in the police report. She was in for a surprise.

Wicks asked, "Okay. And the cocaine that you had, when the police officers came, you threw the bag with the cocaine in it into the backseat; correct?"

"Never," Stevenson replied.

"Never. The coke—you're saying that the cocaine—" Stevenson cut her off.

"Was never in my hand."

"—was never in your hand?"

"No."

"Where was it in the car?"

"In the back—in the back."

"In the back?"

"Right."

"Okay, and so you're saying you never made a throwing motion when the—" Again, he cut her short.

"No."

Everything in the police report about the circumstances of Stevenson's arrest was a lie. He hadn't thrown anything into the backseat, which would justify the police approaching the car. He was just sitting there. All of this seemed like a surprise to Wicks. Maybe she believed her client. I hoped the jury wouldn't.

Keona Holloway, Stevenson's common-law wife, testified right after Stevenson. She also declined to meet with us before testifying. I wanted the jury to understand that she, like Stevenson, was here because she had to be. She wasn't testifying to get back at Taylor.

"Is it fair to say you don't want to be here, ma'am?" I asked.

"Yes," she responded in a voice so soft I had to ask her to speak louder.

She had no trouble answering my questions about what happened the night Taylor and the other officers were at her house on Heathfield.

On cross-examination, Taylor's other lawyer, Christopher Nieto, went first, asking Holloway whether she knew that Stevenson sold drugs. She testified during direct examination that she had not until he was arrested by the Task Force.

Cross-examination questions are mostly designed to undermine a witness's credibility. The theory is that if the witness isn't credible in any one respect, then the jury won't believe anything they say. That's a more effective way to neutralize a witness than trying to disprove the individual facts or events they describe. Nieto's tack seemed to be to suggest that the jury shouldn't believe Holloway because her testimony that she didn't know that Stevenson sold drugs wasn't credible. Though Holloway didn't know, she said she had had her suspicions.

Holloway told the court, "But I didn't—he didn't tell me, like, I'm selling drugs, you know. But just some things, you know, just moving in and out, you know, so." At this point her voice had gotten so soft that Nieto interrupted her: "And I'm sorry, ma'am. My hearing's not that good. When you say you had some suspicions, what were those suspicions?"

Holloway responded, "Because of the way he was moving, you know, in and out of the house some, you know, times of the night and stuff like that. Again, like I said, I've been through this with him before. That was the reason why for my suspicions. But, no, I didn't know for sure."

I understood "I've been through this with him before" to mean when Stevenson had been arrested for selling drugs in the past. She testified that when the Task Force arrested Stevenson he wasn't working. He had been laid off from his job driving a truck. She was working at an assisted living facility and supporting their family, but not exclusively.

Nieto asked her, "And so did Mr. Stevenson in any way whatsoever bring any money or any cash or contributed to the family's finances during that time period?

"Yes," Holloway replied.

"And did you ever ask him about where the money had come from?"

"No."

"Did he ever tell you where the money came from?"

"No."

Rather than undermine Holloway's credibility, these questions, which she answered thoughtfully and honestly, revealed how someone could be in a relationship with a man who sold drugs. She had suspicions but no proof. They both had jobs, but then he was out of work. After that, she didn't ask where the money came from, and he didn't volunteer it. She lived in the borderland between the legitimate economy and the drug economy.

Sergio Summerville testified after Stevenson and Holloway. Unlike them, he didn't seem uncomfortable. In fact, he seemed less nervous than when we had interviewed him. When we met him the first time, he had been friendly and seemed to want to help, but he also seemed fearful that he was being tricked somehow. Now, maybe because he was in front of a judge and jury in a federal courthouse, he seemed more confident that our outreach to him wasn't some ruse to get him to admit to crimes so we could charge him.

In any event, his testimony during direct examination matched what he'd said during the interview. Summerville told the jury that he had been stopped late in the summer of 2016 trying to leave a storage facility where he rented a unit. He kept small amounts of drugs in it, along with money, in a sock. Summerville was homeless at the time. Hersl and Taylor and all the other members of the Task Force had been there that night. Summerville had watched Rayam and Taylor head toward his unit. Then Rayam came out with Summerville's sock and handed it to him—with less money than he knew should have been in it. We also used him to narrate the surveillance video from the U-Store as we showed it to the jury.

During cross-examination, Hersl's lawyer William Purpura asked questions about some of the mechanics of low-level drug dealing. Summerville explained that he kept his drugs in his storage locker but that "when he was working," he "never went back and forth to grab anything out."

"So as a street dealer, would you keep drugs on you while you're dealing?" Purpura asked.

"No," Summerville responded.

"Would you use, what, like a stash area?"

"Yes."

"And could that be an abandoned house?"

"Yes."

"It could be some grass or some trees?"

"Yes."

"And the reason you keep drugs off of you, that's so if you get arrested, the drugs aren't on you; correct?"

"Yes."

"And so if a police officer comes up and says, 'I saw you dealing,' you're going to say, 'Drugs aren't on me'; right?"

"Yes."

The point of this line of questioning would not have been immediately apparent to the jury. I thought it was to set up the Santiful and Tate robberies. Purpura argued that both men were low-level street dealers, despite their denials. While the police reports said they didn't have any drugs on them, in both instances, Hersl claimed to have recovered drugs from stash locations nearby.

Donald Stepp was one of the most colorful witnesses we called. He was also the best dressed, nicely decked out like he had been at his guilty plea. Unlike the other witnesses, he seemed to enjoy the experience of testifying. Perhaps it was the attention, or maybe because he had a good story to tell, and he knew it. Indeed, it was a good story, and it proved the adage that truth is stranger than fiction.

Derek questioned Stepp. He showed Stepp the duffel bag that Ward had said contained marijuana when they robbed two drug dealers in the parking lot of Belvedere Towers. Stepp explained that Jenkins had brought it to him so that Stepp could sell the marijuana. Ward and Stepp testified to the beginning and end of the same story: the former had been present when the drugs were taken, and the latter had received them after the robbery. Both men had recognized the duffel bag the marijuana came in. The story couldn't have been made up, because the two had never met.

At the end of questioning, Derek showed Stepp the watch that he had sunk off his dock, the same watch that Ronald Hamilton, who had just testified, had identified as his. Now the jury understood why we did that. It proved that Hamilton had been robbed. He and Stepp had never met either.

Stepp admitted selling the two kilos that Jenkins stole from Stevenson's basement. He also described how he broke into Armstrong's storage unit before the Task Force had obtained a warrant for it. I could see from the jurors' faces that they were having "aha" moments as Stepp reinforced the accounts of other witnesses and answered some open questions.

During cross-examination, Stepp was even more engaging than he was on direct. Purpura went first. He asked Stepp about Double D., the name of his bail bonds business.

Stepp explained that he and his co-owner, Dennis, both had names that begin with the letter *D*. Purpura put up a picture of Stepp's tricked-out truck, wrapped in an enormous decal not depicting two guys whose names began with *D*, but an illustration of a woman with enormous breasts pushed up out of a low-cut blouse. Purpura tried again.

"Do you see Defense Exhibit No. 23 there," Purpura asked, referring to the picture of Stepp's truck, which was now on screens all over the courtroom.

"I do," Stepp replied calmly.

"And is that one of your bail bond vehicles?"

"It is." Stepp was a model of composure.

"And does that have your bail bond logo on it?"

"It does."

"And who do the Ds stand for?" One might have thought Purpura had him and that Stepp would have to sheepishly admit that his earlier testimony about the meaning of the double Ds wasn't entirely accurate.

"Pardon?" Stepp asked, as if trying to draw out the exchange.

"Who do the Ds stand for on that?"

"Donald and Dennis."

Apparently conceding that point, Purpura pressed on. "Now, is it fair to say that you've got a—you've been a criminal all your life, right?"

"Not all my life," Stepp said.

"Well, let's say past the age of 10."

"Sure. Yes." So only since age 11.

Purpura next tried to establish that in addition to drugs—or, as Stepp would explain, because of drugs—Stepp had gotten involved in fraud.

"And in fact, you were involved in fraud when you were younger. Is that correct, sir?" Purpura asked.

"Yes," Stepp answered. "I was an addict."

"An addict at fraud, or just an addict in general?"

"I was an addict at that time."

"You were a drug addict?"

"Correct."

"And as a result of that, you were involved in a lot of fraud, correct?"

"Much fraud," Stepp responded, not to be outdone.

"And in fraud, you have to lie and you have to deceive. Is that fair to say?"

"Correct."

Purpura's point, as with Ward and Rayam, was that if these witnesses lied in other contexts, they'd lie here. But then Purpura asked one question too many: "And you became very good, adept, at lying and deceiving when you're involved in fraud. Isn't that correct, sir, even as an addict?"

Stepp responded, "Well, I—you know, I wasn't too good at fraud, I'd say, because it put me in prison and destroyed my life as an addict. So I don't—I don't consider that to be too good."

The cross-examination next took several twists and turns that seemed designed to make Stepp sound like a bad guy, but it wound up being dangerous for the defense.

First Purpura questioned Stepp about his overseas drug suppliers.

"In 2008, you're reaching out for Colombian and Dominican sources, right?" Purpura asked.

"Correct," Stepp replied.

"And tell the jury, what do you need a Colombian or Dominican source for?"

"They had the best supply line in the drug business."

"Of what?"

"Cocaine."

The jury's education on narcotics trafficking, from low-level dealers like Sergio Summerville to the best supply lines in the world, continued.

"How does it work?" Purpura asked. "You just pick up the phone and you—well, not Yellow Pages anymore. Do you Google 'Colombian, Dominican traffickers'?"

"It doesn't work that way," Stepp said.

"What do you do? Tell us. Go ahead. Spit it out. You like to talk."

"It takes a lot of years to get up to people like that."

"And that's exactly what happened," Purpura said. "And you were so embedded in the drug world all those years that you got up to people like that, right?"

"Correct."

So Stepp was such a big drug dealer he could access the best suppliers in the world. He readily admitted that, but it certainly didn't undercut his story that he was selling drugs for Jenkins.

Next Purpura asked, "Did you ever think that maybe you should have probably deleted some of those pictures on your camera?" Here he was referring to the pictures that Stepp had taken at Stevenson's house on the day of the robbery. Derek had shown the jury the pictures during direct examination of Stepp.

"Nah," said Stepp. "I kind of liked them as insurance, myself."

"Well, what do you mean by that?"

"Just—I didn't trust him."

"You didn't trust Wayne Jenkins?"

"Correct."

"'Cause he's not truthful. He's not honest. You didn't trust him. Right?" This was one of the themes in Hersl's defense, that Jenkins was a liar and hid his thieving from Hersl. Stepp was willing to agree with that, but Purpura went further.

"So you wanted to have something over his head, right?" Purpura asked.

"Not something over his head; it was just—"

"Kind of blackmail?"

"[It] wasn't blackmail," Stepp said. "I'd have took my stuff to the grave."

Purpura had seemingly offended Stepp. For Stepp, apparently, there was honor among thieves.

"But it was insurance, as you put it," Purpura continued. "You had that information, correct?"

"I didn't trust him down the end. I was starting to worry about my life," Stepp responded.

Purpura didn't follow up. In fact, he changed the topic. It's one thing to suggest that Jenkins was a liar and kept things from Hersl, but if

Stepp feared for his life, it took the criminality of the Task Force to a whole new level. It made it more unlikely that Hersl could blithely go along with them unaware.

As Purpura began wrapping up, he and Stepp had one more back-and-forth. He got Stepp to agree with the obvious—that Wayne Jenkins had pleaded guilty—and then tried to argue that Stepp had fabricated his claims about Taylor and Hersl to get a reduced sentence since Stepp couldn't testify against Jenkins.

"If you don't say something about Taylor and Hersl, you ain't got no cooperation, right?" Purpura said.

Another witness with less confidence might have agreed. That wasn't Stepp. Stepp gave as good as he got.

"Mr. Purpura, I'm just bringing the facts and the truth," Stepp replied.

"I know. That's a good statement," Purpura fired back.

"It's not a good statement. It's a for-real statement." Stepp wasn't going to be cowed.

"Am I right or wrong? If you don't have information—" Stepp shut him down.

"The facts are the facts, Mr. Purpura. You can't change 'em."

Finally, Purpura turned to Stepp's plea agreement. Stepp was facing a lot of jail time if he didn't get credit for cooperating. Again, the point of this line of questioning was to show that Stepp had an incentive to lie. The point was made, but it also produced one of the few funny moments in an otherwise serious trial.

"Your lawyer went through the guidelines with you, the United States sentencing guidelines, correct?" Purpura asked.

"They have," Stepp responded.

"Okay. 'They,' so you have two lawyers." As would become clear in a moment, it didn't seem like Purpura had planned out this question.

"I do," Stepp confirmed.

"It's a great country. The—" Before Purpura could finish his question, Stepp stopped him in his tracks.

"How many does Mr. Hersl have?" Stepp asked, aware of another lawyer sitting at the defense table next to Hersl. So Hersl had two lawyers, too.

"He's got one and a half right now," Purpura, Hersl's lead counsel, shot back. But he seemed to immediately regret it.

"I apologize, Tom." Thomas Rafter was the other lawyer representing Hersl, but he had only come into the case before trial. Purpura had done most of the work.

"He's got one; he's got one *pro bono*, if you want to know," Purpura tried to further explain.

"All right. There we go," Stepp said, triumphant.

The court interrupted. "All right. That's two."

"I'll take the *pro bono*," Stepp said, on a roll.

"Moving on," Judge Blake said politely but firmly.

And we did.

Jimmie Griffin testified next. The only victim in this case who was in custody, he testified in an orange jumpsuit. Griffin told the jury the same sequence of events that he had told us. He admitted to selling drugs in 2014 but testified that selling drugs wasn't his only source of income. He and other members of his family shared money they had received in lead paint exposure settlements. On November 5, 2014, the day Hersl arrested him, he had $6,000 at home in a safe and $6,000 on his person. He testified that his aunt, Samantha Irby, had given him the $6,000 he had on him that same day. When Hersl arrested him later while he was smoking marijuana at a friend's house, he said, Hersl stole the $6,000.

The jury learned about another link in the narcotics supply chain as Purpura cross-examined Griffin, who testified that he had bought grams of heroin for $100 and then sold them. "Were you street-selling those grams?" Purpura asked. "In other words, were you on the street selling out to people coming by?"

Griffin said no, that he sold to other dealers. When Purpura asked how the grams were broken down for street distribution, Griffin said he didn't know: he had never broken one down. He was just a reseller somewhere in between the supply source and the street. That's how specialized the drug economy was.

Purpura next asked him why he had the hydraulic press that police had recovered in the house.

"That's how I double my money," Griffin explained.

"Just quickly tell us how you do that," Purpura said encouragingly.

"All right. For instance, I had a hundred grams. I had another hundred grams of cut."

"What's cut?" Purpura asked. "I know, but [the jury] may not know."

"It's used to stretch the drugs."

"What would you use for cut?"

"Benita quinine."

"Quinine, the same quinine used in tonic water."

"Yeah."

"Then what happens?"

"So I put the hundred together with the other hundred. I make 200 grams, compressed it together. Now you got 200 grams."

"And why would you have to compress it? I guess that's the question."

"So it all could be together."

"And it would look like it's not cut; right?"

"Right."

"And so you could double your profit that way?"

"Correct."

Purpura then waved around a red bandana seized by the police. "Associated with the Bloods?" Purpura asked, holding the bandana above his head.

"No," Griffin said.

"Not a gang member?"

"No."

"Nothing to do with the Bloods at all?"

"No."

Purpura asked him what the "B" tattooed near his eye meant.

"It's a Bugatti sign," Griffin told him.

Purpura next held some digital scales and asked what they were for. Griffin said they were for weighing drugs.

What struck me as I sat there watching this display was the role reversal. Here was the defense lawyer, instead of the prosecutor, asking the drug dealer about all his paraphernalia in an attempt to discredit him. What also struck me was how pointless this was. Griffin had admitted to selling drugs. He was sitting on the witness stand wearing an orange jumpsuit because he was in jail for selling drugs. That wasn't the issue. The question was whether Hersl had robbed Griffin.

EIGHTEEN

Geography Is Destiny

During the testimony of three of our victims—Ronald Hamilton, Antonio Santiful, and Herbert Tate—the defense attorneys focused on geography in their attempt to undermine their credibility.

Tate took the stand and told the jury the same things he had previously told us. He was in East Baltimore Midway on November 27, 2015, the day after Thanksgiving. He was visiting friends. He had finished work and had cash in his pocket from his previous paycheck. He intended to use that money to pay bills. When Daniel Hersl set upon him, on Robb Street, Tate wasn't doing anything wrong. Unsurprisingly, Hersl didn't find any drugs or a gun on Tate, but he got his hands on Tate's money. He turned in $216 of it to the Baltimore Police Department, not the full $600 that he had taken off Tate.

The defense lawyers focused on East Baltimore Midway as they cross-examined Tate. Tate had testified on direct that he wasn't selling drugs when Hersl arrested him. The defense argued he must have been because there was no other reason for him to be in that neighborhood, what they called an "open-air drug market." The obvious inference was that the only people who came to East Baltimore Midway were drug dealers or drug users. The defense's argument boiled down to the idea that if Tate couldn't be believed when he said he wasn't selling drugs, he couldn't be believed when he said that Hersl robbed him.

Hersl's lawyer Thomas Rafter went at Tate this way early in the cross-examination. After some perfunctory questions about the geography of Robb Street, Rafter asked Tate, "But you know Robb Street is basically an open-air drug market?"

"That's what they say," Tate replied.

Rafter pressed him. "And it is, correct?"

"I don't know," Tate said.

"You grew up there!" Rafter retorted, a note of incredulity in his voice.

"Right," Tate responded. Anticipating where Rafter was going, Tate added, "I never seen no one selling drugs myself."

Rafter then brought up Tate's criminal record, implying that anyone who had grown up in East Baltimore Midway and had sold drugs would know that Robb Street was an open-air drug market.

"Have you ever sold cocaine or marijuana?" the lawyer asked Tate.

"Yes," Tate said.

"When was that?"

"When I was in, like, high school, maybe."

Tate didn't try and run from his past. He admitted that there was a time when he had sold drugs, but he remained adamant that that wasn't what he was doing when Hersl had robbed him.

Even though Tate didn't testify about Marcus Taylor—in fact, the robbery had occurred before Taylor even joined the Task Force—Christopher Nieto, one of Taylor's attorneys, decided to cross-examine Tate as well. Like Rafter, Nieto started with questions about East Baltimore Midway.

"This is not a great neighborhood in Baltimore, is it?" he said.

"To me it is," Tate said. "I don't have no problems in the neighborhood."

Faced with Tate's defense of the neighborhood, Nieto went further, saying, "I mean, it's a drug market, right?"

"That's what y'all label it as, but I don't see it as a drug market or whatever y'all label it as," Tate said.

"Well, do you know if people sell drugs in that area?"

"People sell drugs in Baltimore City."

Frustrated by the lack of progress, Nieto tried to explain the phrase "open-air drug market," as if the concept were a source of confusion rather than something Tate didn't agree with when Nieto used it to describe Robb Street: "When I say, 'open-air drug market,' what I'm suggesting is that's a particular area of the city in which people can come to buy drugs because they know drugs are sold in a particular block or area. Have you heard that terminology before?"

Not surprisingly, Tate responded, "Yes." Nieto then repeated his question from earlier: "Okay, in this particular area, right, where you happened to have been when you were arrested, that's considered an open-air drug market; is that your understanding?"

"Yes," Tate said, although I wasn't sure why he agreed with that characterization given what he said next. "I don't see drugs being sold when I'm there, so I can't say specifically."

Nieto tried to insinuate that Tate was there to sell drugs because it was a dead-end street, saying, "There's not much happening on that street; is that fair to say?" Tate agreed, but then, with a note of skepticism, Nieto asked, "So what brought you to that block, not once but twice in the same week," referring to Tate's arrest on November 27 and his encounter with Hersl two days earlier.

"My old friends live in that neighborhood: old basketball teammates, things of that nature," Tate said. When asked to name them, Tate named two friends without hesitation.

Nieto then tried a third time to undermine Tate's credibility using East Baltimore Midway like a piece of evidence.

"So you had been socializing and you're walking down the street, but you weren't sitting on the steps of a vacant building, were you?" he asked.

"No," said Tate.

"Cause there are some vacant buildings in that area," Nieto continued. "Not a heavily populated block, is it?"

"It's a few vacants there, but it's a lot of people in that block I would say," Tate responded.

Like Hersl's lawyer, Rafter, Nieto seemed incredulous. "A lot of people?" he asked.

"Yeah, it's a lot of people," Tate said, refusing to back down. "It's not like a dead zone. That's not a dead zone."

Nieto then showed Tate a photograph of the 2200 block, which Rafter had introduced as evidence. Nieto asked Tate to count the number of vacants. Tate counted five.

Baltimore was once the fourth largest city in the United States. Now it's the twentieth. In 1950, it was home to almost a million people. Now it's home to half that many, according to the 2020 census. Because the population had shrunk so dramatically in such a relatively short period of time, there are boarded up houses everywhere in East Baltimore. In one of the pictures of Robb Street that Nieto showed Tate, there were pumpkins on the front porch of a rowhouse wedged between two vacant ones. The picture had been taken around Halloween. Maybe this was an open-air drug market, but this was also a place where people lived and raised children and loved them enough to put out pumpkins at Halloween.

Antonio Santiful entered the courtroom in a bright orange construction vest. He was either going to work or was on his way home. Unlike Tate, whose movements and speech were quick, Santiful moved and spoke slowly. His cell phone rang when he first took the witness stand startling him—and everyone else in the courtroom. He seemed momentarily embarrassed.

Santiful had never met Herbert Tate, but they had been arrested in the same neighborhood, East Baltimore Midway, one day apart in November 2015. We anticipated that the jury would find Santiful's testimony strikingly similar to Tate's—too many similarities, in fact, to be coincidences.

Santiful testified that Hersl had arrested him for no reason at all, just as Tate had done. Santiful was playing video games on a friend's front porch. Hersl claimed to have found a gun and a small quantity of drugs in the car that Santiful had driven to his friend's house; the car belonged to Santiful's sister. Santiful said the gun and drugs were not his and that he hadn't known they were in the car. Hersl recovered nothing from his person. Before the FBI approached Santiful, the charges against him had been dropped.

Santiful testified that the police took him from his friend's house to a BPD station, where Hersl robbed him. Santiful earned the money that Hersl took from him cleaning office buildings. The police report for the incident listed $218 as having been recovered from Santiful. The report for Tate listed $216. There was no rhyme or reason for the figures being that close—other than the numbers being made up.

Santiful had called his girlfriend from jail the night he was arrested, telling her the police had taken the $700 he had had on him, not just $216.

As Rafter, Hersl's other lawyer had done with Tate on cross-examination, with Santiful Purpura started by showing him a picture of the neighborhood where he had been arrested.

Purpura asked, "You are familiar with this area at Aiken Street, right?"

"Yes," Santiful told him.

"You know what an open-air drug market is, right, where people gather to sell drugs, right?"

"Yes."

"That's a pretty active area, isn't it?"

"Yes, sir."

"And that's an active area for selling drugs, right?"

"Yes."

"And you see that all around that area, right?"

"Yes."

The cross-examination took an unexpected turn when the defense asked Santiful about his criminal record. Santiful admitted that he had pleaded guilty to a state charge of illegally possessing a gun, but he also claimed that a second conviction for the same charge was because a gun had been planted on him. We looked up the records for that arrest and identified the officer responsible: Wayne Jenkins.

Derek Hines, my co-counsel, used his redirect—an opportunity for the lawyer who called a witness to ask questions after the cross-examination—to share this fact with the jury, now that the defense had "opened the door." On redirect, Santiful told the jury that in 2006, when he had been a juvenile, Jenkins had chased him down an alley. Jenkins claimed to have recovered a gun that Santiful had tossed. Santiful said Jenkins had lied and that he hadn't discarded a gun. Santiful told the jury that he pled guilty to the charge because he felt he had no choice: who would believe someone like him over the word of a police officer?

Hopefully they would now.

After Stevenson, the Task Force's other big score was Ronald Hamilton. He was about the same age as Stevenson and spoke with the same deliberateness but there was a heaviness about Hamilton, like the world was weighing him down. The jury would later learn why. Hamilton's trial testimony followed what he'd told us when we interviewed him. He described being robbed twice: once when the police stopped him and his wife after they left Home Depot and again when the police took him to his house in Westminster to execute a search warrant.

The cross-examination of Hamilton provided one of the most dramatic moments in the trial. The defense's theme was that Hamilton was a drug dealer, even though he said he wasn't. Of course, it didn't matter. Cops can't rob drug dealers just like they can't rob people who aren't drug dealers. Jemell Rayam had already testified to stealing Hamilton's money. Momodu Gondo was going to testify to the same thing. Hersl's defense wasn't that it didn't happen, but that Hersl wasn't involved, at least in taking money from the house. Purpura had said in his opening that Hersl did ultimately get a cut of that money later that night. That made attacking Hamilton a puzzling strategy. Regardless, Hersl and Taylor's defense lawyers focused on Hamilton's home in Westminster.

Hersl's lawyer Bill Purpura went first. He began by displaying an aerial photograph of Hamilton's house in Westminster.

"Do you recognize that residence?" Purpura asked.

"Yes," Hamilton responded

"Whose residence is it, sir?"

"My house."

In response to Purpura's questions, Hamilton explained that he had done a lot of work to the house after he bought it. It had sat unoccupied for four years, and there had been water damage inside. Purpura asked him when he'd bought the house. Hamilton told him 2016.

"And you got released from federal prison in—when?" Purpura continued.

"December 2013," said Hamilton.

"So two years later, you were able to do all this?"

"Yes."

Taylor's lawyer Chris Nieto later picked up on the same theme. I was surprised that he'd even chosen to cross-examine Hamilton since Taylor hadn't taken part in the robbery.

"All right. If I may, then, when did you say you purchased this house in Westminster?" asked Nieto.

"May of 2016," Hamilton replied.

"And could you tell the ladies and gentlemen of the jury for how much that house was purchased?"

"Five hundred, like five fifteen, five twenty, something like that."

"And that was less than two years after you've been out of federal prison?"

"Yes."

Nieto then put up some pictures of the home's interior, which looked good, asking if that was the condition the house was in when he bought it. Hamilton told him it wasn't and that he had put a lot of work into it. After some back and forth, it wasn't clear where the pictures had come from or when they had been taken. Nieto described the house as "beautiful" and disputed that there had been any water damage. Hamilton explained the water damage had been in the basement, which made sense, but the basement wasn't in any of the photos Nieto showed Hamilton.

Next, Nieto asked him about how much Hamilton and his wife earned through various sources, including gambling, which, according to their taxes, gave them a combined income of $130,000. Nieto then returned to the house. Hamilton told him that he had put $17,000 down, which didn't sound out of reach for someone making $130,000. When Nieto asked him what his mortgage payment was, Hamilton lost it.

"Does that make a difference? What's this right here destroyed my whole fuckin' family!" Hamilton roared.

Trying to dial it back, he said, "Sorry. Sorry, Your Honor."

"It's all right," Judge Catherine Blake told Hamilton. But he couldn't contain himself. He continued shouting:

This destroyed my whole family. I am in a divorce process right now because of this bullshit. This destroyed my whole fuckin' family, man.

You sit here asking me questions about a fuckin' house. My fuckin' wife stays in the fuckin' Walmart every fuckin' night until I come home.

If you want to know that, worry about that. That's what the fuck's the matter in here, man. Everybody's life is destroyed, man.

My house don't have nothing to do with this. The problem is my wife taking medication 'cause of this.

Judge Blake interrupted. "Sir, sir," but Hamilton kept going.

Man—I'm sorry, Your Honor. I'm sorry to the courts. But the fact of the matter is, man, my house don't have nothing to do with this.

The fact of the matter is, came to my house, destroyed my family. I'm in a divorce process because of this. Because of this.

This has put so much financial pressure on my family. Kids, man, are scared to go in the house because of this.

That's what you want to know. That's what you going to hear, the facts, the truth.

That's what you want to hear is the facts. Worry about the facts. Worry about the facts, sir.

"Mr. Hamilton, Mr. Hamilton, I'm sorry. I really need to ask you to stop," Judge Blake said firmly. And he did. After letting loose with everything about that night and what it had done to his family, Hamilton slumped back in his seat. He looked emptied and slightly embarrassed.

I had no idea the robbery had had such an impact on him, and I had never expected it to erupt out of him in the courtroom. Trials give you glimpses into the lives of people you would have no other reason to know. Like Keona Holloway, the common-law wife to someone whom she thought had sold drugs only in the past, until discovering otherwise. Like Ronald Hamilton, who served two stints in federal prison, but had apparently turned his life around until the defendants destroyed it.

The trial recessed for the day after Hamilton left the witness stand. It was just as well; everyone seemed exhausted. After reconvening the next morning, Purpura made a motion for a mistrial based on what he called Hamilton's "outburst." Judge Blake denied the motion but told the jurors that they shouldn't consider as evidence what Hamilton had said about the effect of the robbery on his family.

NINETEEN

Choices

We decided to end the trial with two dramatic episodes to demonstrate the choices the defendants made and how another officer—one of our witnesses who had briefly been a member of the Gun Trace Task Force—had chosen to do the right thing. That witness, James Kostoplis, or "K-Stop" as he was nicknamed, had joined the Task Force before the arrests in March 2017. Before we got to Kostoplis, however, we had to finish with Rayam's testimony.

"Do you recall being involved in a car chase and car wreck on August 31, 2016?" Derek Hines, my co-counsel, asked Jemell Rayam.

"Yes," Rayam said quietly. He lowered his head and looked at the floor.

"Can you describe what happened that day?"

"It was myself and Gondo and Wayne and Hersl. And we were at a gas station. Wayne pretty much always led the pack. We called it a pack, as far as he led the group of cars. And we pretty much just followed him, and he pretty much initiated all the car stops." Pack seemed like an apt description. It made me think of a pack of wolves.

"So we saw a car at the gas station, and he attempted to stop him," Rayam continued. "And then the car took off, and Wayne followed. And Hersl was in the car, and Gondo was driving the other vehicle. I was the passenger, so we all followed."

What he said next came in a much quieter voice, almost a whisper. The jurors leaned forward in their seats to hear him. "And it was raining out," Rayam said. "And the car wound up turning off on another street, and then it ran a red light and hit—well, another vehicle hit the car that we were chasing and caused an accident."

"What happened to the driver of the car that got in the accident?" Derek said, his voice now lowered, too.

"It was bad," Rayam said. "It was a bad accident. It was—it was a real bad accident. And none of us—none of us stopped."

At that point, Rayam started to cry. The courtroom was the quietest it had ever been, everyone listening intently.

Obviously shaken by what he had been a part of, Rayam said, "I don't know—I mean, none of us stopped to render aid or to see if anyone was hurt. We just listened to the radio to see if someone would call it in.

"And then once we heard someone call it in, then, you know, we just continued to—just to drive on. Wayne didn't want to—he didn't want us to do anything."

"Why didn't you stop to render aid?" Derek asked.

"Cause we were foolish," Rayam said. "I don't know. We just didn't. I had mentioned that we should stop to see if anyone was hurt because I saw it, and it was—it was pretty bad. And it could have been any of us. It could have been any of you guys or my mother or father. But we just we just didn't stop."

Derek played portions of the recording from the bug inside Momodu Gondo's car from that night. It had picked up the Task Force members talking about the accident. Neither Daniel Hersl nor Marcus Taylor testified in their own defense. But the jury got to hear both of their voices on this recording.

"That dude unconscious," the jury heard Taylor say. "He ain't sayin' shit."

Rayam explained that Taylor was talking about the person they had chased who had been T-boned and now lay in the street. Rayam understood Taylor's comment to mean that the victim "won't say police was chasing him, you know, and he may forget; or, you know, we don't have anything to worry about."

Then the jury heard Hersl: "These car chases, this what happens. It's a crapshoot, you know . . . We could just stop the slips at 10:30 before that happened," Hersl suggested. Rayam explained that Hersl was suggesting they falsify their overtime slips to make it look like they weren't working when the accident occurred. "Hey, I was in the car just driving home," Hersl said next, with a laugh, role playing what he would say if anyone asked him about his whereabouts that night.

We were able to identify the accident and its victim. It occurred near the Horseshoe Casino, in the same neighborhood where the Task Force robbed Sergio Summerville. The person was badly injured but survived.

Faced with a hurt and maybe dying man, Hersl and Taylor had done nothing. Even though they and the other Task Force members had caused the accident by chasing the victim. When Derek and I first heard this recording, we thought the Task Force had chased the man with an eye toward robbing him, but it obviously went horribly wrong. They then had the chance to do something to help, but they didn't. That was the choice they made.

The last witness we called in the government's case was James Kostoplis. He had also made a choice.

After the charges against the Task Force members became public, only one police officer ever contacted us to report that they had seen anything or even suspected anything about the unit. That astonished me. The defendants had been robbing people for years with other BPD officers around them all the time and yet no one saw anything?

On March 1, 2017, the day the Task Force officers were arrested, Kostoplis called the FBI. The story he told us then was the same one he would eventually tell on the last day of trial.

Kostoplis arrived to testify at the courthouse in his black BPD uniform. He was small and thin, hardly an imposing presence compared to Jenkins or Hersl. He was 33, but his faint moustache made him look even younger, although I assumed he had grown it to have the opposite effect. Once Kostoplis settled into the witness stand, I asked him about his background.

He told the jury that he had joined the BPD in 2011, but left it shortly after Freddie Gray Jr.'s death in 2015. He went to New Jersey, where he had grown up. He wanted to stay in law enforcement, so he joined the railroad police. Unhappy in that job—he wanted to be a real cop, not a railroad cop—he returned to Baltimore and rejoined BPD. After obligatory stops at the Police Academy and on patrol, a great opportunity presented itself to join the Task Force—or so Kostoplis thought.

Kostoplis had worked with Jenkins before he left BPD, in 2015, and he reached out to Jenkins when he decided to come back. Jenkins recruited Kostoplis to the Task Force at the end of October 2016. During his previous experience with Jenkins, Kostoplis had no idea that Jenkins was taking money or drugs from people. In fact, ironically, he told us that Jenkins had two rules for guys who worked with him: "You don't take money, and you don't put stuff on people." Jenkins had told him that on the first day, and it was those rules that motivated Kostoplis to later seek out Jenkins. Too bad they were more do as I say than do as I do kind of rules. But Kostoplis didn't know that at the time.

Almost immediately after Kostoplis joined the Task Force, Jenkins took leave. His wife was expecting a baby. While Jenkins was gone, Maurice Ward was briefly in charge, then a couple of interim supervisors, sometimes for only a day or two, would oversee the squad.

With Jenkins gone, the Task Force was now Gondo, Evodio Hendrix, Hersl, Taylor, and Ward; Rayam had been assigned to another unit. The remaining officers did little, but Kostoplis wanted to work. He suggested the Task Force develop cases by scouring the logs at local gun ranges for any "prohibited persons"—namely, felons. He was told, "We don't do that here." He didn't understand why not, but as the new guy, he just accepted it. Instead, he tried listening to 911 calls involving shootings to see if the caller gave any contact information, figuring he could reach out and ask who had guns in the neighborhood. So, Kostoplis, perhaps alone on the Task Force, was working during this period. Kostoplis worked so hard that he actually worked some overtime, real overtime, listening to jail calls.

Eventually Jenkins came back. Kostoplis couldn't remember exactly when—around the end of January, he thought. But he did remember, vividly, something Jenkins asked him to do.

Jenkins had asked Kostoplis to take a ride. What Jenkins told him during the ride meant one thing to Kostoplis before the Task Force officers were arrested, and something very different after they were arrested. That shift in meaning revealed something about the nature of the truth, too. Sometimes what something really means depends on what else you know, and that changes over time.

The ride, in Jenkins's van, took place shortly after Jenkins had returned from family leave. Hersl went along with them. Neither Hersl nor Jenkins told Kostoplis why or where they were going. Jenkins drove to a little side street not far from BPD's downtown headquarters. The Task Force's offices had been relocated from the Barn to there.

Jenkins stopped the van and told Kostoplis to leave all his equipment inside: radio, phone, and vest. Jenkins, Hersl, and Kostoplis got out and walked to the back of the van.

"What do you think about this?" asked Jenkins, Hersl at his side. "We start following around a high-level drug dealer, find out where he's keeping all his cash and his money, and we just go and take it."

"No," Kostoplis recalled saying. "That's a terrible fucking idea. You know, you can't have a badge on your chest and do things like that. You know, the fact that law enforcement doesn't do that is what separates law enforcement from criminals." Kostoplis had given our closing argument, two years ago, he just didn't know it at the time.

Kostoplis in his testimony described Jenkins and Hersl's reaction as being "Oh yeah, that's a bad idea." They got back in the van and returned to headquarters. Shortly afterward, Kostoplis was transferred off the Task Force. Jenkins was responsible for the move. Jenkins told Kostoplis that he was under consideration for a promotion from sergeant to lieutenant, and Jenkins confided that he had racked up a lot of civilian complaints. To avoid attracting any more complaints, Jenkins told Kostoplis that he was going to keep the Task Force off the street. Jenkins figured Kostoplis wouldn't want to work in a unit on ice like that given how obviously eager Kostoplis was to work.

What Jenkins had told him was a lie, as Kostoplis soon learned. Shortly after Jenkins transferred Kostoplis to another squad, Kostoplis ran into the Task Force on the street.

On March 1, 2017, Kostoplis saw reports of the arrest of the Task Force members. It was everyone he had served with until just a few weeks earlier. He called the FBI immediately. The last question I asked Kostoplis, and the one that I thought was the most important question in his whole direct examination, was "Why?" Why had he reached out?

"Because I realized that what he had asked me that night wasn't a test to see if whether I could be trusted around large amounts of money," Kostoplis testified. "He was, in fact, asking me to steal money." In other words, Kostoplis had thought Jenkins was giving him an integrity test and that when Kostoplis told him he wouldn't steal, he had passed. Except he hadn't. Jenkins was looking for the opposite answer. That's why he transferred Kostoplis off the Task Force.

During cross-examination, Hersl's lawyer William Purpura returned to Kostoplis's decision to contact the FBI. Purpura tried to discredit Kostoplis by implying he should have come forward sooner.

"Obviously, you could go down to [internal affairs] at any time if you had some information involving a police officer who suggested something wrong, is that fair to say?" Purpura said.

"I suppose so," Kostoplis said. "However, if you're referring to the meeting that we had, I didn't believe at the time that he was being serious. I thought he was testing me to see if I could be trusted around money."

Trying again, Purpura began, "So from the time whenever that happened, up until March 1st of 2017, you—obviously you had the opportunity—" But Kostoplis stopped him.

"I had the opportunity if I believed—" the officer said, before himself being interrupted.

"Okay. Hold on. Relax," Purpura said. "You had the opportunity to go into [internal affairs] or to speak to anyone else in the hierarchy at BPD about what occurred in this conversation, correct? Just yes or no, and we'll let you explain."

"I don't really understand how that would be correct, because that's not what I believed at the time."

"Fair enough," Purpura said. "What you believed at the time was that Jenkins was just testing you or just being Jenkins fooling around. Is that fair to say, then?"

"Correct."

In the end, Kostoplis didn't budge. He didn't concede that he could have reported the incident earlier because, as he said on direct examination, he took one meaning from Jenkins's question before the arrests and a totally different meaning from it after the arrests.

When Kostoplis finished his testimony, he left the stand without fanfare. He was just another witness, but he had shown the jury the path not taken by the defendants. When Jenkins had asked him if he'd rob a drug dealer, Kostoplis had said no. He told Jenkins what separated police officers from criminals was that they didn't give in to that temptation. And when Jenkins and Hersl were arrested, Kostoplis didn't keep quiet. He stepped forward and told the truth about what had happened on that day. He was the good cop.

When Kostoplis finished testifying, we rested our case. That was it. We hoped it was enough. Kostoplis made his choice. Now the jury had to make theirs. The date was February 6, 2018.

While the jury deliberated, we simply had to wait. I actually like the wait; it's stressful but exciting. At that point there's nothing more we can do. That brings a kind of peace that I don't feel during the trial when we're working around the clock. As we wait, it feels like we're on the knife's edge. The jury will either tell us we got it right or tell us we got it wrong. That's the exciting part.

As we waited, I thought back to when the case started. When Andi Smith called me upstairs for a meeting, and I heard about Antonio Shropshire and the belief, and that's really all it was at that point, that he had a cop protecting him. I was open to the idea, but I had no idea if it was true or, if it was, if we could prove it. I certainly didn't anticipate where we would end up—discovering not only that Shropshire had a cop protecting him but that that cop and the cops on his squad were robbing people, planting evidence, writing phony search warrants and police reports, and selling drugs.

I also never thought we'd arrive at the truth by going on the journey we went on. It introduced us to people I had never met before—people who sold drugs or lived with people who sold drugs or lived in neighborhoods where drugs were sold. And we encountered these people on terms that were different from nearly every other criminal case. They weren't the ones in trouble; they weren't sitting on the stand in an orange jumpsuit, brought in from jail. They weren't being called to testify against their family members or friends or people like them. And, of course, most notably, the police weren't testifying against them.

They were testifying against the police.

And we believed them.

We believed them because, it turned out, they were telling the truth. We knew they were telling the truth when we charged the case because we had more than just their word to go on. We had their jail calls. We had recordings from phone calls and from the bug in Gondo's car. We had video from the CitiWatch cameras and CCTV from the U-Store. We had their overtime records and their cell phone locations. And we had the pattern that we saw across the individual robberies that meant all these people, none of whom even knew the others existed, couldn't be making it up. Then after we charged the case, and in many ways, this was the gratifying phase of the investigation, the Task Force members who cooperated, the perpetrators themselves, told us the victims weren't lying. Not a single one.

With that proof we had tried to do something that rarely happens—deliver justice when the police abuse people in neighborhoods that our society has every incentive to overlook.

On February 13, 2018, my cell phone rang while I was in my office. It had been two days since the jury began deliberating. I answered, and Karen Moye, the courtroom deputy, told me the jury had a note. Once a jury starts deliberating, the only way they are allowed to communicate with the court is in writing. So, if they have a question about the law, they send out a note. And when they reach a verdict, they send out a note. But the courtroom deputy can't tell the lawyers what the note says. We only find out when we get to the courtroom, where a copy of it is waiting for us on our table. So, every time we get a call about a note, there's added suspense. I went to Derek's office, and we walked across the street to the courthouse together.

When we got there, we saw the note. It read, "We have a verdict."

Every juror must agree on the verdict: the only two choices are guilty and not guilty. Both turn on whether the government has proven its case. Guilty means that the government has proven, beyond a reasonable doubt, that the defendant broke the law. Beyond a reasonable doubt doesn't mean beyond all doubt. The word "reasonable" means that jurors can harbor some doubt, a theoretical doubt, a far-fetched doubt, and still vote to convict.

To conclude that a defendant is not guilty—and this is very important—the jurors don't need to conclude that the defendant is *innocent*. The question is one of proof. Even if the jury believes the defendant committed a crime, they should acquit if the government doesn't prove the crime beyond a reasonable doubt.

I am always amazed that twelve people who likely have little or nothing in common can reach a unanimous decision even though they don't know each other, come from widely different backgrounds, have diverse life experiences, politics, ideologies, and have conscious and nonconscious biases. But unanimity is what the law requires they achieve, whether the verdict is guilty or not guilty.

If the jury can't reach a unanimous decision, the judge must declare a mistrial. In that case, the government can try the defendant again. One prosecutor in my office compared trying a case a second time to eating cold, leftover eggs for breakfast. I've never had to try a case twice, and I didn't want to do it here.

There is always a delay once a jury reaches a verdict. The lawyers need time to get back to the courthouse. The US marshals have to bring the defendants from the lockup to the courtroom if they're in custody. Because of the public's interest in this case, reporters and other members of the community were given time to file into the gallery. Other prosecutors from the US Attorney's Office and a large contingent of prosecutors from the Baltimore City State's Attorney's Office also came to the courtroom to hear the verdict.

We arrived before the US Marshals brought in the defendants. Derek and I stood behind the prosecution table. I was too nervous to sit down. I decided to share something with Derek that was going through my mind.

I want you to stop and think about what we have done, regardless of what the verdict is, I told him. We had followed the facts wherever they led us, and I believed we had done everything we could to hold these officers accountable. We had acted in the best traditions of the US Department of Justice. It's the only government agency with a virtue as its name. That meant we had been guided by the principle, as Derek described in his closing argument, that "the police officers on trial weren't above the law and their victims weren't beneath it." If ever a case demonstrated that justice should be blind, this was it. The victims had told the truth. They deserved justice. That they sold drugs or lived with people who sold drugs or lived in neighborhoods where people sold drugs didn't mean the law shouldn't protect them, too. Even if the verdicts were not guilty, I wanted Derek to be proud of that work. I was.

As I stood there in 2018, I remembered how I had felt in 2005 at the end of the Enron trial, my first criminal case. I vividly remember sitting at the government's table in the courtroom as the jury filed in to deliver their verdict. I thought at the time how lucky I was to experience that moment, regardless of the outcome. I had been given the chance to play a small part in a big case. I felt that way again.

In a podcast describing the scene in 2018, *Baltimore Sun* reporter Jean Marbella said the defense table looked "stricken," and Derek and I were "beaming" as we all waited for the verdict. Although I don't think we were "beaming," I think what she saw on our faces was the sense of accomplishment we felt for having brought the case to that point.

When everyone was finally in the courtroom, the process of taking the verdict began.

Moye asked the jurors if they had reached a verdict. They all said they had. Then she asked them, "Who shall speak for you?"

"Our foreperson, they replied," in unison. And then juror number two stood up.

When he rose, it sent a jolt through my body. He was a young Black man, the only one on the jury. Nearly all of the Task Force's victims who had testified at the trial were Black men. While a number of them were older than the foreman, several were right around his age. The moment he stood up, I thought, they're going to convict. They wouldn't have picked this man, who looked like the victims, to send the message that they didn't believe them.

In a loud, clear voice, juror number two said, "Guilty." He said "guilty" again and again, as the courtroom deputy asked him the verdict for each count in the indictment.

The jury had believed the victims.

The truth had revealed itself to them, just as it had revealed itself to us.

Afterword

During a trial, the jury must decide whether a defendant broke the law. Who the defendant is as a person or what the defendant did in their life apart from what's relevant to the charges isn't considered. The sentencing phase, however, is different.

At sentencing, the court takes the full measure of a defendant—the good and the bad. Defense lawyers call witnesses in an effort to get their clients lower sentences. They ask witnesses to talk about what a good parent a defendant has been or to describe their involvement in the community and things like that. Such presentations can be heart-wrenching, and they're meant to be. In every criminal case, there is collateral damage to a defendant's family, whether it's their children, their spouse, their elderly parents, or their siblings. The tragedy is that these people did nothing wrong but will suffer the consequences of the defendant's choices.

Sometimes defendants try to recast themselves as victims, as if prosecuting them caused the harm. I always respond to that argument the same way—we're here for sentencing because of the defendant's actions, not because he got caught.

For the Gun Trace Task Force trial, Daniel Hersl and Marcus Taylor had family members speak for them at their sentencing hearings. They both had young sons, and their families pleaded for them to be given short sentences so they could be around to see them grow up. They won't be.

Hersl and Taylor each got eighteen years.

Wayne Jenkins got twenty-five years, the longest of any of the Task Force defendants.

Thomas Allers, the Task Force's other sergeant, got fifteen years.

At Jenkins's sentencing, the grown children of Elbert Davis, the elderly man killed in the high-speed chase of Umar Burley and Brent Matthews spoke. They talked about how much they loved their father and how much they missed him. They asked Judge Catherine Blake to impose a sentence that reflected what Jenkins had done to their family. Jenkins cried and begged the family to forgive him.

None of the cooperating defendants had anyone speak at their sentencings. They each addressed the court and asked for forgiveness in their own way. Jemell Rayam was the most emotional. Momodu Gondo continued to project strength, like he was ready to take whatever the court gave him. Maurice Ward and Evodio Hendrix spoke in quiet voices, like they had done at trial, showing neither the emotion nor the strength of Rayam and Gondo. Their contrition came across in what they both said, not how they said it. All of the cooperating defendants got lower sentences than Hersl and Taylor.

The consequences of the investigation and prosecution of the Task Force members reverberated far beyond the courtroom. Baltimore mayor Catherine Pugh fired Commissioner Kevin Davis, head of the Baltimore Police Department. Davis had stood with US Attorney Rod Rosenstein when the charges were announced, but he didn't survive the scandal.

Pugh chose an internal candidate, Darryl DeSousa, as the new police chief. He was, for a short time, a popular choice. The trouble was he hadn't paid his taxes for three years. We learned this not long after he was sworn in and brought tax charges against him. At first, he resisted resigning, and Pugh even seemed to back him up, saying his taxes were "personal matters." DeSousa resigned not long after that and ultimately pleaded guilty. He was sentenced to ten months in jail.

Soon after the trial, I was asked to work on an investigation of Pugh herself. Her comments on taxes being a "personal matter" took on a new light when we discovered that she wasn't paying hers either. In fact, she was hiding income from a lucrative children's book deal she had struck with the University of Maryland Medical System, on whose board she also sat. Except that it wasn't just a tax case. She was also defrauding UMMS by not providing the books she had promised would go to Baltimore City school kids. She resigned in May 2019.

After the sentencings of the Task Force officers, our investigation continued. The cooperators told us about other BPD officers with whom they had robbed people or planted evidence or officers who they knew had done those things. We pursued those cases as well, bringing new indictments and convicting all the officers in another plainclothes unit, run by a sergeant named Keith Gladstone.

One of the questions that our investigation didn't answer, and wasn't asked to answer, was what happened to BPD officer Sean Suiter. As Gondo testified to at trial, Suiter had served with him earlier in his career. As was publicly acknowledged at the time, Suiter was scheduled to be a witness before the grand jury in our case when he died on November 16, 2017, the night before he was supposed to testify. The medical examiner determined Suiter's death to be a homicide, but the BPD, which investigated his death, was never able to identify a suspect. An Independent Review Board created by the BPD concluded that he had committed suicide. We didn't investigate his death, and what I know about the circumstances surrounding it is drawn largely from what I've read in the media and in the IRB's report.

Suiter's death shocked the city and divided it into two camps—those who believe that Suiter had been murdered and those who believe he committed suicide. There is even a group who believe police officers murdered him because he was going to testify against them. Because Suiter died before he could testify, we never learned what, if anything, he knew. Unfortunately, there doesn't appear to be any prospect that definitive proof will emerge to resolve what in fact happened to him. And ultimately, regardless of how he died, his death was a terrible tragedy for his young family.

The Task Force case also had an impact on policing itself in Baltimore. Most significantly, the BPD disbanded all its plainclothes units. Now all police officers are in uniform, and citizens know they're BPD.

The state legislature created a special commission to study the origins of the Task Force scandal. After months of taking testimony, they issued a report chronicling what led us to the courtroom. The city commissioned a similar study that also made recommendations for reform. I met with the lawyers who ran both of those efforts. They asked me, in so many words, what I thought had led to the Task Force's lawlessness. Answering that question was easy—they weren't supervised. And that's the issue. The only way to prevent another Task Force is to properly supervise the police. The hard part is actually doing it.

The Task Force case had a profound effect on me personally and professionally. I came to know the East and West Baltimore neighborhoods where the Task Force operated and the communities they were supposed to serve. My previous pursuit of financial crimes and public corruption cases never brought me into contact with either. I saw firsthand that people from these communities told the truth about what the police did to them. That knowledge is where I would start any future police corruption investigation I might be involved with.

Information provided by people who live in East and West Baltimore is essential to solving crimes. Most criminal cases are not built on forensic evidence like DNA but on information provided by eyewitnesses and other people who live in the communities affected by crime. To get people to cooperate with the police and provide that kind of information, however, they have to trust the police. Given that, what the Task Force did was not only destructive because it victimized people, but because it also further undermined confidence in the police, which, in a kind of negative feedback loop, meant that crimes would go unsolved, and the communities the police served would be further victimized by their misconduct.

More than anything else, the case opened my eyes to the reality that people living in East and West Baltimore faced in dealing with the police. For these folks, the police didn't protect them from crime. Instead, they exposed them to daily indignities. Traffic stops for imagined violations—tint violations on cars that didn't have tinted windows; seat belt violations when the driver was wearing a seatbelt—and searches for no apparent reason. That's what happened to Herbert Tate. Imagine what it would feel like to have another grown man stick his fingers in your mouth? Or run his hands around your waistband? These things happened repeatedly to Black men in Baltimore. That's why Tate left the city. Who could blame him?

And then, of course, our investigation revealed not only bad policing, but much worse—parasitic lawbreaking by the police toward the very people they were supposed to be protecting the community from. Drug dealers flush with cash were supposed to be arrested. Instead, they were robbed and let go. Perhaps what was most shocking was that what we discovered, what seemed so surprising to us, wasn't all that surprising at all. It wasn't a surprise to the people who had had to live with it. One day after the trial I was waiting for the elevator in the lobby of my office building. One of the elevators was out of service. As I stood there, an older Black man left the elevator that he was repairing and approached me. I had never met him before. I can only presume he knew who I was from a news story that had my picture in it.

"I'm from East Baltimore," he said. "We all knew about Hersl."

Now I did, too.

Acknowledgments

In the spring of 2018, I had a conversation with Matt McAdam, who would become my editor at Johns Hopkins University Press, about writing a book on the Gun Trace Task Force case in Baltimore. When Matt explained to me that the way you get a book published is to hire an agent, who gets a percentage of your royalties to shop your book proposal to publishing houses, my heart sank. I knew I couldn't get paid for this book because I was and wanted to remain in public service, and the rules prohibited me from making any money off of it. That meant that no agent would want to work with me. But then Matt told me, "The reason you hire an agent is to get an editor's attention, and you have an editor's attention." Without Matt, this book never would have happened.

I'd like to thank Alec MacGillis, whom I met because our sons played on the same baseball team in Baltimore. He was kind enough to share his book proposal with me when I was working on mine.

Thanks as well to Lawrence Lanahan, who Hopkins Press engaged to work with me on the book proposal. After a fruitless year trying to come up with a proposal on my own, collaborating with Lawrence was a breakthrough. He helped me figure out the story within the story, as well as the book's themes. When I choked up describing the scene in the courtroom when the jury announced their foreperson, Lawrence exclaimed, "That's the opening scene!"—and the title of the book. He was right.

ACKNOWLEDGMENTS

I wrote this book while working full-time at the US Attorney's Office, writing only at night and on weekends. The only way I was able to do that was because of my wife Anne's generosity with her time and her understanding about how I was spending mine. When the grass was knee-high, or the million other things I was supposed to do weren't getting done, she didn't complain, because she knew I was writing. Simply put, this book never would have gotten written without her giving me leave to ignore all the other things in our shared life so that I could pay attention to it.

Lastly, I want to acknowledge my son, Joe, and my daughter, Claudia. I wrote this book for them more than anyone else. They're a little too young for the subject matter, but they motivated me more than they know. Long after I'm gone, I hope they will hear my voice in these pages and understand why I worked as hard as I did when they were growing up and what public service meant to me. I won't leave them a lot of money but I leave them this.

Index

ABOUT THE AUTHOR

Leo Wise is a lawyer who has spent his entire career in public service.

He graduated with a BA in international studies from Johns Hopkins University, where he was a recipient of the Truman Scholarship. He went on to earn his MA in international relations from the Johns Hopkins School of Advanced International Studies and his JD from Harvard Law School.

The summer after finishing law school, Wise received a commission as an intelligence officer in the US Navy Reserve and served in that capacity for eight years. He clerked for a US District Court judge in Philadelphia before joining the Department of Justice through the Attorney General's Honors Program.

In 2008, Wise was recruited to be the founding staff director and chief counsel for the Office of Congressional Ethics, an independent entity within the House of Representatives that investigates allegations of misconduct against members of the House.

In 2010, he joined the US Attorney's Office for the District of Maryland. In partnership with the American Bar Association, Wise trains anti-corruption prosecutors from other countries, and he has worked with and mentored prosecutors from Croatia, Serbia, Bosnia–Herzegovina, Jordan, the Philippines, and Mongolia. He also served as an adjunct faculty member at American University's School of Public Affairs for eight years.

Wise is a three-time recipient of the Attorney General's Award and has received the Director's Award from former FBI director Robert Mueller, among other honors.